NOW WHAT?

Navigating an Unimaginable Divorce

Nancy Stevens

Clovercroft Publishing
Franklin, TN

Clovercroft Publishing
307 Verde Meadow Drive
Franklin, TN 37067

Cover design and interior layout by Anita Jones, Another Jones Graphics

ISBN 978-1-950892-50-1 print book
ISBN 978-1-950892-60-0 ebook

Publisher's Cataloging-In-Publication Data
(Prepared by The Donohue Group, Inc.)

Names: Stevens, Nancy (Writer on divorce), author.
Title: Now what? : navigating an unimaginable divorce / Nancy Stevens.
Description: Franklin, TN : Clovercroft Publishing, [2020] | Includes bibliographical
    references and index.
Identifiers: ISBN 9781950892501 (print) | ISBN 9781950892600 (ebook)
Subjects: LCSH: Divorced women--United States. | Adultery--United States. | Army
    spouses--United States. | Stevens, Nancy (Writer on divorce)--Marriage.
Classification: LCC HQ834 .S748 2020 (print) | LCC HQ834 (ebook) | DDC
    306.8930973--dc23

Printed and bound in the United States of America

Dedication

To my son and daughter: You are my greatest gifts; you've been an eternal source of love and fun, and I'm proud of your accomplishments and the way you've conducted your lives. Teasingly my daughter-in-law and my son try to catch me referring to him as my favorite child. It must mean they listen very carefully to everything I say.

Contents

Preface vii

Acknowledgments xi

1. I'm Divorcing You... 1

2. Time to Reminisce.....................................10

3. Must Have Been Blind 17

4. The Phone Call 21

5. Screw Him!...28

6. My New Best Friend..................................34

7. Know Your Enemy 38

8. Inspector Clouseau and Me......................43

9. The Search for Tumbleweed.....................48

10. Keeping Up With the Jeffersons 53

11. The Cold Call..61

12. "The Pillow"...69

13. The Deposition..77

14. Unprepared to Divvy Up My Life 87

15. Headwinds Make Flying Solo Difficult.....93

16. Showing Respect to His New Wife..........99

17. My Son's Deployment 109

18. War, Love and R&R.................................115

19. Where, Oh Where, is the Alimony?........122

20. A True Brats' Love Story 129

21. The 29th Returns 142

22. Contempt of Court – and Stalking.........147

23. Texas, Here I Come...154

24. Cocktail Napkins Say the Darnedest Things......166

25. His Net Worth...170

26. The Battalion Commander 182

27. Meltdown with Milou..187

28. Maximilian and Me...195

29. Deutschland and An Officer's Wife......................206

30. Moving Onward and Upward...............................212

31. The Ex Husband Strikes Again 218

Glossary 224

Resources..233

Preface

Five months after my husband and I celebrated our forty-fifth wedding anniversary, I received a phone call from a woman claiming to be engaged to him. Normally, I'd have hung up on the rude, malicious person; however, I'd never had an abusive call from a mistress—my husband's mistress, at that. Until that moment I had no idea that anyone in my family had a mistress, and I was dying to hear her sordid explanation. Her goal was to make sure that I knew my husband was hers—in essence, a shot across the bow. I couldn't wait to call her alleged fiancé and ask, as nonchalantly as possible under the circumstances, "So what's going on?" When the philandering husband calmly responded to my call he said, "I'm divorcing you" and hung up. In his haste he forgot to say, "I'm also abandoning the kids," considering that that's exactly what he did.

My husband had some challenging personality traits, but I'd never thought about divorcing him. Also, I'd never had a reason to analyze the word "divorce;" however, its two syllables sound harsh, and no matter how softly you say it, the word can't be fluffed up.

When did the adulterous relationship begin, where did the mistress come from, what was her agenda, and more to the point, how in the hell did I get to la-la land and who were these evil strangers?

Becoming a divorce statistic at sixty-seven was an event I hadn't prepared for. My husband and I had prepared for "Till death do us part" by having our financial holdings, medical directives, and wills placed in a trust. This was time consuming and costly, but our intention was that it would be a gift of sorts for our kids, a roadmap of our final wishes for them in what would otherwise be a time of sorrow, so worth the expense; as it turned out the papers remain, but the trust died first.

Financially I was unprepared for going through a divorce of any duration, much less ten years of financial drain. Over the years, I've listened to talk shows that address divorce and the need to be financially prepared, and I suppose that would make sense if it were a planned event. It would never have occurred to me to perhaps take ten dollars out of the grocery money each week and hide it away in a container marked MISTRESS PROTECTION. Had I been diligent for most of our forty-five-year marriage, without stealing a dollar here and there, it might have covered the initial retainer, but you could never save enough to cover the full financial impact of divorce. It's a widely accepted fact that women are more often the ones who experience financial disadvantages, and I was panicked the moment he said, "I'm divorcing you," because my intuition was warning me that my life was about to be challenged as never before.

In truth, my life and that of my family changed in the blink of an eye. I knew nothing about the trauma of divorce, so a week or so later, when I'd collected myself, I headed to the nearest large bookstore and its divorce section. I spent an hour looking through books that defined divorce, but I was looking for one that told me where to begin, how to deal with the betrayal and devastation, how to protect myself, how to retain the best attorney, going to court, the cost of the drama, and what life would look like after divorce. I left the store with several books, but none of them took me through the day-to-day, month-to-month, or years of "getting a divorce."

Within a week I began to experience outrageous and disrespectful actions taken by my husband that I couldn't have imagined, and I began to say to myself, "I've got to write a book." As the drama escalated, I became more emphatic, saying, "I'm writing a book," and now "It's in my book."

The challenge of putting my real-life drama on paper was so compelling that I couldn't wait to get started; however, my creativity lay in the interior design field and with regard to computers, all I knew was how to send emails. Eventually I clicked on the Microsoft icon; up popped something that looked like a sheet of paper, and I started typing, but if you don't know to click on SAVE, forget it—your words have vanished and you can't even remember them.

During those forty-five years of marriage to an army officer, I, as an officer's wife—which came with its own protocol—supported and participated in my husband's career. With mentoring from the senior officers' wives, I learned what it meant to be a successful officer's wife, and I'm convinced that I mastered the challenge.

There is no way to prepare for a deployment, a separation of a year or more; however, as military wives we've faced the test, perhaps more than once, of being in the unique position of surviving a deployment. During those months we customized our survival skills, most likely without even being aware of it. I never thought about a deployment as being a training camp for a divorce; however, they certainly weren't vacations.

Divorce was not an assignment I wanted to accept, as I loved being a wife and mother, but my husband's affair had advanced beyond the bounds of marriage, and he wasn't interested in anything but being in love with someone new.

I drew strength from knowing that I had persevered during deployments dating back forty-five years to Hanau, Germany. I wasn't about to let him tread on me. I was prepared to win with strength and dignity. I just didn't know quite where to begin.

I was, however, combat-ready.

Acknowledgments

I have been blessed with enduring friendships that have enriched my life for years. They became the glue that held me together during my most challenging days, and when I said, "You're not going to believe this" it was a heads-up for another outrageous action committed by Roi.

Unlike my daughter, I cannot claim any friends from kindergarten, so fortunately for y'all, I won't have to bore anyone with all the playmates and activities I participated in.

When I met Joy Starner in 1963, she was the battalion commander's wife, of the 6/40 Field Artillery Battalion. She took me under her wing and became my mentor for the next fifty-one years from 1963–2014. No matter where we were stationed, we started our days with an early morning call, often made challenging due to time zones.

My lifelong Scottish shopping buddy and I met at a nursery school in Springfield, Virginia, in 1973 when our little guys were four. She and her husband were my saviors when they flew to Seattle to share the drive to Virginia in the winter of 2009.

The Fairfax County Adult French class created friendships far beyond le premier jour de la classe, so when le professeur moved to Florida, IHOP became our classroom.

In 1974 I was ordering fabric from Darr-Luck Associates, just chatting with the showroom manager when she said, "I could sure use some help." On a whim I said, "You're looking at help." Within a day or two I had an interview. Despite finding a babysitter, traffic, and parking tickets, it was such fun. One of my favorite memories is trying to explain to people in the industry that real cowhide is not sold by the yard but by the square foot. They still keep me laughing with their daily emails.

Seattle Design Builders became friends during the remodel of my 1925 home in 2004 and created a piece of art out of the nearly 3,000 structural components that go into making a fabulous home. In my opinion they are the best.

My longtime neighbors in Seattle became single ladies, and we sold our homes within six months of each other. I will forever miss having hors d'oeuvres and wine in front of my fireplace, talking late into the night, or crossing the alley to my other neighbor's, sometimes in jammies, as she had a huge television and we'd watch Netflix while eating ice cream and sipping champagne. Almost like college days, when you thought your only challenge was what time to get up.

My niece, Lorrie, helped me with punctuation, and her family has given me visiting rights to some of my treasures, which now reside in their home.

I often hear disparaging remarks about attorneys. Fortunately, I had two of the best family law attorneys. I'll always be grateful for Mr. McGarry and his associates who calmly led me through the drama of divorce with their professional guidance, friendship, and sense of humor. The divorce that occurred in Virginia didn't stay in Virginia. I needed a referral to a law firm in Texas, debunking my suggestion about being comfortable with the commute to the firm. Ms. Vance of the Law Office of Lisa Vance, San Antonio, came to my rescue in 2012 and again in 2015. Ms. Vance and her associates are the best in Texas, and I was blessed with their guidance and friendship and their ability to find humor in the bizarre turn of events.

I am grateful to each of you.

I'm Divorcing You

One lovely day in the Pacific Northwest, I was in my garden, enjoying the last day of summer and the beautiful flowers I'd planted in the spring. Flowers grow well in Seattle, with its cool temperatures, salt air, and a little rain, and mine were no exception. The city is known for its rain, though "real" Seattleites claim they don't carry umbrellas; still, local artists make a business of painting pictures of open umbrellas gathered together in a rainbow of colors. When summer brings blue skies and fluffy white clouds, it's the perfect time to sell those paintings to visitors at the Pike Place Market.

It was Saturday, September 20, 2008, and instead of wandering around in my garden, I should have been preparing to close up our summer home for my return to Virginia and my husband and our kids. We'd called Northern Virginia home since 1972 when my husband was assigned to the Military District of Washington and our son was three years old. When he was six, we were on the move again, this time to Fort Leavenworth, Kansas, where we were blessed with the birth of our daughter. After that posting, we four returned to Virginia and my husband's last army assignment at the Pentagon. Fifteen years after his retirement and a successful civilian career, we took the first step toward moving to Seattle permanently by selling our home and moving into an apartment near our neighborhood. Deciding to leave his job in Virginia and sever our ties proved more difficult than being reassigned by the army to a location of their choosing, so we began commuting coast to coast.

I heard the phone ring and ran to catch the call, thinking it might be my friends wanting to change our dinner plans. When I answered, an unfamiliar voice said, "I'm looking for Roi."

> *When I answered, an unfamiliar*
> *voice said, "I'm looking for Roi."*

Instantly on alert, as no one knew my husband by that name, I asked, "And whom am I speaking with?"

"My name is Bunny," she said, "and I'm looking for Roi."

In a heartbeat I went from the joy of the beautiful day to sheer panic. *Who is this woman, and why is she asking to speak to my husband?* Before I could get a word out of my mouth she said, "How are you related to him?"

For a fleeting moment I thought a bizarre question deserved a flip answer, and I almost said, "I'm his girlfriend," but on second thought, after forty-five years of marriage, what the heck—"I'm his wife," I said, and she slammed the phone down.

I hurried upstairs, as I had just enough time to prepare to go out to dinner, when the phone rang again. I grabbed the nearest handset, giving no thought to who might be calling. "It's Bunny again," she said. *Oh, great! Now she thinks we're friends.* Bunny said, "I think you need to know what's been going on for the last few months."

I'd barely had time to get upstairs, much less give her first call any thought other than that I might mention it to my friends over dinner; however, my instant reaction was *Oh, I can't wait to hear!*

I had absolutely no idea who this woman was, but she was obviously angry, filled with hate, and intent on spewing venom. Bunny, my new best friend, told me that she and my husband had met in Orlando, Florida, at the American High School Reunion on April 10, 2008, just five short months ago. From 1946 through 1971, American High was a Defense Department school for American military and other US government dependents living in Europe. Bunny told me she had attended American twelve years after my husband graduated from that school; their first meeting was at the reunion, and they hit it off immediately. She didn't use the word "intimately," but I have yet to fall off a turnip truck, so I knew exactly what she was getting at.

I didn't accompany my husband to the reunion, as just days before it was discovered that my right wrist, which I had broken seven months earlier, hadn't healed on its own, and I was immediately scheduled for surgery. I left the hospital with a huge cast covering my hand, and there was just no way for me to look cute in a sundress or at the pool, much less be able to feed myself gracefully, so I stayed home—evidently a really big mistake!

In her attempt to explain or justify her affair with my husband, Bunny said, "He told me his wife died five and a half years ago, and in July he proposed to me and I accepted."

> *He told me his wife died five and*
> *a half years ago, and in July he*
> *proposed to me and I accepted.*

Grappling with the concept of being dead, I really can't remember all the fun stuff she told me they'd been doing in the five months since their meeting, though one of those months my husband was in Seattle with me. I recall Bunny mentioning spending weekends at bed and breakfasts in Virginia, attending a reenactment at the Sharpsburg Battlefield in Maryland, the site of the Battle of Antietam, and picnicking at the National Zoo in Washington, D.C. The zoo, how absolutely appropriate! A romantic little picnic at the zoo, and let me guess—they didn't notice that they were covered in sweat. It dawned on me that we hadn't taken our kids to the National Zoo in August because it was too darn hot and unbearably humid.

Bunny said, "I'm out in front of his apartment." Then I heard, "Hi, Bun." Just before she hung up, I had the opportunity to ask, "Were you at our apartment last night?" She answered yes and hung up. That explained why he hadn't answered my endless phone calls the night before.

As the dial tone rang in my head, I pressed the number for our apartment, and when my husband answered I calmly asked, "What is going on?" Bunny was now inside the apartment and undoubtedly in his face. My husband's rather blasé response was "I'm divorcing you." As calmly as I could, I said, "You must be kidding." Instead of an apology or an expression of regret, he too hung up on me. I've been stunned on several occasions, but those three words had me in an immediate state of panic; time stood still for a few seconds until I realized that I hadn't moved a muscle or taken a breath. I've never been one to go off the deep end and carry on half-crazy, but after what I'd just been told, who could blame me? Then again, I was alone and needed to think straight, as my thoughts were all over the map. What to do first?

I called my friends, who are also neighbors, to tell them, "I don't believe I can go to dinner tonight, as I was just told I'm being divorced," as at that moment I was feeling timid and unsure. By the next morning, that timid feeling was gone. Already, my husband's Christian name was stuck in my throat; in an instant, I began to think of him as "the Deviant," and was thereafter unable to think of him as anything else. My friends suggested I come over and we'd sit around and talk and drink wine. That sounded like a good plan, as I surely didn't have one of my own, but was wine going to be enough? I don't remember if I changed clothes, but I was calm enough to leave cell phone messages for my son and daughter, grab one of my best bright blue plastic glasses, and fill it to the top with bourbon before heading to their house.

I was not only panicked and fearful, I was on the verge of crazy. For some inexplicable reason, I remembered as I crossed the alley, that Canadians refer to their alleys as lanes. It sounds so sophisticated, suggesting that it's not a place for gigantic recycle bins like your average alley. I had never been told, "I'm divorcing you," so I had no idea how to respond, but at that moment divorce didn't sound like a good idea.

I had never been told, "I'm divorcing you," so I had no idea how to respond, but at that moment divorce didn't sound like a good idea.

In Dr. Phil's opening salvo, he says, "Today is gonna be a changing day in your life," and believe me, he's not kidding.

My neighbors and I just sat smiling at each other while sharing a drink. We were clueless about what to say: maybe we should just laugh; it was, after all, the most bizarre moment in my life, or were they wondering if I was going to do something exotic like hyperventilate and roll up in the fetal position on their floor? I was in no mood to fall apart; I needed to get my head straight and talk about the phone calls I'd received less than an hour before. I was beginning to put all the details together. Had my new best friend, Bunny, whom I subsequently always thought of as "the Trollop," really said that my husband had told her I'd been dead for over five years? And did my husband really tell me he was divorcing me? How could I have not suspected something was going on?

I shared my fears and frustration about my inability to contact Roi for hours the night before, having called his office, his cell, and our apartment in an attempt to reach him. At about 10:00 p.m., I called my daughter to ask if she would drive by our apartment, less than a mile from her home, as I was afraid something serious had happened to her dad, and I couldn't get to sleep. I must have fallen asleep for a few hours though, because I awoke to realize that I hadn't heard from her. In desperation I called her again about 1:30 a.m., and she told me, "His car is parked at the apartment."

That was all she said, and for some divine reason I went back to sleep. When I awoke Saturday morning I was beyond pissed, and felt that it was up to him to call me. We hadn't talked at all the day before, which was very unusual as we usually touched base with one another several times a day. He always called just before leaving the office to say he was on his way home. I figured that if he did call, he'd offer a cheap excuse and then lie, leaving me even angrier. We would be back together in Virginia in two days, which would give me time to cool off and be able to confront him in a calmer frame of mind.

My daughter didn't tell me that she'd caught her dad and his lover in our apartment the night before; she'd said only that his car was there. She and I had talked several times that Saturday, and at no time did I detect anything amiss in her voice. I'm thankful that by the time I knew what was going on, Nicole and a very good friend were at dinner, and our daughter wasn't the one to give me the devastating news.

If I hadn't been going to dinner with friends Saturday night, I probably wouldn't have called anyone. Instead, I'd have wandered around my home, waiting for my kids to call and wondering what in the hell had just happened. I believe things happen for a reason, and my friends were there to offer an immediate haven. I was comfortable being with them, as they knew my husband, and I wanted to stay with them until my daughter's call before I went home alone. When she finally called, I told her about the call from Bunny, and that her dad had told me he was divorcing me. Nicole said that she and her friend were at a restaurant right around the corner from the apartment and would go there right away. She still didn't mention having caught her father and his paramour in my bed the night before. I later found out that she'd called her brother on the way to the rendezvous with the adulterous pair, and he had told her that he too would head to the apartment.

It was late, and the bourbon was gone. I really needed to go home and be alone while waiting for my daughter's account of the situation at the apartment, and would then, I hoped, be able to go to sleep. When she eventually called, it was time for her to unload all the details of the last twenty-four hours. She had told me earlier that she'd seen his car at the apartment the night before, but that wasn't the whole story. The lights were on, so he was home, but not answering the phone, so she went to the door. He answered wearing pajama bottoms and no shirt. He didn't let her in, but rather came out on the porch in his abbreviated outfit. Trust me: he's not Michelangelo's *David*. Nicole told him that "Mom" had been trying to call him for hours, at which point she saw a figure move behind the drapery-covered windows. She realized that her dad was entertaining, and that's when she became unglued and screamed,

"Does she know you're married?" She immediately called her brother for advice about what to tell me; they agreed that it was too late and that they had to come to terms with the situation.

Does she know you're married?

My husband had all day Saturday to call and apologize for not answering my calls the day before, but he remained silent, wrongly assuming that Nicole had spilled the beans about the slumber party at our apartment. Roi had earned the honor of Eagle Scout and attained the rank of lieutenant colonel, but in actuality he's nothing more than a devious coward. He let his mistress do his dirty work by calling me to tell me of their affair. She might have believed that he was a widower and that I'd been long dead, but knowing my husband as I do, he had also exaggerated his life story beyond belief, and she'd be damned if his wife was going to get in the way of her living the fairytale.

Despite the severity of the crisis befalling our family, my daughter's description of her arrival at the apartment was truly hilarious. Roi and his lover were in for a scene and a berating, as she was furious with her dad for his contemptible behavior.

She has described herself as a mama bear needing to protect her cub, so her first instinct was to remove as many of my things as possible. With her friend stationed at the door, the unloading began. My daughter characterized herself as a whirling dervish, emptying my clothes from closets, taking artwork off the walls, and carting out two end tables, leaving the lamps sitting on the floor. Finally, she told Bunny to get off the couch where she sat sniveling, so that the floral needlepoint rug could be rolled up. She told me that at that point her dad asked if she was going to leave him anything; with that, her parting salvo was to remove the faux white tulip wreath from over the master bed.

Leave him anything? Well excuse me! He already had something new in our apartment, and from what I've gathered she'd already been in my bed, and I don't think she was interested in the décor.

I've been associated with the interior design field since college, and as an army wife have lived in some very interesting and challenging quarters. To make a sow's ear into a silk purse on a shoestring is just something those of us who move every two or three years learn to do. What I'm trying to say is that everything about the apartment said, "Married man;" however, not everyone is observant or detail oriented, and maybe some people have other things on their minds when they come a-callin'.

My son, Gary, arrived at our apartment that night at about 10:00 p.m. The apartment was still lit like a Christmas tree. He knocked, and his dad answered the door with a gin and tonic in his hand. He told me that it was evident that it wasn't the first. Bunny had left to lick her wounds somewhere else. Roi said, "I don't want to talk to you."

Gary replied, "If we don't talk now we may never talk again." Truer words were never spoken. Roi then became belligerent and defensive, and said that if he wanted to speak to him, he'd have to sit down. That was when Gary saw that his dad was holding one of his two handguns, and questioned, "Why do you have that gun in your hand?"

Roi replied, "I'm afraid of you."

Gary opened his jacket to prove that he hadn't come to threaten his dad with any type of weapon, and asked him to remove the gun from the room. Instead of returning it to the bedroom, where the guns were kept, he slid it into the seam of the chair he was sitting in. An uncomfortable standoff ensued while Gary waited to hear his dad's explanation for allowing his mistress to tell Mom about the infidelity. He eventually acknowledged that he was having an affair and had fallen in love with the woman. Gary was convinced that his dad was more concerned about losing his mistress than about destroying the family and losing his relationship with his kids.

A coward, Roi might have thought he'd be better off dead, but he did give his son one of the guns and swore up and down that the other wasn't in the apartment. As Gary was leaving, his dad asked him how to "fix the mess." Gary replied that he could begin by telling the truth. Roi exhibits traits of a compulsive liar. I knew he was given to lying, but not to what extent until this episode. I had buried my head in the sand, but that's a lame excuse—I take responsibility for my unawareness.

As Gary was leaving, his dad asked him how to "fix the mess." Gary replied that he could begin by telling the truth.

Chapter One Take-Aways

- ◉ You'll NEVER be prepared to hear "I'm divorcing you."
- ◉ You'll NEVER be ready to share your husband with a mistress.
- ◉ Start keeping daily notes.

2
Time to Reminisce

Life can change in an instant, and my children's and mine did that Saturday afternoon. I vividly recall where I was standing when my husband said, "I'm divorcing you." I was gazing out at our beautiful lake, cluttered with small sailboats from the yacht club, bobbing around, looking for wind to fill their sails. The scene was serene, but I was anything but calm, and I desperately needed to hold myself together so I could concentrate on closing up the Seattle house so as to head to Virginia and deal with the unraveling of a marriage.

First things first, however: drain the outside water pipes, set timers on lamps, take as much cash out of our joint checking account as I dared, and of course pack, just mundane stuff that kept me focused.

A friend drove me to the airport for my flight to Virginia, and I managed somehow to appear normal, just like every other time she had dropped me at SeaTac. I was experiencing emotional overload, and just wanted to board that plane and wait for it to back away from the gate before anything else happened. I'd share the bombshell with friends another day.

I had five hours to sit on the plane and wonder, would my husband pick me up at Reagan International Airport in Washington, D.C.? Should I go to our apartment? What about the money wasted on his airline ticket for our family Christmas in Seattle? And speaking of money, how soon would he cut me off from our joint checking account? It had taken us forty-five years to get to this point, and in the blink of an eye he was engaged and severing all family ties.

We'd met at Seattle University in the fall of 1960, when I was a freshman majoring in art and he was a junior majoring in engineering. By chance we were simply two Episcopalians who found ourselves in a Jesuit University. On the day I met him he was in his army uniform as a member of the Reserve Officers' Training Corps (ROTC). I thought he was pretty cute, and we started dating. At some point in the relationship he told me that he had attended the United States Military Academy at West Point, New York, but had been dismissed for lying. I thought I was terribly sophisticated, but in truth I was a mere babe from the far Pacific Northwest. In retrospect, even as a mere babe, I knew lying was wrong and a deal breaker. If I'd been several years older, I might have seen his acknowledgment of lying as a sign of future behavior, but even with the benefit of that knowledge, would I have been able to point to clear signs of a pattern of lying?

Though our dating years were rocky, as my parents didn't approve of his career, and their disapproval influenced my siblings, we were married in May 1963 at Saint Mark's Cathedral in Seattle. We honeymooned in New York City, visiting all the tourist spots, but the highlight was attending a taping of *The Ed Sullivan Show* before heading across the Atlantic to Germany. We boarded the USNS (United States Naval Ship) *General Simon B. Buckner,* a 608-foot navy transport, for the nine-day crossing to Bremerhaven, Germany. It was hardly the *Queen Mary,* but it was a big ship. We'd barely left the dock and were just passing the Statue of Liberty when I found myself reaching for one of the little brown bags that lined the handrails. When we boarded the ship, I'd asked, innocently, "Why are all of those paper bags hanging on the handrail?" While still in New York Harbor, I became well acquainted with the little brown bag. I had grown up cruising Puget Sound and the San Juan Islands on my family's boat and have a few memories of my dad saying, "Get your life jacket on" due to rough water, but New York Harbor didn't have so much as a ripple. After bobbing up and down aboard ship on the Atlantic for nine days,

I absolutely knew the difference between rough water and really rough water. During those nine honeymoon days I was so seasick and dehydrated I just wanted to die and was afraid I wouldn't. I wound up in "sick bay," and after twelve hours of intravenous drip I'd recovered enough to ride the train from Bremerhaven to Hanau, Germany, where we spent the next three years with the 6th Battalion, 40th Field Artillery, attached to the 3rd Armored Division.

Suddenly I was being introduced to military life and the demands on an army wife, and at the same time getting used to living with a husband who left at ungodly hours for days or weeks of patrolling the border at the Fulda Gap between East and West Germany. The corridor would offer an easy route for the Warsaw Pact forces, undoubtedly led by Soviet forces, to reach Frankfurt and the Main River. Frankfurt was and is Germany's financial capital, and at that time was the heart of the United States forces in Western Germany.

All adult dependents were required to attend evacuation exercises every six months in preparation for such an invasion. We were instructed to keep all our important personal information—passports, medicines, C-Rations (known today as Meals Ready to Eat, or MREs), clothing, and the map of the evacuation routes out of Germany—in a safe but accessible place in order to be able to leave at a moment's notice. I was skeptical, even in my twenties, that a convoy of cars with "Allied Forces" license plates wouldn't cause a mass exodus of Germans and French, as it would've been apparent that we Americans had been given a heads-up. Most dependents attended the exercises simply because it was mandatory, and if you weren't there you'd better have been on leave or have had an airtight alibi, because your absence was going to be called to your military sponsor's attention. Fortunately, preparations for an evacuation were never activated, but there were many in attendance who paid no more attention to those instructions than today's airline passengers give to the evacuation procedures on every flight I've ever been on.

Those years as a second lieutenant's wife were eye opening. We were all young, new wives, new to the military, newly arrived from towns and cities all over the United States, and living huddled together in a foreign country. I found living in Germany an immediate challenge, but it didn't take me long to learn the driving customs and how to spend deutsch-marks (replaced today by the Euro). Those years gave me the opportunity of a lifetime, not only to live in Germany but also to travel extensively in Europe. Those were defining moments of my life, as the experience gave me confidence, strength, and above all determination. When you're twenty-two you might think you're well educated and worldly—how wonderfully naïve. It's comforting, however, to know that uninformed immaturity can be overcome through experience and, I'm sorry to say, age, giving one the ability to handle enormous obstacles.

> *Those were defining moments of my life, as the experience gave me confidence, strength, and above all determination.*

The battalion commander's spouse, "the colonel's wife," is titular head of all the wives in the battalion; in other words, head camp counselor. Each colonel's wife brings her own style to the position, and should you be a battalion wife one day, you'll find that some "heads" inspire emulation, while others make you feel you can't wait for the colonel to receive orders for a new assignment—in army lingo, to rotate. My first experience with the colonel's wife turned into a lifelong friendship, and we remained dear friends until her passing not long ago. I would have patterned myself after her had I been the colonel's wife, but when Roi was in a command position his tour was an unaccompanied one. Truthfully, I'm not sure I could have filled Joy's shoes. She was so gracious to the junior officers' wives, and able to rise above all the pettiness that went on among us. We reminisced about our memories of the 6/40 Field Artillery Battalion for forty-eight years, laughing about the funny stuff and boo-hooing over the sad while holding hands through it all. Ours was an irreplaceable, once-in-a-lifetime friendship.

Enough reminiscence! I hear "Please put your tray tables in the upright and locked position and prepare for landing," music to my ears. I had so many new experiences to face that my memories of the past would have to stay hidden for a while.

Upon landing I still had no idea who would pick me up, but knew that my kids would make sure I didn't have to cab it. I called Nicole, whose office was near the airport, but she was unable to get away, so Gary would be along soon. To tell the truth, I was relieved that I wouldn't have to face my husband, but at the same time I was sad. After forty-five years of marriage, following him from army post to army post, standing by for two deployments—one in Vietnam and one in South Korea—and his long-term injuries from Vietnam, it would have been appropriate for him to at least show me some respect and decency. He, however, chose to show his true colors as neither an officer nor a gentleman: as if brushing the dirt off his hands, he was just going to walk away.

I waited patiently at the curb of Reagan National Airport, having already retrieved my luggage. It was a wee bit warmer than Seattle; in fact, it was downright hot. My cell phone rang; it was my son, who said, "I'm at Dulles in front of Alaska Airlines and I don't see you."

I burst out laughing because I was now the star in my own comedy of errors. "I'm at Reagan, and it's not a problem, so please don't drive like a crazy person." Dulles isn't exactly around the corner, and at rush hour the traffic would move at a snail's pace. The last three days had been surreal, so a little quiet time off that plane and on a sun-drenched bench was relaxing. I'd been traveling about nine hours, and a drink would have been nice at that point, but the airport doesn't offer cocktail service at the curb, in fact the airport police hardly let people stop long enough to load or unload luggage, let alone passengers.

Fortunately, they weren't shooing me off. I sat there alone, on a bench I'd never sat on, at an airport where my husband had for years dropped me off or picked me up regularly. It was unbearable to think that I had dropped off Roi, someone I thought I knew, at Reagan National Airport only five months before to attend a reunion in Florida, and picked him up two days later; he looked just the same, but he had already changed in those forty-eight hours. My trust has made me feel vulnerable on many occasions. While your feelings might be right on, without solid proof you're stuck, while he runs around like he's covered in a nonstick coating.

Gary arrived, so I could shut down my memory, which was stuck in the past, for a little while at least. On the way home he said, "Mom, Nicole and I have kept something from you for many years, and now you need to know the truth."

> *On the way home he said, "Mom, Nicole and I have kept something from you for many years, and now you need to know the truth."*

When Nicole was home from college one weekend and was at the family computer, she found a series of sexually explicit emails between her dad and a woman named Lydia. She printed them out for her brother, and he made a surprise visit to his office. Roi denied the accusation, at which time Gary presented him with the emails. A short time after that visit, Roi told Gary that the affair was over. That affair at least!

Gary said, "I told Dad that if he didn't stop the affair immediately I would tell you." It breaks my heart to think that both of my kids protected me, but in so doing they protected their dad as well. I understand why they did it, and I love them more than I can express. I'll never understand how they put up a front for him, but we've always been a close-knit family and enjoyed being together for all the important family events, including several trips to Europe in the approximately ten years since Lydia. I never detected that they were uncomfortable around their dad, but since I hadn't known about that affair, I wasn't looking for signs of their disapproval of him. It disgusts me, just thinking about what they were masking in order to maintain a united front, while he was waiting for the next opportunity to engage in adultery and just be cleverer and more devious.

My husband has never taken responsibility for anything personal, as he never viewed his infidelity as his fault. In the early years of our marriage, if an argument cropped up it could never be settled, as he was committed to winning at any cost and did so by walking away. At first, I didn't pass up an argument; after all, I'm Irish. I learned over the years to not take the bait as quickly, and as I gained maturity, he had to work harder before I'd explode, but I have yet to hear an apology. Years into the marriage, I just sadly accepted that behavior.

My husband has never taken responsibility for anything personal, as he never viewed his infidelity as his fault. In the early years of our marriage, if an argument cropped up it could never be settled, as he was committed to winning at any cost and did so by walking away.

I believed him when he would tell me about an upcoming business trip or an evening office event, as questioning him was not an option. As I look back, however, I silently questioned almost everything. I had become an ostrich, so to speak, to avoid accusations and arguments because guilty people are masters of manipulation, which certainly describes how he pulled off this affair with his Bunny.

I was so happy to finally change out of flying clothes, sit down in the comfort and security of Nicole's home, and sip bourbon with my kids. I was going to need every ounce of their support, as I wanted them to be proud of the way I would approach the divorce. Also, I wanted to be proud of myself. What defines us is how well we rise after falling.

Chapter Two Take-Aways

- In whatever position you find yourself, bring your own style.
- Rise above pettiness.
- Surround yourself with the support of loved ones.
- "What defines us is how well we rise after falling."

3

Must Have Been Blind

I'd been in Virginia for two days, and Roi hadn't had the decency to get in touch. Evidently, just saying, "I'm divorcing you" with no explanation gave him the privilege of living at our mutual expense in our marital apartment. It was outrageous of him to assume he could use our apartment as a place to brazenly carry on an adulterous relationship. How very convenient for him that our daughter lived down the road from the apartment, and afforded me a place to hang out. The lease wouldn't be up for another six months, and believe me—a one bedroom was not going to be big enough for cohabitating, though several friends thought I should move back in just to make his life miserable. I thought it might be a hoot just to see what would happen, but then I was reminded that my bed, my pillow, and my down comforter had been slept on or under by my husband's mistress.

Nicole had been in Croatia on business for a few days, and her cat and I were home alone. It was about 9:30 p.m. when I heard knocking at the door. I was already in bed, so I didn't go to see who it was until the knocking became louder and more insistent. I went to the door and asked, "Who is it?" Roi said, "Open up." I told him no, but he kept yelling, "Open this door."

Afraid that the neighbors would be alerted, against my better judgment, I opened the door. I could see that he'd parked his car at the curb, headlights on and motor still running. Angry and scowling, the SOB thought he could say, "I'm going through with it" while standing on the stoop? Even though I was wearing a nightgown that he'd seen many times before, I suddenly felt naked and sleazy, but I wasn't about to stand in the doorway and let him get away with such evil treatment. I told him if he had something to say he'd come in and sit down and say it. He came in, sat, and repeated, "I'm going through with it," clearly unable to use the word "divorce." An overwhelming sadness came over me as I sat there, realizing that our marriage had just died without my having a say, much less having a clue about his illicit affairs.

"I'm going through with it."

With that, he got up and walked out. It was perfectly clear his whole life was being ruled by one organ—and that organ was not above his neck. A Judge Judy-ism. It was also clear that he wasn't about to do anything to save our marriage. It was so dark that I couldn't be absolutely sure whether Bunny was waiting in the car, but at that hour and given his insistence that I open the door, I'd put money on the fact that she was making sure he carried through with her ultimatum. His actions were those of a cunning, nasty bitch, and my instinct was that his mistress must be a woman with an agenda and fully capable of destroying her lover's family. Let's see: He lies to her about being a widower, and then she gives him an ultimatum, and I'm the one to suffer her ruthlessness? My only regret that night was that I hadn't dialed 911. It took me several months, but on one garbage pick-up day I donated that nightgown to the local landfill.

Until that night I had never considered my husband abusive, but abuse comes in many forms, and perhaps I had just become accustomed to his toxic behavior. He knew our daughter was out of the country and that I was alone, but he was under the spell of his mistress and willing to be vicious to a wife who had stood by him through all his military assignments: a year in Vietnam and another in South Korea, and numerous periods of civilian unemployment, not to mention his affairs and lies. It had been just ten days since he'd said, "I'm divorcing you," and that night he said, "I'm going through with it."

Just say *divorce*, for heaven's sake. Get used to saying *divorce*, and learn how to spell *divorce*, and above all, use it in a sentence, because you're going to be using that word for the rest of your life!

Just say divorce, for heaven's sake.
Get used to saying divorce, and learn
how to spell divorce, and above all, use it
in a sentence, because you're going to be
using that word for the rest of your life!

That was without a doubt one of the worst nights of my life, though I also vividly remembered another night when we were stationed in Germany. Roi came home with a manila envelope containing his orders for Vietnam. I was so frightened I thought I wouldn't live through the night, but here I am talking about another night forty-two years later.

Sleep was impossible; the moment I laid my head on the pillow and turned off the light I couldn't stop going over our life together. It was like a lousy movie playing over and over again. What in the heck had brought us to this breaking point? I thought that my husband and I were a team, whether it was family activities, a house project, or the love of travel, but maybe I'd been going through the last forty-five years in a daze.

We lived in Germany during the first three years of our marriage; then I lived with my parents during my husband's tour in Vietnam. That tour was cut short when he was injured and medevaced to Fort Lewis, Washington, where we lived for eight months while he underwent several surgeries to repair the head injuries he'd sustained. We then moved to Fort Sill, Oklahoma, for a year, and Gary was born there. With his new orders for a Reserve Officer's Training Corps (ROTC) assignment at the former Southwest Missouri State University, we moved to Springfield, Missouri. After eighteen months there, he volunteered for a thirteen-month deployment in South Korea. A minor detour on the way to Korea put us in the Wildcat Creek Apartments in

Manhattan, Kansas, outside of Fort Riley, for six months, where Gary turned two. Then, Kirkland, a suburb of Seattle, and near grandparents, became our stomping ground while we awaited the next move.

Chapter Three Take-Aways

- Get used to saying divorce, and learn how to spell divorce, and above all, use it in a sentence, because you're going to be using the word "divorce" for the rest of your life!

- Sleep is important. You might need support in this. Consider natural remedies first but don't hesitate to speak with your doctor. You will need rest and recovery throughout this journey.

- The mistress could very well be the puppet master in your story, as much as she was in mine.

The Phone Calls

With orders for the Military District of Washington, we moved to Northern Virginia and bought a home. It would be the first time in our married life that we could paint or plant to our hearts' content. If you wanted to find us on a Friday evening, we'd be at Hechinger's, a forerunner to Home Depot. Our three years in Springfield, Virginia, were spent playing with our new home and watching my son go from nursery school through first grade. I had a great job with an interior design showroom in Georgetown, D.C., and hated to leave it for parts unknown in the Midwest.

Our move to Fort Leavenworth, Kansas, was uneventful; when I was six months pregnant, however, the baby decided to arrive three months premature, putting us in a state of panic, but when our daughter was four months old and out of danger we were on the move back to Northern Virginia to our home and an assignment at the Pentagon.

We knew before we returned to Virginia that our house and yard had taken a beating. Our neighbors acted as forward observers, and their first impression was that the rental might not go well based on their observing the renters' four kids, one boyfriend, and one dog all exiting the car through the car windows. The lease clearly stated NO PETS, but said nothing about teenage boyfriends.

The poor condition of the house was overwhelming, and wasn't something that could be fixed in a week or a month. With our baby hardly weighing in at seven pounds and our son starting school in less than a month, not to mention 20,000 pounds of household goods piled up waiting to be unpacked, I was beside myself! Did I mention we had an Old English sheepdog?

As I hurried to fix breakfast, dress Nicole, and make sure Gary had his coat and tie on for the drive to school, the phone rang. In 1976 we didn't have caller ID, and I answered. The unidentified woman wanted to inform me that my husband was carrying on with a woman who worked at Fort McNair, Washington, D.C., just across the Potomac from the Pentagon.

OMG! Despite my heart racing, I managed to let the dog out, get both children into the car, and drive the nine miles to school in sheer panic. I spent the next six hours, until it was time to pick up my son, wandering from room to room, clutching my baby and desperately trying to remain calm while deciding whether to confront my husband. I decided against it, as he'd deny, deny, deny, and I wouldn't be able to keep it from my son, who was a third grader. Truthfully, I was scared to death! The one good thing was that I never received another call; however, it only took one such event to shatter my trust forever.

When we moved to Fort Leavenworth, I'd had to put my interior design career on hold, so upon our return to Virginia I came back on a part-time basis. By 1979 there was a gas crisis that had us waiting in long lines for hours for more expensive gas, making going to work and day care unaffordable. I loved the guys I worked for, but I also loved being a stay-at-home mom.

A year or so later, I found a receipt on Roi's dresser for a local motel on a night he was supposedly attending a class at Catholic University where he was enrolled in a master's-degree program. I remembered that he'd worn a suit that evening and had asked me to pick out a tie to go with it. I've never forgotten that strange request, as he'd never asked me to pick out a tie before that night, and since I bought them, they were all fabulous. I questioned him about the date on the receipt and his class and he sloughed it off, but I was not about to be deterred, so

I pointed out that Catholic University is located in D.C. and the motel was ten miles south of our house in Virginia, nearly thirty miles apart. Once again, he acted like I was delusional. He tilted his head to one side and gave me that *I don't know what you're talking about look*. By the way, I didn't need to call the motel to ask about their dress code, as I could tell by the address and the quality of the receipt that it was an older one-story, park-out-back motel.

It seemed like my husband was becoming less and less involved with the three of us, demonstrating an air of not giving a damn. With no concrete evidence that he was fooling around, I was not about to make our family life more uncertain, but my lack of trust sadly kept me pulling away from him. I, not he, was the one who suffered with distrust, so why would he want to waste time and money talking to a counselor about it?

In 1983 Roi received orders for Izmir, Turkey. The experience of living in western Turkey with a NATO assignment would have been exciting and challenging, though after weighing the pros and cons, and with twenty-three years in the army, the decision was made that my husband would retire. We stayed in Northern Virginia, as we had a nice home and our son was in a great school. With a Rolodex filled with contacts, Roi transitioned into civilian life with ease. The move was scarcely noticeable, with the exception of changing from a uniform to a suit—and a larger paycheck. There was still travel, late nights, and weekends away from home, though he did participate when it came to the kids' activities. Life moved along smoothly for eight years until 1991, when he was let go from his first civilian job and I experienced my first bout with unemployment.

In those eight years Gary had graduated from high school and Valley Forge College, and had been commissioned a second lieutenant in the army. On his return from basic artillery school at Fort Sill, Oklahoma, he became a full-time student at American University in Washington, D.C. Our daughter was a high school freshman.

We were financially secure for a time, but what exactly did unemployment mean? What was going to happen? How long would it be before my husband had a new position at the level he thought he deserved? I had never experienced financial insecurity; at the same time,

I knew I needed to stay positive to support him, as he was probably experiencing insecurity as well, but we never expressed our feelings of anxiety. I was afraid and frankly embarrassed by the situation so I didn't share my anxiety with anyone, not even my mom. That unemployment was the first of nine or ten in a period of seventeen years, and with each new position I became less and less confident that the new job would last until my husband's retirement. One of his periods of unemployment lasted about eighteen months, during which time Mom became critically ill, so I was flying back and forth trying to keep everything together on both coasts. In 1996, Nicole was a sophomore at Sweet Briar College in Virginia, and had just been accepted for her junior year in Paris. Within days, however, her dad was looking for another job, and the $38,000 tuition bill was due. I will always be grateful to the college for the scholarship they offered, as studying in Paris had been her dream from about the age of ten, creating an unquestionable Francophile.

Losing my mother was huge, and Hospice suggested counseling, which I accepted. My mother named me as executrix of her estate and co-trustee of my dad's trust, which came with the challenge of dealing with my brothers, who thought that they should be in complete control. Their argument was that they had more experience with everything, and I lived 3,000 miles from Seattle. If they weren't enough to deal with, my husband was again searching for a job. I pride myself for taking on a monumental task and completing it with dignity. Perhaps it was a precursor for handling an unexpected divorce while maintaining my self-respect.

Having spent seventeen years of anxiety and uncertainty over Roi's employment ups and downs, it was impossible to share my fears with friends, because I could hardly deal with his actions myself. I couldn't understand why someone who appeared to be giving his complete devotion to the company with the hours and days he spent working—often at the expense of his family—would be let go in a matter of months or maybe a year or two. I've never been able to understand his firing time after time. Being with friends afforded an escape from my real situation, and I just wanted to enjoy that time and their friendship.

In 1997, I inherited my childhood home in Seattle, and had the intention of our retiring in Washington State. By 2000 we'd finished renovating our Virginia home, and made the decision to sell it and renovate the Seattle home. My parents were married in 1936, and my grandmother gave them the 1925 home, in one of Seattle's historic neighborhoods, as a wedding gift. The home has always been our anchor regardless of the army assignments, and for our kids it's still a special place to go for Christmas and summer vacations. We enjoyed a spectacular view of Portage Bay, a lovely large cove surrounded by two yacht clubs and houseboats. Since they're no longer cheap student rentals, and were now priced well over $1 million, those houseboats have become known as floating homes. The University of Washington School of Aquatic and Fishery Science share the shoreline, adding to the ever-changing water activity. With the Cascade Mountains framing the majestic scene to the east, it's as soothing as sitting on a beach without leaving home, especially in the summertime, 3,000 miles from the Virginia humidity.

The renovation was complete in 2005 and we moved into the home—sort of. My husband reneged on his decision to fully retire, and for the next several years our lives turned into a long commute. We moved into the lower level of Nicole's townhouse with a few clothes, and that worked to some extent; however, Roi wasn't forced to make the decision to retire as planned. He and I then leased a garden apartment about a mile west of our old neighborhood and one mile closer to Seattle. At that time, I was completely clueless that he might have no plans to move to Seattle.

In the summer of 2007, just a year before he met Bunny, Roi's dream workshop was about to take shape. With me as general contractor on the project, my crew and I and tore down an old garage and rebuilt a beautiful new structure resembling a New England carriage house complete with cupola. The interior of the workshop would make any professional woodworker jump for joy, and let's face it—it would've been a great place for my husband to spend his retirement days. It even afforded him the ability to call the house via intercom if he needed something.

On the final day of the workshop project, I tripped and fell headfirst onto some concrete pavers, catching myself with my right hand just before my forehead made contact with them. My hand was slightly scraped, and I had a black-and-blue knot on my head, but nothing hurt and I gave no thought to the possibility of a broken wrist or a concussion. For Pete's sake, the new 12×18-foot structure needed at least one coat of paint before I headed to Virginia, and when my wrist didn't hurt and my mental acuity checked out, at least to my standards, I just kept going.

A few weeks later I was having my knee replacement checked when I casually mentioned to my orthopedist that my wrists didn't match. (I'm all about symmetry.) "Of course not," the surgeon said. "One's broken." In the two months since the fall, I had painted the new structure, flown to Virginia, and done a few hundred other things without any pain, but the two wrists just didn't match. Frankly, I don't recall whether they matched before the fall, but for some reason I thought they should.

The doctor said, "Follow me."

Whoa, follow you where," I asked?

"To the cast room"

"Oh, no! I'll come back tomorrow—I have to get home for Halloween."

He paid no attention to me and suggested I might like an orange cast as a Halloween costume. Had I been ten, I'd undoubtedly have left with a colored cast; instead I left with all but my fingertips encased in a white cast. We celebrated Christmas in Virginia while waiting for my wrist to heal on its own, but it didn't, and several days before Roi's April 2008 high school reunion in Florida, I had surgery on that wrist.

I had hoped that the new workshop would be the carrot that would entice my husband to Seattle, but it wasn't until June 2008, almost a year after the workshop took shape, that we installed the first sheet of pegboard so he could organize his collection of tools. While we unpacked enough tools for a small hardware store, he, obviously behind my back, was emailing to order enough flowers to fill Bunny's bathtub. He already had his eye on the next goal, and it had nothing to do with hammers, saws, and routers. He was short-tempered and not much fun to work with, but my years as an army wife had taught me to be flexible and I tried to ignore the unpleasant stuff. I admit, I wasn't always successful, but like really good bourbon, I've improved with age.

Little did I know when I drove him to the airport for his return to Virginia that it would be the last time I would hug him goodbye and say,

"I love you." He was going to be met by his mistress, who was going to take him home to his very classy uptown apartment.

Little did I know when I drove him
to the airport for his return to Virginia
that it would be the last time I would
hug him goodbye and say, "I love you."

I spent that awful night reliving years of good times and the gradual unraveling of a marriage. It was time to "hit the deck," as my dad said each morning to my brothers and me, and get on with a divorce.

Chapter Four Take-Aways

- It's time to "hit the deck," get on with a divorce.

- Reminiscing is all well and good, but don't dwell too long on what you thought to be good times. Put your battle gear on and prepare to ensure your rights are protected.

- Plan immediately as you have no idea how quickly your future ex is working with their attorney.

- The mistress will play a major role in your divorce story.

5

Screw Him!

My husband's cruel late-night attack simply to announce he was "going through with it" was uncalled for. The moment he said "I'm divorcing you," I knew I'd never put up with him again, but I spent over eight hours, and lost most of a night's sleep, wallowing in past history. Then, strength and resolve took over during the wee hours, and I instinctively knew that I needed to form a plan to screw Roi. Enough reminiscing already, get on with the new program! By daylight I was in full war mode. I knew that as a military wife I'd be entitled to benefits, but I had no idea what they were. Again, instinct was my guide. I called the office of the Judge Advocate General (JAG) at Fort Myer, Virginia, and by the grace of God was able to make an appointment for the next day.

> *By daylight I was in full war mode.*
> *I knew that as a military wife*
> *I'd be entitled to benefits, but I had*
> *no idea what they were.*

The JAG explained that since my husband and I had been married well over twenty years, I qualified for the 20/20/20 rule. Under federal law, all ex-spouses are entitled to full military benefits, including medical care and commissary and exchange privileges, provided they met the following qualifications: 1) They were married to the military service member for a period of twenty years or longer; 2) the military service member had twenty years of service; and 3) the twenty years of marriage overlapped the twenty years of service. That would give me 49 percent of his army retirement, lifelong Tricare (a health-care program of the Defense Department that provided civilian health benefits for US Armed Forces personnel, military retirees, and their dependents) and Post Exchange and commissary privileges. The one benefit I wouldn't be eligible for was burial in a national cemetery alongside my husband. I'd just bet that I could deal with that inconvenience! Those benefits are in no way controlled by the service member, and I was advised that as the ex-spouse I would be the one to file paperwork with the military to ensure a claim to the benefits when the divorce was final.

The colonel asked whether I knew how complicated the divorce would be, whether we had young children, whether we had financial assets, whether there'd been involvements with other women or other men, and whether we'd lived in other states or countries. By the time I left the JAG office, I was on information overload, but I also left with the names of two nearby law firms that were familiar with military benefits. I drove home as fast as the speed limit allowed, which on Interstate 395 South is at least 15 mph over what the sign says, convinced that I'd need a very good lawyer and that my wallet was about to shrink.

> *By the time I left the JAG office,*
> *I was on information overload.*

No one I knew had been through a divorce, so I couldn't call anyone for advice. Little did my cadre of friends, let alone I myself, know how much drama was about to take over our lives. I called both law firms, and was able to get an appointment with one for the next day. What a small world! The law firm was located next door to Nicole's office in Old Town Alexandria, Virginia. The other firm wasn't available for an interview for another week, and I was anxious to know what getting a divorce looked like.

Later that same day, my ex's therapist, whom our priest had recommended he meet with, contacted me. The priest told me sometime later that my husband had been contrite when he asked for guidance—quite possibly his only moment of contrition in the whole sordid experience, and certainly not a moment I had the pleasure of experiencing. I did agree to attend a counseling session with Roi, and as it turned out the therapist was also located in Alexandria, efficiently allowing me to kill two birds with one stone.

I was a nervous wreck as I walked into the counselor's office, but was also curious about what might come out of the session. My husband, "the new stranger," didn't disappoint me. He was seated in the lobby, his bulbous nose in a magazine, and when I said, "Hi," he grunted. I've never been treated so rudely and with such disrespect by anyone, anywhere, at any time. Evidently falling in love doesn't make one civilized. I sat there wondering, *How could I have thought he was cute, and how could I have ever loved him?*

In the three weeks since he'd told me "I'm divorcing you," I hadn't even begun to understand the meaning of those words. I didn't know why we were meeting with a therapist in the first place. Could he be having second thoughts and wondering how to make amends? If that was why we were there, I was not about to get over it and return to being the affable wife he had known.

We were ushered into a very small parlor with an assortment of chairs; Roi claimed the tallest one in the group, which put him in a position of authority and intimidation—and believe me, he used that tactic. I was surprised that his feet touched the ground, as he's not the tallest person in any room. I had an immediate flashback to Lily Tomlin as Edith Ann rocking back and forth in that gigantic rocking chair. I wanted to laugh, but instead began to feel like I was at a sideshow. It was apparent that the therapist and the furniture were contemporaries, so this was not going to be her first rodeo. She and I were stuck sitting in small, rickety, over-stuffed chairs, which were in desperate need of new springs and upholstery. From our position we had to look up to have eye contact with my husband, and I'd be damned if I was going to let him avoid eye contact with me. Sitting scrunched in the chair, my butt just barely above the rug, made me feel like I was about the size of a dust bunny. If I could've gotten out of that chair gracefully, I'd have left, as I could already tell the session was going to be a bust.

My husband wasn't there to work anything out; he had no intention of working it out, and he was determined to dominate the session. The therapist already knew how long we'd been married and that we had two children, so the blame game began. Roi came out of the starting gate running; he launched into his justification for adultery by accusing me of lacking sexual intimacy. I listened to him explain how he hadn't been sexually satisfied since our daughter's birth, thirty-two years before, so his frustrated need took him outside the marriage with affairs and Internet sites. He was bubbling over with happiness as he went on to describe meeting Bunny at the high school reunion. In a matter of forty-eight hours they were physically and emotionally connected. Then he said, "The last four months have been the happiest time of my life."

Each time he expressed how magical his new relationship was, the therapist would ask me, in that condescending "therapy speak" tone, "Wouldn't you like to comment?"

I'd known this guy for forty-eight years and it would be pointless to express how I felt. Frankly, I just wanted to barf—preferably all over him. I had an entirely different version of our life, and as I recall, sexual intimacy is a two-way street. I also recall him saying night after night, "I'll be there in a minute," or "My favorite program is about over," or how about "I need to finish this proposal (RFP) for tomorrow." Aware of how he'd respond, I just shook my head no; however, it was offensive to listen to him gloat about his newfound joy. He wanted out of the marriage as fast as possible, and I was an obstacle to his happiness. He used the therapy session to be as cruel as he could, blaming me for his philandering in an attempt to feel free of guilt and responsibility. Pushing me into a corner was a threatening move, and just because I wasn't responding to his ugly claims didn't mean he would not be in my crosshairs. The irony of that worthless therapy session is that Roi didn't pay the counselor; she sued him for nonpayment, and became one of the forty-nine people on the list of creditors in his federal bankruptcy case. Just get in line, lady!

I couldn't get out of her office fast enough; on my way out, however, she suggested that I would have an emotional crash eventually. She said, "You're angry, and you're using a sense of humor to cope and stay focused, so you might want to make another appointment."

Wow! Maybe next time I could sit in the big chair. After that fifty-five-minute session, I knew that I didn't have time for an emotional meltdown. I didn't make another appointment, and after meeting my husband in several legal situations, I can attest to the fact that the therapist did not fix him—he remained the same ugly, selfish, insensitive, narcissistic jackass he'd always been.

Within weeks of his announcing at the therapy session that he had used inappropriate Internet sites, I found a list of thirty websites he had email connections to. He used his kids' names as passwords, while his online handle was a configuration of busy executive. I had always been a trusting person, not inclined to suspect anyone, including Roi, and completely unaware of how he was using our family computer. Knowing him, even if I had discovered what he was doing online, he'd have cleverly dismissed my disgust and continued on down that path.

Chapter Five Take-Aways

- Educate yourself about your rights, especially your rights to military benefits.

- Make a game-plan, go speak with the Judge Advocate General (JAG) to learn more. They will give you your entitlements and then help you to identify law offices in your area who will be experienced in military divorce.

- Depending on how long you have been married, understand the 20/20/20 rule (in my case) or other aspects of the Uniformed Services Former Spouse Protection Act (USFSPA).

- Identify several family law attorneys to interview and make your appointments. Do your research on each attorney and select the one you feel will best represent you.

- Your initial consultation with a divorce attorney should be free.

- There are a number of sites when searching online that advertise military marriages, divorce, support, tips, benefits, inexpensive and quick divorces (no such thing!).

6
My New Best Friend

On the way to interview my prospective attorney, I went over the session I'd just experienced. My memory of our marriage was entirely different than Roi's was; it was clear that in order to embrace the excitement of his new life, he utterly dishonored the former one. How deplorable that he blamed his unhappiness on the premature birth of our daughter, the joy of whose life completed our (then) family of four.

When I arrived at the law firm I was introduced to Mr. Demian J. ("Dem") McGarry. I liked him immediately. I wasn't exactly interviewing for a young, tall, good-looking elegant lawyer with a nice personality and a great memory. I needed a pit bull, and I needed representation in Virginia. I knew nothing about family law, but I wanted to win, and Mr. McGarry was interviewing for the job. I was going to receive a quick tutorial about the ugly side of divorce, complete with new laws, rules, sentences, and paragraphs that don't make sense and words you've never had on a spelling test—unless, of course, you've been to law school. I caught a word that sounded familiar: "analogous." In my world of interior design, the word is defined as two colors adjacent to each other on the color wheel, but I was quite sure that *analogous* in law lingo would have nothing to do with pretty colors, except, of course, the color green. Mr. McGarry explained how the firm could represent me, and the costs involved in the process. He told me about the retainer, which is an amount of money the client puts into a trust with the law firm to cover expenses—known as billable hours—that the firm incurs from month to month. It's a standard bookkeeping procedure for most legal services, but *billable* was one of those words I'd never had on a spelling test, and neither did I ever have to use it in a sentence.

> ### *I needed a pit bull, and I needed representation in Virginia.*

I now understand the meaning of *billable hours,* and I can use the term in a sentence. At that point I was trying to remember if I had taken my blood pressure medicine that morning. Spending large sums of money makes me very uncomfortable; my goal, however, was to live the same comfortable life that I had been always blessed with. The thought of becoming a bag lady just because my husband couldn't keep his pants zipped was repugnant.

I was desperately trying to stay focused on what Mr. McGarry was explaining, but in all honesty I was thinking, *OMG, I had planned to use my investments for travel and retirement with my husband, but due to his adulterous behavior, I'm about to spend those funds on a divorce from him.*

While trying to wrap my mind around parting company with my money, I said, "I personally don't need a divorce." Fortunately, Mr. McGarry didn't roll on the floor in hysterical laughter, as I was embarrassed to be there in the first place. Law school must surely offer a course in "How Not to Laugh at Virgin Clients Who Say Inane Things." He kindly explained something called "divorce from bed and board" (a legal process by which a married couple can formalize a de facto separation while remaining legally married), but of course that wasn't an option and we never discussed it again. I left with a brochure, and was told that if I decided to become a client, I should just call for an appointment.

I walked next door to Nicole's office to share the ABCs of divorce with her, also mentioning that I had just told Mr. McGarry that I didn't need a divorce. We couldn't stop laughing, just picturing him thinking, *What a nutcase, she really thinks she doesn't need a divorce?* Maybe he even went so far as to wonder if they wanted me as a client.

The other law firm kept rescheduling, which helped me make the decision to become a client of Mr. McGarry's. I felt a rapport with him and the approximately 200-year-old townhouse where his firm is located. I am in no way suggesting that a firm should be selected on the height of the ceilings or the width of the crown molding or museum-quality art or for that matter red walls and a fireplace in the conference room, but the whole ambiance spoke to me as an interior designer, and it was going to make going through this life-changing experience more comfortable.

I was utterly clueless about how to move forward with a divorce, but I have to believe some higher power had led me first to the Judge Advocate General's office and then to Mr. McGarry. The divorce process is a long-term commitment, something else I had no idea about; however, after becoming a client and parting with my retainer fee, I began to call Mr. McGarry by his first name, Dem.

> *I was utterly clueless about how to move*
> *forward with a divorce, but I have to*
> *believe some higher power had led me*
> *first to the Judge Advocate General's office*
> *and then to Mr. McGarry.*

My team, as I refer to them, included Dem's assistants. They were always available, even if Dem was in court, and they knew how to pass on a Mayday message, as there were many. They made going to the firm for appointments a pleasure, almost like being a guest in someone's gracious home. A divorce is a team effort, and to have people who can make a deplorable situation easier to wade through is a gift to a client. There's nothing funny about divorce, but when the opposition is made up of stars like Bunny, Roi, and his attorney performing comic relief, laughter comes easily.

The first line of defense was to provide Dem and my team with every aspect of my forty-five years of married life, which included charge accounts, bank accounts, mortgages, my husband's military discharge papers, and on and on. It's truly amazing just how much paper it takes to establish who you are, where you've been, and what you're worth. I was determined to leave no stone unturned, and it took hours to search files for that information. As an overly organized person, I'm a filing failure, simply because I hate to file. Let's hope I've learned that not filing wastes time.

Chapter Six Take-Aways

◉ Your divorce attorney will become your new best friend, you will want to make sure that you are comfortable with him/her, and that you trust this person to look after your best interest. Make sure that you can easily communicate with them.

◉ The ABCs of getting a divorce:
  • how the firm could represent me.
  • the costs involved in the process.
  • Retainer = an amount of money the client puts into a trust with the law firm to cover expenses.
  • Billable hours = a standard bookkeeping procedure for most legal services, expenses the law firm incur monthly to handle your case.

◉ Keep extremely detailed notes on a daily basis.

◉ Gather all personal information you can imagine, make several copies.

◉ File the copies away for easy access; you never know when you'll need to produce a copy.

1
Know Your Enemy

Simply telling me that he was divorcing me seemed to have absolved my husband of any need to behave respectably toward me or his kids. He had moved on, and wasn't about to waste his time with regrets or explanations. Nonetheless, he and I had a marriage contract, which was going to complicate both of our lives. My own battle plan required me to become a private investigator, and my first target was our apartment. I resented the marital money that was being used to pay the rent on what had become his "bachelor pad."

Fortunately, the apartment was only a short drive from our daughter's home. The manager told me that my husband and his paramour had tried to have my name removed from the lease; however, they could not do so without my permission. Something tells me she'd like to have moved in, even with some of the decorative touches removed, as her agenda called for dominating the battlefield. My name on the lease gave me legal access to the apartment and the mailbox where all our mail was delivered, such as credit card accounts, car leases, mortgages, and utility bills.

In addition to the mailbox, the kitchen garbage can also became a treasure trove of evidence of adulterous activity. For instance, Monday's garbage told me what they had done or where they'd gone over the weekend and our credit card bills gave proof of the extravagant spending.

*In addition to the mailbox,
the kitchen garbage can also
became a treasure trove of
evidence of adulterous activity.*

My son repeatedly encouraged me to find the second gun because he was worried that, if the affair ended, my husband might take his life, though I thought it would be too cowardly of him to do so. I searched the apartment and found the pistol among the underwear in a dresser drawer. I carefully removed it and checked to make sure it wasn't loaded, then placed it in a brightly colored gift bag and put the bag on the floor behind the driver's seat in my car. I didn't exceed the speed limit on the way to Gary's office that day. I've never been stopped for speeding, though my car just automatically goes five miles over the posted speed, but with a gun onboard and no concealed weapon license I wasn't about to risk ruining my record. As I approached my son's office I called and told him I'd be out front of his building in about four minutes with the gift. He told me to drive to the back of the building, where he'd meet me. We then drove to the outskirts of the parking lot, where he parks so no one will scratch his car, and completed the handoff. For a novice, my first clandestine act went well—and what a rush it gave me!

My investigative work became a full-time job, and I scheduled visits to our apartment each day to coincide with the mail delivery. We were, after all, still married and owned everything jointly, and for forty-five years I had paid all the bills. I wasn't about to have my credit rating taken down a rat-hole, as I knew my husband wouldn't pay the credit cards, car leases, or mortgage on time, if ever. When there were bills, I'd take them home, steam open the envelopes, make copies, then iron the envelopes closed and put them back in the box the next day. I've since heard that putting a sealed envelope in the freezer works, though now that I'm out of the private investigative business I can't verify the technique.

By keeping track of our bank withdrawals and credit card charges I was able to make monthly spreadsheets to "follow the money," as my husband spent amazing amounts of marital money and charged up a storm with utter disregard for anything but his own pleasure. I continued to pay off the credit cards he was using to wine and dine his lover, along with his car lease, as they were still joint accounts and I still had access to our joint money. Talk about crazy! He may have earned the bulk of the money, but I was a banker's daughter, and from an early age my siblings and I were taught to save. I could stretch one dollar into two, so we always had money for extras, even on a military salary, and when it came time for private schools, colleges, and travel, we could, within reason, write the checks.

The credit card expenditures were a glowing indicator of what was really going on. My husband had been generous with the three of us, but showering his lover with expensive dinners three or four times a week, destination weekends, sex toys by the dozen, and enough "flowers by wire" to strip the tulip fields of Holland was an indication of what she was all about. I didn't need to be a rocket scientist to recognize a gold digger.

> *I didn't need to be a rocket scientist*
> *to recognize a gold digger.*

In reading about divorce I learned that the person who wants the divorce often tries to hide joint assets, which makes retrieving those assets almost impossible. I decided it was vital to track the expenditures as long as possible. My husband eventually changed the addresses on all our mail, including the joint accounts, or placed them online, making it impossible for me to have access and monitor them without his online passwords, even with my name on the accounts. I tried to have mail readdressed to me, but the post office said no, so I had to notify each business of the name and address change. He then redirected his army retirement pay and his civilian paycheck to a joint account with Bunny, which gave her access to all of our marital money over a year before we were officially divorced. Judge Judy often asks, "Do you see the word 'stupid' on my forehead?" and then she asks the plaintiff, "Why would you commingle monies if you're not married?"

I'm sure my husband would say he did it because he was in love, and I can almost guarantee that she encouraged him to open the account with her to protect him from me. A little pillow talk and my name vanished from the accounts, replaced by hers. As my husband said so many times over the years, "I make the money and it's mine." He had moved on, and they were spending it faster than he could earn it.

It was critical to open a new checking account and apply for a credit card in my name. I had had a checking account of my own and had put 50 percent of our joint checking account monies into it, but it took me longer to realize that I needed my own credit card. As a member of the United States Automobile Association (USAA) and the spouse of a military member, I was able to apply for a credit card and auto insurance as soon as I got my act together.

One of my dear friends and I had been meeting every Thursday at a local coffee shop conveniently located just around the corner from the apartment. One afternoon I stopped at the apartment as usual for the mail, and found a plain wrapped package sitting at the front door. I wrestled with the option of leaving it there or taking it with me; the "taking" option won out. My friend and I had caught up on the latest news, finished our coffee, and were headed to our cars when I mentioned the package. I was driving Nicole's SUV, as my car was in Seattle, and as I was about to climb into the driver's seat my friend insisted we get into the back seat with its tinted windows. It crossed my mind that two mature women sitting in the rear of an SUV parked at the neighborhood coffee shop really looked like we were doing something illegal, but we both climbed in. Our instincts told us that something in a plain white bag might be something we wouldn't want anyone to see us looking at. In her Scottish brogue, my friend asked, "What do you think it is?" Those little words sent us into a round of laughter, and we hadn't even opened the package. She kept saying, "Hurry up and open it," but with tears of laughter clouding my vision I couldn't get it open any faster. As I pulled out three cellophane bags, she asked, "What are those?"

> *Our instincts told us that*
> *something in a plain white bag*
> *might be something we wouldn't*
> *want anyone to see us looking at.*

"I don't know," I said. "You read what it says."

You'd have thought we were innocent teenagers just out of the convent; in fact, we were acting like teens hiding in the back seat of an SUV and laughing hysterically. The picture on each package caused us more laughter. Just thinking about the nipple jewelry made us "Ooh," and we didn't know that pearl rings could be worn in so many places. The third package had a rubber finger cover. I'd seen such things at the stationery store, but they didn't come in a plain-wrapped package.

To this day we're convinced that the funniest part of the whole caper was that as mature, well-traveled women we'd never seen stuff like that up close and personal. Barbara Bush often used the phrase "Learning never ends," and my friend and I can attest to that. I eventually turned the toy exhibit over to Dem and my team. We shared a moment of laughter, but my hunch is that as younger people in the divorce business they probably had knowledge of those things. The stuff added to my growing collection of evidence, and should it be needed during questioning of my husband under oath, we had the goods.

Recently I received an email from Dem with the subject line "Guess what we found?" The firm was packing up former clients' records for archiving, perhaps hidden deep in a cave somewhere, and my loot included that plain white package. To reveal what Dem told me they'd done with it might violate attorney-client privilege.

Chapter Seven Take-Aways

- ◉ Keep detailed notes.

- ◉ Realize that your spouse may not only walk away physically and emotionally from your marriage, but your children as well.

- ◉ You need to become your own personal investigator and advocate throughout the entire process.

- ◉ Be battle-ready.

- ◉ Unfortunately, there is an interloper directing your former husband.

Inspector Clouseau and Me

On a visit to our apartment, I felt mixed emotions when I spotted a new army dress-blue uniform in the closet. My husband had been retired from the army for twenty-two years, and his original dress uniform hung there until my son, then a member of the Virginia Army National Guard, needed one. Our son was carrying on the family military tradition, so it was then handed down to him. Overwhelming sadness and anger poured over me when I saw that my husband had purchased shoulder boards with the rank of colonel instead of lieutenant colonel. It was all I could do to stop myself from tearing them off the blouse and throwing them in the garbage; instead, I unloaded the closet and carefully put everything on the bed except the uniform. It was my one and only fall from the high road, and it gave the amorous duo a real reason to call me a bitch over dinner.

My husband's army career had been honorable, and I thought it pathetic that he needed to impress by pretending a rank above the one he'd rightfully attained. I knew that he and his lover were going to a formal affair, and was pretty sure it was the Association of the United States Army (AUSA) in Washington, D.C. The event always takes place in the fall, and I hoped they wouldn't run into friends of ours. Within weeks a photo of the formal evening appeared on the Internet. My husband wore his new uniform, and Bunny was in a strapless floor-length gown with a tiara in her hair. As far as I know, she doesn't have royal roots, though I must remember they'd met at the high school reunion. When I showed Dem the photo, he assured me he would stipulate, in the divorce agreement, that I would be awarded a tiara.

My son kept encouraging me to hire a professional private investigator because frankly, "What the hell was going on?" I didn't know where to start looking for an investigator, so where else but the *Yellow Pages?* In the old days, say 2008, *Yellow Pages* referred to a phone directory of businesses organized by category. A rather thick book printed on yellow paper, it took up lots of space; the Internet was, of course, so much more efficient.

I read several ads, made a choice, and within minutes had an investigator on the case. Armed with the information I'd given him, he knew where my husband worked, his physical description, where our apartment was located, and the make, model, and license number of his vehicle. It was a Friday evening, and the inspector showed up at our apartment at approximately the time I told him my husband would arrive home. The inspector called to inform me that Roi had arrived at the apartment, changed clothes, and was leaving, and he would follow him. I was going to get my money's worth that night. How bizarre! I was actually spending money that I didn't really want to, for someone to investigate my husband and his mistress. The threat of divorce had me doing things that would never have crossed my mind, though if the information I was gathering guaranteed a foolproof case, I was willing to do just about anything.

My Inspector Clouseau was taping as he followed Roi's car to Bunny's apartment. A week later I met the investigator at his office to view the tape, and sure enough, Bunny lived within a few miles of our apartment. After driving around the circular drive, Roi got out of the car and waited to open the door for her as she exited the building. I hadn't experienced such chivalry in years, but there's a perfectly simple explanation: out with the old and in with the new. Their destination was a well-known restaurant in Washington, D.C., that overlooked the Potomac at Haines Point—a restaurant that we hadn't been to together in years. The couple was seated near a window, and though I'll never know exactly how, Inspector

Clouseau caught the entire meal on tape. I'd seen the photo of them at the formal, but it was my first opportunity to see how Bunny really looked and acted. I've read that men don't necessarily choose a woman taller, thinner, or more attractive than their wife, and trust me: she and I have nothing in common. Once again, she was wearing a strapless dress, and it was obvious she was very proud of her assets and didn't mind sharing them with Roi, the other patrons, and the private investigator. They sat side by side at the table instead of across from one another, and by the time the tape ended, I'd seen every sip of wine, every bite of hard roll, and every kiss.

During one of my investigative visits to the apartment, I decided to take a pair of lamps from the master bedroom, but not before finding replacements. Based on our joint credit card, I knew that the lovebirds had gone to IKEA for something to hang over the bed after my daughter had taken the tulip wreath. They replaced it with a three-by-five-foot picture of a red rose. Shopping for my design clients could often be challenging, but that red rose was the inspiration for my shopping trip.

I was looking for two inexpensive lamps with bordello flair, hopefully red shades with fringe, and voila—I found them at the local Goodwill store. The saleslady complimented me on my purchase, nearly causing me to burst out laughing. Such a deal! For sixty bucks I had two lamps and thirty minutes of therapy. I took those beauties directly to the apartment and swapped them for the ones I wanted; the new pair pulled the room together as only an interior designer could!

Several weeks after Clouseau's first success, he caught the loving couple at the Dulles Hyatt Hotel, attending a formal dinner dance sponsored by a group of aging military brats. If your mom or dad was career military, you could call yourself a military brat, and once one, always one. The hotel was within thirty minutes of each of their apartments, but spending the night at a hotel is so much more fun than going home after an evening out. Those raging hormones create the most amazing cocktail, making even seniors feel like they're eighteen-year-olds in love (or lust), floating on cloud nine and wanting to never get off. It's a wonderful high, and when we first experience being in love we think it will last forever, but inevitably that feeling changes, like watching a beautiful cloud that changes shape and then vanishes.

I'll never know how Inspector Clouseau managed to spend the night in a room directly across the hall from Roi's, which allowed him to record their comings and goings through the peephole in the door. One recorded moment was of the pair in the hall outside their room, with Roi adjusting the necklace that I knew—based on the credit card statement—he'd purchased earlier in the day at the Fort Belvoir Post Exchange. That statement also showed three charges of fourteen dollars, so I checked with the Hyatt and was told they were for movie rentals. Something tells me they weren't Westerns. Despite the cost of Inspector Clouseau's services and hotel stay, I had seen enough to prove adultery in court should it become necessary.

During that time, I had also continued my own investigation, and that was when I found phone numbers at our apartment for a Washington State law firm that Roi had retained. Washington is a common-property state were the only grounds for the dissolution of a marriage is that the marriage is irretrievably broken. The state holds no one accountable for the divorce, which is therefore considered "no fault," and the property and debts acquired during the marriage are split equally. In my book, adultery and abandonment is a deal breaker, so I wasn't about to accept some namby-pamby fluff like irreconcilable differences or irretrievably broken and then split the baby. The filing requirements for a divorce are that one of the parties is a resident, or married to a resident, of the state. It may have been hard to prove that we were not residents of Washington, as we were both on the title to the home, but neither of us claimed Washington State as home on either our tax returns or voter registration, and as far as I was concerned the divorce was not going to happen in Washington.

Finding those phone numbers was timely, as it appeared that Roi was trying for an end run. I recalled his having mentioned at our counseling session that he and Bunny had already made plans to be married on April 10, 2009, the one-year anniversary of their meeting. With the wedding date only four months off, Roi had found that a Washington State divorce could be finalized in a matter of months, and the speed with which he was moving scared the hell out of me. I immediately called Dem with the new information, as I felt it was time to set something legal in motion to keep the divorce in Virginia. If not for their ages you might think Bunny was pregnant, but let's face it, she's a clever, conniving woman, and in her world everything is fair game, even a married man who's risking everything to achieve a change without changing himself.

I feel fortunate to be able to enjoy the beauty of Seattle and the history of Virginia, but I didn't have time to think about the beauty or the history of a state; instead I needed to know which state had the most equitable divorce laws. In Virginia, the residency requirements for a divorce state that both parties cohabitate in the city or county in which the defendant lives, or at the option of the plaintiff, the defendant qualifies for fault such as adultery. Virginia is one of the few states that recognize adultery, and Roi was unarguably an adulterer.

> *Virginia is one of the few states*
> *that recognize adultery, and Roi*
> *was unarguably an adulterer.*

Fearing that he might already have filed for divorce in Washington State, I gave him my Christmas gift in the form of a complaint for divorce on December 22, 2008.

Merry Christmas and HO, HO, HO!

Chapter Eight Take-Aways

- ◉ Do your best to monitor everything and keep on top of your spouse's actions. Hire a private investigator if it will be of help.

- ◉ Tips on hiring: you may not get to keep the information you "paid" for.

- ◉ If you reside in multiple states, understand the state divorce laws before selecting which state to file in.

9

The Search for Tumbleweed

Christmas is such a magical time of year, and as a couple we started our Christmas tradition in Hanau, Germany. Around the first of December, Germany becomes the land of Christmas enchantment, with festive *Christkindlemarkts* popping up all over the country to offer fabulous ornaments and traditional German decorations. It's nearly impossible not to want one of everything, but fortunately I had two more Christmases in country. Our Christmas trees are loaded with German ornaments that Roi and I purchased years ago, as well as many new ornaments that the family has traveled specifically to Germany to buy. The kids and I are quite possibly addicted to purchasing ornaments, as we believe there's no such thing as too many.

I flew to Seattle right after Thanksgiving 2008 to decorate the house for Christmas, determined to celebrate the holiday in the same festive way we always had. I was absolutely determined to not let Roi's disregard for his family, especially his kids, alter our traditions.

When we remodeled the Seattle house, I had several very important details that I wanted to incorporate into the remodel. I wanted the front of the house to be symmetrical, and I wanted to increase the height of a portion of the living room ceiling to accommodate my twelve-foot faux

Christmas tree. Pete, my contractor, told me that when the crew looked over the plans stipulating a ceiling height change for a Christmas tree, they burst out in laughter and a version of "You must be kidding."

We had a wonderful Christmas, though different, as it was our first without Roi. Snow had turned Seattle into a perfect wonderland, a rare white Christmas, as snow in abundance is uncommon in the city, though about fifty miles from my driveway I could be skiing (if I still skied), on the rugged slopes of the Cascade Mountains. Prior to the divorce, our plan was to leave my car in Seattle and share Roi's car in Virginia; however, I was going to need my own car. It was January 2009 and the car was 3,000 miles from Northern Virginia, a five-day drive in good conditions. Roi and I had driven cross-country many times, but never during the winter months, so it was going to be an experience.

Dear friends offered to fly to Seattle and share the drive east, as they'd never driven across the country. We packed my SUV for the trip, but getting out of Seattle and over the mountains was our first challenge: Interstate 90 East was closed due to heavy snow. Even though we didn't have an estimated time of arrival in Virginia, it was disappointing, on our very first day, to fall behind what I'd anticipated our time on the road would be. We were able to make it as far as eastern Washington, thinking we could make better time the next day, though snow preceded us to the outskirts of Washington, D.C., and we never picked up time.

As balls of tumbleweed flew across the highway in front of the car, I shared with my Scottish friend, who had never seen tumbleweed, how my mother had collected several tumbleweed balls in eastern Washington, sprayed them white, and strung little white Christmas lights around the weeds to use them as a Christmas decoration. Tumbleweed grows in dry, hot, barren areas in the West. The aboveground part of the plant disengages from the root during the winter, tumbling into a ball-like shape that blows around in the wind. Suddenly our mission was to spot the perfect large balls of tumbleweed and take some home with us. It's a very prickly, brittle, unattractive weed, but it has decorative potential. Some might question our good sense, but my friend's husband, a lawyer and a gentleman, did not—besides, he'd had years of experience with our projects.

Our drive took us south through eastern Oregon, then into Idaho and farther southeast to Utah. Snow and tumbleweed followed us, but in all those miles we hadn't seen the perfect specimen. When we reached Wyoming we ran into heavy wind-blown snow that often shuts down the highway; fortunately for us it was still open, and we made it safely to Sydney, Nebraska, and a restaurant that I'd been to on other cross-country drives. When we parked, we found that the wind had blown so many tumbleweeds in front of the entrance that we had to push the stuff out of our way just to get inside. Talk about hitting the tumbleweed jackpot! It's always windy out on the plains, but that day it was bitter cold as well, so we spent little time selecting pieces of it, and even less time shoving then into the SUV.

The remainder of the trip was uneventful, though the weather caused very dangerous driving conditions. I delivered my dear friends safely to their home and then drove on to my daughter's. As the adventure came to an end, I couldn't stop thinking how very blessed I was to have friends who would rescue me at an unimaginable time in my life, friends I will forever be grateful for.

Talk about timing! I could hardly believe that I'd driven 3,000 miles leaving just enough time to park, get in out of the cold, and call my daughter's office. As I stood at the glass storm door, complaining about having to go back out in the freezing weather to unload my SUV, I noticed a car go by. As it started a second pass around the circle, I realized it was Roi. Perhaps he had to go around twice: like the proverb states, "Trust but verify," to make sure it was my SUV. I'll admit it was hardly recognizable, having obviously been through a snowstorm or two. Surprise, surprise!

I hadn't noticed there was a package near the door, and naturally, Roi didn't approach the house with me standing there. The next day he emailed, asking to have the box put on the porch so he could come by and pick it up. He had assumed (and you know what that means) that no one would be home and he wouldn't be caught. The man just exudes *chutzpa!*

What a deceitful person! Why couldn't he have it sent to our apartment? He didn't know I was on my way to resume my daily visits to the apartment and the mailbox, but let me guess: he was hiding something by using his daughter's address. He assumed correctly that "little Nancy" as he'd begun to call our daughter, was at work, but "big Nancy" was standing in the doorway watching him. Wives, and I was to remain the wife for another year, have a way of screwing up the best of intentions. Since I didn't recognize the address on the box, was it possible that in the four months since he'd announced that he was divorcing me, the old job had divorced him?

The billing records from Roi's attorney indicated that he had called the firm within minutes of seeing me; they also showed that the Washington State law firm was still involved, and that Roi and his attorney were trying to change the complaint for divorce from Fairfax County, Virginia, to Washington State. They were counting on my being in Seattle, waiting to be screwed over in a common-property state, but I must have missed the memo ordering me to stay put. I hadn't met Roi's attorney at that point, but Google provided all I needed to know about him and his firm. He'd graduated from a military college in Virginia and been commissioned as an army officer, and he advertised his military experience to clients with military backgrounds.

As artillerymen they were undoubtedly positioning their large-caliber weapons for a fight, but they might have miscalculated the army wife who'd be damned if he was going to get away with a ladylike divorce. I too, could muster my troops!

Roi's plan was to walk away with as much money from our home as he could, after all, lust and a new wife was going to be expensive. He didn't care whether I'd have to buy him out or have to sell the home, just as long as he had money. In his state of hormone-induced amnesia, he must have forgotten that selling the house would mean paying off a mortgage, realtor's fees, taxes, and my inherited value. Under that scenario, neither one of us would be a winner, but I had the most to lose.

Roi's plan was to walk away with as much money from our home as he could, after all, lust and a new wife was going to be expensive.

Then again, when he said, "I'm divorcing you," it was because he'd been caught. I don't doubt for a minute that he thought he was in love and was doing things he hadn't done in years, all because he was caught up in his lie about being a widower. So, within three months after the high school reunion, he and his new love were engaged. Fooling around hadn't left Roi much time to consider all the ramifications of divorce; I can surmise, however, that after saying, "I'm divorcing you," he didn't have the courage to slow the process down and leave on a civilized note.

Roi was raised in a family with a long history of military service, starting with his grandfather and father, both West Pointers. "Duty, honor, and country" was ingrained from birth. Roi was a member of the Anglican Episcopal Church and active as an altar boy. He was an Eagle Scout, and he served twenty-three years in the United States Army, which included a tour in Vietnam. With the knowledge that military doctors have today, he might have been diagnosed with posttraumatic stress disorder (PTSD), but PTSD wasn't officially recognized as a mental health disorder until 1980, thirteen years after the severe head injuries he'd sustained. With a diagnosis of PTSD and treatment, Roi might perhaps have dealt with his life in a more positive way. On the other hand, he's lied all of his life to everyone, himself included.

Chapter Nine Take-Aways

- Try to celebrate holidays as normally as possible. Your spouse made the choice to leave. Find the joy in small things.

- You will learn who your friends and closest supporters are throughout this journey. They will be there for you when you least expect it, e.g., to drive across the country through snow storms.

- Be prepared for the unexpected.

- The process is time-consuming and emotionally draining but you must remain always vigilant.

- Always take the high road, even though that is easier said than done at times.

Keeping Up With the Jeffersons

It had been a week since my return to Virginia, and the bitterly cold weather continued. I wanted the snow and road mess cleaned off my car, but the local carwashes were closed due to freezing temperatures. My dealership told me to run it by, and though they couldn't guarantee showroom perfect, they'd do their best to remove the grime so as to protect the finish. When I returned, an email awaited me: it said that Roi would be moving to a new apartment, so if there was anything I hadn't already taken, I should come and remove it before February 9, 2009.

Wow! West Springfield Terrace Apartments was going to allow him to break a lease with my name legally on it without officially notifying me? Maybe he used the "she's dead" story, but breaking the lease would affect me and my wallet, as Roi was using 3,000 marital dollars for the early release. Rather than prolong the whole sordid incident, I made an arrangement with him to help me carry my Pilates equipment to the car, which we did in complete silence. There was nothing to say, and he wouldn't have answered my questions about breaking the lease. As I was getting into the car, however, he said, "I'm a little surprised," a phrase his mother had used often to indicate that you had done something unexpected or unacceptable. I should have ignored him, but instead I asked, "Surprised about what?"

"Oh, just surprised," he replied.

Having been married to him had prepared me for all kinds of innuendos, so I knew exactly what he was getting at. I had driven to Virginia and foiled his Washington State caper; how thoughtless of me—don't you just hate it when that happens?

My daughter and I couldn't pass up the opportunity to watch the lovers moving out of our soon-to-be former apartment. On our way to the event we stopped at Starbucks and bought coffee and a little something sweet, as we had no idea how long we'd be waiting for the move to begin. We arrived early in her SUV, as it was less flashy than mine, and were fortunate enough to park near a large bush that shielded the car but afforded a direct view of the apartment. Forty-five minutes later our coffee was nearly gone, the goodies were history, and we'd decided that neither of us had the patience to apply for a professional private investigator's license. Up to that point our "stakeout" had been beyond boring, but wait, a moving truck pulled up and Roi and Bunny jumped out—our mission was finally getting off the ground. Then the Goodwill truck arrived, and Nicole said, "I'm out of here." She leapt out of the car and headed toward the action. I determined it would be best for me to stay put, as she was more than capable of handling the situation. Still, it would have been satisfying to sit on the garden wall and watch what Bunny was giving away, while making them both uncomfortable with my presence.

Instead, I loaded the SUV with stuff I hadn't gathered earlier. On her third trip to the car she told me that Bunny was hiding in a closet. Nicole, a former camp counselor, had spent several summers being challenged by nine-year-old girls, so she had no trouble identifying Bunny's immature behavior. "Bunny, come out of the closet," she shouted, whereupon Bunny opened the closet door a crack and said, "I won't come out because I'm afraid you'll yell at me." Nicole told Bunny that she wasn't worth it.

Does Bunny actually think she should be treated like someone special? My daughter then told me that she had accused Bunny of helping break up her family, and Bunny said, "No, I didn't. Your dad and mom did that." Nicole said, "Well, you didn't help the situation."

Knowing Roi's haughty attitude as I do, I'm sure he was angry to think that his daughter would treat them so disrespectfully.

When I thought the car was loaded, she brought a small TV that we'd given her to take to college, and some picture frames that were being given to Goodwill. She told me that when she informed the men loading the truck that her dad was divorcing her mom and that the woman with him was his mistress, they gladly handed over the frames. As the Goodwill truck drove by the car, they tooted their horn and gave my daughter the thumbs-up sign—evidently just another interesting day on the job. For the two of us, it was another day in the divorce process.

Shortly after the move I was informed of Roi's new address. Sure enough, they were moving into Bunny's apartment building. She had lived on the first floor, but the new address indicated that they were moving into an apartment on the sixteenth floor. It reminded me of *The Jeffersons,* an old TV series whose theme song was "Well we're moving on up, to the east side. To a deluxe apartment in the sky. Movin' on up, to the east side. We finally got a piece of the pie." There was just one minor problem with that picture: Roi was still married to me and was using marital "pie" money to pay for shacking up.

Good grief, Bunny's expertise in moving her agenda along suggests that she might have had prior experience. They met in April 2008 and were engaged in July 2008 and I was dumped in September 2008, and then they moved in together in February 2009. It's amazing how much can be achieved in just ten short months, though if I believed Bunny's deposition of October 2009 and how they'd met, it was more like the lyrics to Renee Olstead's song *What a Difference a Day Makes* - "*just twenty-four little hours.*"

Moving to the sixteenth floor was costly; the rent was more than that of our apartment, but according to the credit charges the apartment needed some decorative touches by a well-known national fabric store. It was such a shame to see the red bordello lamps board the Goodwill truck to be recycled right back where they came from; I'm not positive they had much of a future. I didn't see the big red rose picture go into the truck, so it must have been moving to the apartment in the sky. As the saying goes, "There's no accounting for taste," or "To each his own."

While I watched two joint checking accounts dwindle, my attorney told me to take a portion of the balance for myself, so I did. One of those banks was local, and when I tried to cash a check I was told that the account had been deactivated. I learned that day that if your husband has done something behind your back you might as well be gracious at the bank, say, "Thank you," and walk out. I sat in my car in front of that bank and used every four-letter word I could think of that would describe the embarrassment I felt when the teller looked at me like *I* was the bitch. I could not change an address, close an account, or break a lease even if it was owned jointly, but Roi could and did. He even tried to have his name removed from the lease on my car. He was advised that he could have his name taken off the lease, but the Ford Motor Company would still hold him responsible if I failed to pay. He most certainly was receiving advice about changing addresses, closing accounts, breaking leases, and heaven knows what else Bunny was manipulating, but of course, she had his best interests in mind and was only trying to help him move forward and break all ties with his past so he could be happy again. The feeling of betrayal is incredible: it's like being robbed, though there was no time to wallow in my feelings, because I didn't know what might happen next.

> *I could not change an address,*
> *close an account, or break a lease*
> *even if it was owned jointly,*
> *but Roi could and did.*

It didn't take long for the next shoe to drop. It happened right after I'd eaten something delicious containing almonds, and I knew I'd better take advantage of all the dental benefits that I was still entitled to as Roi's wife. The crown was going to cost about $1,000, so I went ahead and made an appointment. Walking out of the office without a care in the world, believing that I still had dental benefits, I vowed to never again eat almonds. About three days later my dental office called to verify the number on my insurance policy, as the one the office had on file had been refused. Just hang on, give me a minute to check my member number, and, of course, it matched the one they had on file.

Something was not credible or ethical, and I knew my husband had screwed me again.

Sure enough, when the office checked with Human Resources (HR) at Roi's *new* employment, she was informed that I was not listed as spouse; rather, Roi had listed a partner, evidently a selection from column A on the list of coverage choices. My attorney also made a call to the HR department, and I'd bet he wasn't the first attorney to call an HR department seeking employee verification. He was told that Roi claimed he was a widower when he filled out the paperwork for his new employer. Naturally, the company wouldn't hire a lying, dishonest, immoral, cheating manipulator to work for them.

Money was becoming an even more serious issue for me, and I needed to address it immediately—like yesterday if possible, so Dem filed a motion for *pendente lite* relief with the court. *Pendente lite* is a Latin term meaning "while the litigation is pending." It's used for court orders or legal agreements entered into while a matter such as a divorce is in its early stages. Our joint account had been depleted primarily due to the fact that Roi's army retirement, his civilian pay, and his disability checks were now going to a joint account with Bunny. The *pendente lite* order would require Roi to maintain a current level of dental insurance and stop using marital monies, and it would specify an award of attorneys' fees. Roi's attorney and his client received the invitation to attend a court hearing scheduled for May 22, 2009, just one day before our forty-sixth wedding anniversary.

Money was becoming an even more serious issue for me, and I needed to address it immediately— like yesterday if possible.

Oh, my gosh! Dem and I were going to be joined in court by a representative from my dental office, as my husband's law firm had subpoenaed that office. What an odd turn of events in the divorce process, but at that point, I was still a clueless divorce virgin. It was after all going to be my first foray into a courtroom. I suppose that if the receptionist could verify that I was no longer covered by Roi's dental insurance then I could understand why she was there. A letter from Roi's attorney to the dental office attempted to explain the need for a subpoena as follows. The attorney's letter states:

> The information required from the receptionist was so technical that he could not obtain it by deposition, although the reasons for that are rather technical and, frankly, they would be beside the point because I had offered Ms. Stevens through her counsel, Mr. McGarry, the opportunity for our respective clients to stipulate what I expected the dental office representative would be and, in so doing, spare my having to enforce a subpoena requiring her appearance at the hearing. Mr. McGarry would not enter into any such stipulation though, although he did eventually stipulate to other, unrelated things from another witness.

What in the heck did the opposing counsel say? That letter was the biggest pile of expensive manure, and I do recognize a pile of manure when I see one, having spent lots of time around a barn. I've not only mucked stalls but have piled the muck myself. That letter, copied verbatim, would be just the first example of what would become a regular encounter with that attorney, so welcome to the seamier side of divorce.

The two attorneys, my husband, the dental receptionist, and I were all present and accounted for at court. I don't know if comedy follows all divorces, but we've had our share, and when we've least expected it. Roi's lawyer, supposedly a reputable Northern Virginia attorney, mistook the receptionist for a lawyer representing the dental office, even though he himself had subpoenaed the receptionist. Does anyone know who's on first? It must be nearly impossible to defend someone with narcissistic traits while he clings to his indignation—"How dare you do this to me!"

The attorneys went before the judge while the defendant, the rep, and I remained seated and within a blink of an eye the judge approved the motions in the *pendente lite* order. It required Roi to maintain dental insurance for me until the divorce was final and to pay attorney fees. Sounds good, but not so fast! Roi never honored even one of those court-ordered motions. He hadn't made those rules and he didn't intend to comply with them regardless of the judge's order. Perhaps a moral person would take such a judgment seriously, but a seriously flawed little man like Roi would just give it the finger.

My dental office consists of the doctor, a hygienist, and a receptionist. When the dog-and-pony show at the court was over, my dentist wrote a letter to Roi's attorney requesting that his client pay for the receptionist's time and travel to the court, as they were the ones issuing the subpoena. Naturally, Roi's attorney didn't see eye to eye with her, and claimed that his client owed her nothing; she should instead be requesting the money from me, as I was the one who needed the dental work. Now the three of them were involved in a patient's divorce because of the patient's husband generously giving his mistress his wife's dental insurance benefit. One more thing Bunny could cross off her list of must-haves.

This is a good time to mention that there are attorneys for everyone, every personality, and every dishonest client. There are attorneys who represent adulterers and murderers, and do everything in their power to vindicate those jackasses who roam with impunity. In my opinion, Roi and his attorney were a perfect match. In his attempt to defend a lying, cheating, dishonest jackass, that lawyer looked like one himself. I wish to apologize to all the four-legged jackasses that roam among the tumbleweed, minding their own business, while their two-legged cousins roam around destroying the lives of individuals and families.

> *This is a good time to mention that there are attorneys for everyone, every personality, and every dishonest client.*

Chapter Ten Take-Aways

- Realize that while the lease may be in both of your names, the other party can break that lease without your signature and at your expense (assuming all monies are joint).

- Be prepared for nasty treatment, your future ex-spouse may easily remove you from certain benefits such as dental insurance, in my case.

- Prepare for your first day in court. Your attorney should spend time with you reviewing what to expect, questions you might have to answer, and how the day may go.

- Try to be emotionally and physically prepared for your first day in court. I prepared by ensuring I looked and felt my best which meant getting my hair done, nails done and dressing smartly. Be yourself.

- Keep notes and dates. Use a calendar as a quick way to refresh your memory as there will be too many details to remember.

- Remember, he wants to please his mistress and not you.

The Cold Call

The hazy, hot, and humid season in Northern Virginia was oppressive, and Seattle's cool summer weather beckoned. It was June 2009, and I'd been away for several months, remembering the ever-present responsibilities of owning a home. As an army wife with two unaccompanied tours to draw strength from, I knew I could handle just about anything—with the exception of six perfectly synchronized screeching smoke detectors at 3:00 a.m. OMG, what a noise! Fortunately, I had my wits about me and remembered to turn off the security alarm before heading to the electrical panel, lest a siren have added to the noise. With silence restored, I decided to deal with the problem in the morning and went back to bed.

> *As an army wife with two*
> *unaccompanied tours to draw*
> *strength from, I knew I could handle*
> *just about anything.*

One of my brothers suggested I remove the batteries from each detector and vacuum inside, just in case spiders had made a nest. Since I'm not six feet tall, it required a ladder, a vacuum, and new batteries, and it might have been nice to have that brother show up to hold something. Just days before, I'd found sugar ants on my kitchen counter, and that same brother said, "Nancy you can't live alone." And he's suggesting what? So much for brothers!

It was quiet on the western front for about five days; on the sixth night, however, the security panel began to beep and lights flashed that shouldn't have. I told myself, "You can handle this, stay calm." Truthfully, I really didn't want to have to handle that one. The next morning, I called the alarm company, and they offered me a choice: I could pay them ninety dollars for a service call and battery replacement or I could buy a battery and install it myself—"But you won't find that battery in the drugstore." I hate to admit it, but I had no idea that the security system had a battery, like the smoke detectors. I thought the fact that they were all hardwired meant I'd never have to deal with batteries. Even though I thought I knew every square inch of my house, the battery box was no longer where it had been for years prior to the remodel. I searched everywhere for it. The only place I hadn't checked was the attic, and you might know that it was one of those rare 85-degree days in Seattle, which made the attic very toasty. I removed the old battery, found a store that sold specialty batteries, and reinstalled the new one, saving the ninety dollars. Oh, for the days I lived in military quarters and could call the post engineer to come and fix something.

On my daughter's first night in Seattle, several weeks later, the unwelcoming screech of the smoke detectors awoke us shortly after midnight. What is it about electrical devices acting up after dark? This time tripping the electrical panel didn't shut them up, so once again up the ladder to remove the "new" batteries. Eventually, we identified and disconnected the culprit, but the fear of it happening again still haunts me.

Nicole and I also unloaded Roi's "man cave," which was located in the basement, placing all of his belongings in what he called his workshop. We meticulously took photos to document the condition of those items so there could be no accusations of damage. We were approaching a year since the divorce threat, and the case was slowly moving toward the nitty-gritty of the lawsuit, at which time he would find out that his stuff had been moved. I anticipated that he would find some reason to create an issue.

Her stay was over and I was visiting with my neighbors, talking about nothing terribly important, when Peter said, in his Czech accent, "I borrowed one of your husband's tools and they are all shit." It was like a verbal slap, and I reacted by saying, "Peter, you've gone over the top!" With that I ran home. It was the first time in almost a year that I had shed any tears, and I allowed myself to cry all afternoon. While Peter's comment was something I'd normally laugh at, I just hadn't had time to cry in the past ten months; I was obviously overwrought, and on top of that, for some demented reason, I felt protective of Roi's damn tool collection.

> *It was the first time in almost a year*
> *that I had shed any tears, and I*
> *allowed myself to cry all afternoon.*

The next day Peter arrived with a lovely dinner, and I hope I expressed that my meltdown really had nothing to do with his comment about the tools but everything to do with my need to let go of pent-up feelings. The meal was just fabulous, and no wonder, as Peter and his wife, Susan, owned Seattle's number-one restaurant. Tragically, Peter has passed away, but I'll always be thankful to him for giving me a reason to cry. Those tools, and the fact that Roi had inherited some of them from his father, had been in our home for years, and represented another step in letting go of the past.

When the divorce process began, I was determined to do everything in my power to try not to become depressed or stressed—those emotions are unhealthy and could cause me serious health problems, and Roi just wasn't worth it. Unfortunately, I've experienced a whole list of emotions that at times were frankly out of my control. So much for well-meaning people who talk about reducing stress!

It was late summer of 2009, and my time in Seattle was again winding down. It had been a good summer despite my new status, and of course my daughter's stay was a highlight. I did have some spare time, though, which allowed my curiosity to escape its bounds. I recalled the day I was at the private investigator's office reviewing the video of the dinner date in Washington, D.C., and the weekend event at the Hyatt Hotel in

November 2008. The PI was surfing the Web for information about Bunny, on a site that the average person doesn't have access to, and suddenly said, "Look at this—she has three Social Security numbers and several outstanding judgments against her." He then said, "This woman has the profile of a predator."

I left his office convinced that Bunny was giving Roi advice that was about to make the divorce more difficult! I gave that information to Dem, and later that day signed up with an online identity theft protection company because so much of our joint mail had gone to their apartment, including copies of our joint federal income tax records, complete with my Social Security number.

My computer-savvy kids had found Bunny on Facebook, where she'd posted a photo of herself, a daughter, and two grandchildren along with her personal information. She gave her last name, which turned out to be her maiden name; her bio indicated that she had moved to Northern Virginia from a western state, and she gave her status as "engaged." She'd had the chutzpah to put *engaged* in her Facebook biography even after finding out that I wasn't dead?!

I couldn't keep myself from doing a Google search, and truth be told, I didn't try. I knew from the private investigator and Facebook exactly which state to begin my search in for anyone who might have known Bunny. Knowing which large western state had judgments against her, I started my search in its biggest city, simply because it's the biggest city in that state.

I typed in her name and it repeatedly popped up with a list of other people she was connected to, including her two other daughters and two husbands. She'd been one busy gal, wreaking havoc on others! Now I had more names to work with, and cross-referencing those names narrowed my search, which turned out to be lots of fun. As I Googled, I found information about Bunny's connection to American High School, the same school Roi had attended years before. As military dependents, they were qualified to join an organization for military brats who attended American overseas schools.

When I started the search, I was looking for answers to what type of woman would stay with a married man after he had lied about his wife being dead and abandoned his children? Over several days I narrowed the search and then wrestled with what to do with the information. Being a novice in the investigative business and an utter failure at lying, I needed a plan. If I were going to make calls, who would I say I was? What was I going to ask? And what should I tell them if they were family? I wrote a script so I wouldn't screw up, as I was incredibly nervous about calling random people I'd found online. It might be something a kook would do, but it's definitely not my *modus operandi*; facing a divorce, however, turned me into Joe Friday, and I was looking for facts everywhere.

I mustered my courage and, script in hand, made the first call. I told the woman who answered that I was doing research for a law firm in Virginia in an attempt to locate a Bunny. She gasped and said, "The family's been trying to locate her, as we didn't know where she had moved or what she was doing."

The woman turned out to be the daughter in-law of Bunny's second husband, and the excitement in her voice gave me a ray of hope that I could possibly find out who Bunny really was. She asked me if her father in-law could call me, and I said I'd be very happy to speak with him, as I was eager to hear about his experience with Bunny.

Thank goodness I'd had a stroke of beginner's luck, as I didn't want to make any more cold calls. I had no idea whether Bunny had left the family on a positive note, and I surely didn't want the daughter in-law to report that I was a nutcase, as the soon-to-be ex-wife of her father in-law's ex-wife's lover. It does sound a wee bit convoluted, and it took me a moment to get the succession of characters straight. I hadn't told anyone that I was planning to make a cold call to people who might know Bunny, as I didn't want to be discouraged, but I was excited to share my beginner's luck with my daughter. When I told her about the script, which in the end I hadn't used, she burst out laughing, and to tell the truth, I found it hilarious myself. I was taught that lying was never permitted, though facing divorce changes all the polite rules.

I was taught that lying was never permitted, though facing divorce changes all the polite rules.

Several weeks passed, and I thought that perhaps the family had decided they weren't really that curious about Bunny's whereabouts or what I knew about her. One boring Sunday morning the phone rang, displaying the area code I'd been waiting for. I was excited and a little apprehensive, but above all I wanted the opportunity to speak to Bunny's second ex-husband. Goodness, where to begin? He sounded like such a nice man, and of course he was interested in my situation and eager to share the details of his marriage to Bunny. We set a time for a conference call with his daughter, and as crazy as it sounds, I felt a bond with this man who had experienced the wrath of the same woman.

Bunny's former husband and his daughter listened to my story about Bunny and Roi, and then they explained their relationship with her. There were so many parallels between our stories, though they were through with her, while I was just getting a taste of what was to come. When her former husband met Bunny she was a single mother of three young daughters. They were married for ten years, and the divorce had taken three years to settle, so when we spoke, they had been officially divorced for only three years and he was still paying alimony.

He told me that when he'd married Bunny, he was heavily invested in real estate for his retirement years and to pass on to his children, but she had persuaded him to liquidate that property. His daughter said, "We tried to discourage Dad from selling, but Bunny had a way of being very persuasive." The proceeds from the sales became joint property. His daughter went on to tell me that Bunny was able to keep her dad isolated from the family, and particularly from her. Almost in unison they said, "Her must-haves are travel, jewelry, and money."

Right from the start of Roi's affair, he cut off any contact with his kids, was even a no-show at a birthday they'd planned for him. Let me see: Bunny moves in on a family, breaks it up, and then keeps her new guy separated from his family—just what the second ex-husband's family told me she'd done to their family.

The longer that marriage went on, the more desperate the daughter became to do something about the way Bunny was treating the family and especially her dad. He was in his early seventies and completely unaware of what was going on behind his back. His daughter tried to tell him that his wife was telling people that she didn't love him but he didn't believe it. She didn't share how she was able to record Bunny's phone calls to her mother, but the tapes proved what Bunny was telling others. The tape was inadmissible as evidence in the divorce proceedings because permission hadn't been given to tape Bunny's conversations, but it was enough evidence for her former husband to file for divorce and give his family vindication. When the litigation ended three years later, Bunny walked away with half a million dollars and fourteen years of alimony. Over those fourteen years, at $2,000 a month, her ex-husband would be on the hook for $336,000. In order for him to meet the obligations of the divorce, he was forced to sell the last home he'd shared with her plus pay additional cash. I had met Bunny's former husband only through a phone conversation, but my blood just boiled thinking about what Bunny was capable of, and I rightly feared for the outcome of my divorce.

I talked with that family from time to time and was able to give them information they needed to legally discontinue the alimony payments. Bunny's divorce decree included the standard language, which stated that alimony would no longer be paid to her if she were living with someone in a relationship analogous to marriage or with the intention of marrying. Bunny and Roi had moved into an apartment together in anticipation of marriage, and had by then lived together for five months. I shared the address and phone numbers with them and the fact that the apartment was listed under Roi's name. At $2,000 in monthly alimony, Bunny had already pocketed a nice little sum. Obviously, I shared that information with my attorney, and gave him permission to share some documents we'd obtained, so as to help the former husband prove Bunny's new living arrangement, which could nullify his alimony obligation.

Chapter Eleven Take-Aways

- You may need to maintain your home as it is your biggest investment, and may be your biggest financial pay-off in the end.

- This is an emotional roller coaster, yet you need to be strong for yourself and those around you. Yet, allow yourself those moments for a really good cry even when you least expect it.

◉ Look into services that will protect your identity, such as an online identify theft protection company.

◉ Never let your guard down, and continue the investigative process.

◉ Sometimes you'll have to be a little creative and crafty to obtain information.

"The Pillow"

Meanwhile, back in Virginia, a spending marathon was taking place. The credit card charges were on fire, and had begun to look like what Bunny's former husband and his daughter had described. In the first six months of the affair, Roi's spending records were those of a high roller: a trip to Disney World to introduce Mommy's new fiancé to her three daughters and five grandchildren for a mere $7,000—of which $1,500 was for Disney merchandise—was a drop in the bucket.

We'd never taken our kids to Disney World, but I'd have drawn the line at one set of Mickey Mouse ears each; of course, I wouldn't have been trying to make nice to kids I wanted approval from.

By July 2009 hormone-induced amnesia was once again skewing Roi's behavior—or maybe he had just plumb lost his mind. On one Saturday at Tysons Corner, Virginia, they bought a $21,000 necklace and then purchased airline tickets for two to Paris and Vienna for late August. Spending like that would have had me headed to the nearest pub, but evidently it made them hungry, so they stopped for lunch, then realized the car was dirty, so a quick run through the carwash, and $25,000 later they must have called it a day. With a month before going to Europe, however, they had some spare time to fill, so they took wedding dance lessons, purchased a wedding gown, bought two custom-made suits for Roi, new eyeglasses, and heaven knows what else. All these expenditures took place months before the divorce proceedings had even begun. Squandering thirty-seven thousand dollars in two months is exhausting. A relaxing weekend getaway to Virginia Beach, Virginia would be a perfect place to stroll along the sandy beach and forget spending.

> *By July 2009 hormone-induced amnesia was once again skewing Roi's behavior—or maybe he had just plumb lost his mind.*

Lust is expensive!

Roi's deposition was scheduled for October 2009. A deposition is the out-of-court testimony in a civil or criminal proceeding taken before trial, usually in an attorney's office. I offered to help Dem's legal assistant collate the data I'd given them, which amounted to a years' worth of paper piled high on the conference table. Every page needed to be examined and filed according to topic, just in case it was needed for verification, perhaps in court. By that date we'd been legally married for forty-six years, those years now reduced to a mound of paper littering a conference table.

> *A deposition is the out-of-court testimony in a civil or criminal proceeding taken before trial, usually in an attorney's office.*

The day of Roi's deposition and that of his mistress would be long and stressful, and I needed an outfit that would bolster my self-confidence. It's not every day you meet a stranger who called himself your husband for forty-six years and the woman who was replacing you. I bought a beautiful navy blue double-breasted suit and scheduled an appointment at Salon Ilo in the Georgetown neighborhood of Washington, D.C., where I've been a client for over thirty-six years, along with others you've seen regularly on the national news. Clients, myself included, rarely walk out saying, "I can't wait till it grows out."

One of the owners is my special hair guru, therapist, clothing consultant, and good listener. Nicole occasionally works at the salon on Saturdays, so we both have hair that looks like a million bucks. When I told my hairdresser about my new suit, he suggested that I should have some hunky pearls that would complement the buttons on the suit. I mentioned his suggestion to my daughter. She said she had a Junior League function at Neiman Marcus in a few days, so I asked her to look for a strand of faux pearls. She came home with the perfect set of hunky rich-bitch pearls.

It had been nine months since I'd seen Roi at our apartment on that moving-out day in February. I'd only seen Bunny on the private investigator's tapes or photos of her on Facebook. I hoped she wouldn't arrive for the deposition in a strapless dress or a skimpy animal-print camisole without a bra. Her second ex-husband and I had spoken several times prior to the deposition, so while I didn't know what Bunny looked like in person, I had the sympathy of her former family. I arrived early at the law firm on the day of the deposition so I could calm down, get my blood pressure under control, and review the strategy for the day. There is absolutely no way to prepare yourself to face a scowling husband of forty-six years across a five-foot-wide conference table and not be disgusted with his disrespectful and dishonest actions. He wasn't even capable of showing me respect as the mother of his children.

There is absolutely no way to prepare yourself to face a scowling husband of forty-six years across a five-foot-wide conference table and not be disgusted with his disrespectful and dishonest actions.

From the moment Roi and his attorney—two of the cockiest, most arrogant little men I've ever had the displeasure of being in the same room with—entered the conference room until they left hours later, the tension was enough to power the whole electrical grid of Old Town Alexandria.

Placed under oath, Roi promised to answer truthfully. There's that pesky word "truth." He swore to tell the whole truth and nothing but the truth. I could be wrong, but I don't recall that stretching the whole truth was an option.

Roi hung his head, unable to make eye contact with Dem or me. That bolstered my confidence, and I sucked in my stomach and tried to increase my five-foot-two body to at least five-three. The questions weren't difficult, but when truth is a foreign word it makes answering every question more difficult. Roi remembered the day he and Bunny met, but he couldn't remember the first time they'd had sex. How disappointing for her had she heard that answer. Many questions dealt with Roi's credit card charges and his joint checking accounts with Bunny. Roi was very uncomfortable responding to the questions about the exorbitant amounts of money the two of them had spent in just seventeen months. When he was asked about a $21,000 purchase at a jewelry store, just months before the deposition, he couldn't remember that purchase until Dem jogged his memory with a copy of the credit card statement.

Roi admitted to having had just one other affair, but he said, "No one knew about it." Well, hello! His kids knew about at least one of his affairs. You see, affairs aren't so much about with whom you lie but to whom you lie. Nearer the time of this particular affair, Gary had gone to Roi's office with the evidence he had found, but it was not until the time of the Deposition that Roi was faced with having to attest to the truth of it. Depositions are serious somber meetings that seek the truth, the whole truth, and nothing but the truth, though that can be embarrassing, especially when the questioning turns to sex or sexual paraphernalia. Some of Roi's answers were hilarious. He was asked to explain the weekly charges for adult outfitters such as Frederick's of Hollywood and a laundry list of others. "Do you know if those catalogs sell men's clothing?" He responded, "They provide a great deal of clothing, from shoes to lingerie."

The last question along sexual lines was about an eighty-dollar charge from one of those outfitters and was designed to embarrass Roi. My attorney handed him a copy of the credit card statement; after reviewing the charge Roi said, "It was for a pillow." At that moment his attorney said, "Off the record," turned to Roi, and said, "I'm sorry, a pillow?" Roi responded with a quivering yes. I'll never know whether he gave his attorney an explanation for the pillow, but it must have been one mighty fine pillow.

The questioning turned to Roi's health, and he described a list of ailments he was being treated for. In forty-five years, outside of his wounds from Vietnam, which were severe and lifelong, he'd never had so much as a yearly checkup. Surprisingly, he said, "I'm seeking psychiatric therapy for my needle phobia."

No foolin', this guy needs a checkup from the neck up! He testified that a portion of his tour of duty in Vietnam was not public knowledge. His response to the question about being held by an enemy combatant was yes, and that the needle phobia might have been a result of that experience. He turned to his attorney and said, "I want to talk to you privately, as I want you to stop that line of questioning."

> *He testified that a portion of his tour of duty in Vietnam was not public knowledge.*

Dem said, no, and the next question was, "In what country were you held?" Roi whispered, "In Laos." Again, he attempted to have his attorney end the questions about Laos. Again, Dem said no. His last question was "Were you tortured?"

Roi mumbled, "I can't remember."

Throughout the deposition I had tried to pull off a poker face, but what I had just heard him say turned that expression into one that clearly said, "Oh, you have got to be kidding!" It was such an egregious claim that I shook my head, silently screaming, "You're a blatant liar."

Dem looked at me and perhaps realized my head was about to fall off, so he said, "No further questions," and everyone scattered, maybe for a breath of fresh air.

During the break I walked next door to my daughter's office to vent. The first words out of my mouth were "You're not going to believe what he said. He claimed he was in Laos during his tour in Vietnam, was held captive by the enemy, and was possibly tortured." I knew both of my kids would be filled with disgust. Neither of them is ever at a loss for words, but when your dad is deliberately telling out-and-out lies about being a captive in a country he was never in, it's breathtaking. Roi might have brought up Laos during his deposition as a preemptive move, in case Bunny might perpetuate the lie while under oath.

My son was convinced that his dad had told the incredible lie about Laos when he met Bunny. The two claimed under oath that their first meeting was at the high school reunion, though they might have met online. Roi had to have had some information that caused him to invent his Laos story and share it with Bunny at their first meeting. It's a claim one could not make up on the fly. I don't know how many times he told that lie prior to the deposition, but it didn't end there; unbeknownst to the three of us, we would hear that story again in greater detail. But it would take almost two years.

The deposition was exhausting, and had yet to face my replacement, so I replenished my makeup, checked my hair, and returned to the law firm ready to sit across the conference table from my husband's fiancée— another bizarre moment!

Bunny was the perfect example of a woman Roi would look up and down with such an air of superiority that I'd be embarrassed by his offensive manner. At least appropriately dressed for fall weather, Bunny took her seat across from me at the table, a permanent smirk plastered on her face, and never broke eye contact with me. The questions she was asked all pertained to where and how they'd met, what they'd been doing since meeting, and sex. Bunny took delight in relating how they'd met at the American High School reunion in Orlando. She stressed that she was twelve years younger and hadn't yet been a student at the school when Roi was in attendance. Unlike Roi, Bunny knew that they'd had sex within twenty-four hours of first meeting. She continued to gloat with each answer, explaining that she lived in Alexandria, Virginia, about nine miles from his apartment, and that they'd had sex within days of his return from Orlando. Her smug demeanor continued, while Roi sat at the far end of the table, his head hung in his hands and as near to being under the table as he could get it. Dem asked a final question: "Did Roi tell you that his wife was dead?"

"Yes," she answered. "He told me she'd been dead for five and a half years."

It was obvious that she wanted my soon-to-be ex-husband, but I was the problem she had to eliminate; my marriage and family meant nothing to her. On her way out of the conference room, Bunny had the temerity to want to shake my hand, mistakenly believing that she had scored a "gotcha" moment. She is the epitome of a mistress who comes in and takes over a life, ruins others, and thinks nothing of it. Oscar Wilde said, "A man who marries his mistress leaves a vacancy in that position."

The day was emotionally draining and I was exhausted, the questioning having gone on for six long hours. My head was swimming in details, and frankly I couldn't remember the questions asked or the replies, though I felt secure in my car heading home, and would try to sort out the Laos mess another day.

For years Roi accused me of remembering our first argument. Also, I vividly remember my Vietnam experience. We were stationed in Germany from 1963–1966 and detached from the United States and "the war." We received our news from the American Forces Network (AFN), the only English-language radio station, and the depth of coverage was limited. Vietnam was not one of our vocabulary words until, little by little, our friends received orders to Vietnam, creating fear among us. When Roi came home with his orders to Vietnam, I was terrified and hardly able to point to that country on a map. Now I would need to go chronologically through his tour there to see if I could separate truth from fantasy.

Roi left for Vietnam in late June 1966. He commanded A Battery, 1st Battalion, 21st Field Artillery of the 1st Air Cavalry Division in Pleiku, near the central highlands from July 1966 to March 1967, when he was severely injured. The long journey from hospital to hospital began in the Philippines, then to a hospital on the Japanese island of Okinawa, the hospital at Travis Air Force Base in California, and finally to Madigan Hospital at Fort Lewis, Washington, in May 1967. He underwent two cranial surgeries during our eight months there. In March 1968 we moved to Fort Sill, Oklahoma. In the forty-two years since Roi's return from Vietnam, he rarely talked about his experience other than occasionally showing his slides taken at different landing zones (LZs), including a photo of Landing Zone Bird where he was wounded. I don't know whether he exchanged war stories with other military officers, but I do know he was never ever in Laos. Truth has a way of surfacing.

Chapter Twelve Take-Aways

- Be prepared for your future ex-spouse to continue spending like there's no tomorrow even though it's still marital monies.
- Be prepared for the outrageous to be said during the deposition.
- You won't be allowed to speak during the deposition unless you are being deposed and under oath. You have to remain quiet even though you would love more than anything to shout from the rooftops.

The Deposition

I was not looking forward to being interrogated on my day in the hot seat. I was positive Roi's attorney would make it as uncomfortable as he could. After all, he was retained to defend the betrayer, who'd made the decision to have an affair on his own; it was, however, the attorney's job to somehow make it look like my fault. Evidently my deposition wouldn't be enough, so my kids were subpoenaed to testify, causing Gary to be outraged to think that their dad had drawn them into the middle of a divorce they had nothing to do with.

> *Evidently my deposition wouldn't be enough, so my kids were subpoenaed to testify, causing Gary to be outraged to think that their dad had drawn them into the middle of a divorce they had nothing to do with.*

That caused my kids to hire an attorney, and don't think for one moment that the cost of their testimony was going to be on their dad's next invoice. Fortunately, one of my son's fellow Virginia Army National Guardsmen is a family law attorney and was able to represent them. Nonetheless, it was an expense that neither of them should have had to incur. The divorce was not about Roi's being a good father; it was about sexual infidelity and abandonment. He *had* been a good father, past tense, and that was now the only quality he could honestly claim. Just in case the divorce went to court, the kids would be recorded saying that he had been a father who supported them and provided the money that allowed them to live a charmed life.

I know I planned an outfit as exciting as the one I'd purchased for Roi's deposition, but I can't remember too many of the details up to the time I was sworn in. I was chosen to go first—after all, I might say something the kids could refute. After being sworn in I was asked if I was on any medication that would cause me to be incapable of answering questions. I said no. Who would say, "Well, I took something and can't remember how I got here, but I'm here, so fire away"? I did remember driving to the inquisition. I was determined to keep my eyes riveted on Roi and hopefully make him uncomfortable. The grilling began with a question that set the tone for the entire session. Roi was the adulterer, but I was going to be the reason for his sexual addiction and his need to go outside the marriage.

The first question asked of me was "Where did you consummate your marriage?" While seated in front of four men—two attorneys, an adulterer, and the court recorder—I calmly said, "The Marine Club in San Francisco." His attorney asked, "Not Hawaii?"

> *"Where did you consummate
> your marriage?"*

My answer was no. I wouldn't expect Roi to remember, as he's always suffered from convenient memory loss. He'd testified that he couldn't remember the tryst with his mistress that had taken place a mere eighteen months before he was questioned, so it's no wonder he couldn't remember forty-six years back. I don't believe the answer to that question is one a woman would forget, especially a woman with an exceptional memory. If Roi thought I was going to be unnerved by the attorney's question, he could think again! I admit it wasn't pleasant to be asked something so profoundly personal in front of three guys and one adulterer, though the audacity of the question emboldened me—and we were just getting started.

Their strategy was to paint me as a cold fish incapable of intimacy. The questions for the most part were about sex: Did I like sex, how often did I want sex, did I say no to sex, and did I ask for sex? Keeping on topic, Roi's attorney continued, "Can you describe the sex toys you claim to have?" The gotcha question! I answered yes. I've never been bullied, even though I grew up with four brothers, and now this vulgar attorney wanted to embarrass me by asking me to describe the toys. I felt powerful standing up to the two little men who wanted to justify having affairs and committing adultery by making me cower. That wasn't going to happen! I boldly described the nipple jewelry, the cock ring, and the rubber finger cover. While describing the finger cover I unintentionally placed my elbow on the table, wiggled two fingers, and said, "It was covered in wart-like bumps." *You asked, you pervert!*

The opposing counsel moved on to question the birth of our daughter, who'd arrived three months premature. He asked, "How did you handle the stress of a premature baby?"

Whoa, another question of the kind that gives attorneys the reputation of being slimeballs. I had, however, formed that opinion when I searched his website prior to the phony "dental insurance case."

Forty years ago I handled her birth like any other mature mother who desperately wanted a baby, but let me tell you about that stress. I desperately wanted a second child, having had a miscarriage when Gary was three, and by the time I was pregnant again he was seven. In the fifth month I experienced "leaking membranes" and was immediately admitted to the hospital at Fort Leavenworth, Kansas. I was a wreck, as any expectant mother would be, and for the next eight days I begged God to let the baby survive. Military families pull together when someone needs help, as it's not often that one lives near one's blood family. My neighbors—who became Nicole's godparents—and their kids watched out for my little boy after school until his dad came home from classes at the Command General Staff College, now known as the Army Combined Arms Center.

When my white blood-cell count went above normal about six days after being admitted, I was medevaced to the University of Kansas in Kansas City, about an eighty-mile roundtrip from Fort Leavenworth. Roi followed in our car, arriving in time to be with me in the emergency room before I was placed in a very small room, about the size of a closet, with a student nurse attending me. It grew late, and Roi left to go home to be with our son. Talk about being alone! I'd been alone during labor with my first baby, but a birth at twenty-six weeks was something else. I had to be strong for my baby and me, and in the end you just do what you have to.

About 9:00 the next morning I was experiencing labor pains, but the student nurse insisted they were false labor pains. Believe me: If they were false, I wouldn't be back for the real thing! Someone with a little more knowledge finally came in at about 11:00 a.m., and in a panic said, "Don't push" as they wheeled me to the delivery room at record speed. The baby was born about 11:30 a.m. She weighed just 900 grams, or two pounds. Roi arrived while I was in recovery; I was ecstatic to think that we had a little girl, but scared to death that because she was so tiny that she might not survive.

The baby was taken to the Neonatal Intensive Care Unit (NICU), and I was once again placed alone in a dingy little room, but at least it had a phone, so I could call my parents and family in Seattle. One of my sisters-in-law said, "You always have to do things with such flair." She became affectionately known as "Sisty Ugler."

The next morning the student nurse who'd been with me the day before came to take me to the neonatal unit to see my baby. I admit I was afraid to bond with her because I feared for her survival. My hesitancy was reported to the nursing staff. It sounds terrible, but I wanted her so desperately I was terrified! The nursing staff was very understanding and most encouraging. They explained that I'd need to put on a gown and scrub my hands for what seemed like an hour. There were four or five other incubators in that room, each with a tiny baby hooked up to monitors. As I sat on a barstool looking at my baby I couldn't believe just how small she was. She had a tube on her forehead, one in her tummy, and one on her foot. The nurse told me that I just needed to stroke her in order to bond with her, but my hand seemed almost too big to touch her, so I used one finger. Her foot measured from the tip of my little finger to the first joint. Except for tiny, she was perfect.

When I returned to my room someone arrived with paperwork for me to fill out, and encouraged me to give my child a name besides "baby." Since her birth was premature and we didn't yet know her gender, we hadn't decided on a name, thinking we had several months to choose one. A favorite movie that we'd seen in 1964 in Germany was *If a Man Answers,* starring Sandra Dee and Bobby Darrin. It was filmed in Paris. Roi and I loved Paris, and had seen Bobby Darrin perform in New York on our honeymoon. The character of Bobby Darin's wife in the film was Sandra Dee (also his wife in real life), and she had a French name. I named my baby after Sandra Dee's character and wrote that name on the birth certificate and voila—*Elle adore Paris!*

I went to the NICU several times before I was discharged two days after my baby's birth, but we had to go home without her. It was like being in la-la land! Her dad had seen her just twice, and her brother hadn't been able to see or touch her, as children weren't allowed in that unit, though he could see through the window that she was there. On our way home to Leavenworth we swung by the Kansas City Airport to pick up my mom, who was arriving from Seattle to help hold us all together.

It was an eighty-mile round-trip to the University of Kansas, which made a daily visit nearly impossible because my son, then a second grader, also needed me. Our calls and visits to the NICU were monitored, and the data was reported to a state agency. A representative from that agency made a visit to our quarters at Fort Leavenworth to interview us. It was explained that preemies require more feedings round the clock and daily doctor visits, and they wanted to be satisfied that we were stable, loving parents ready to bring a baby home. In truth, we weren't really ready, as our son's baby furniture was in storage in Virginia, but as I've said before, military families come to each other's rescue; our friends showed up with a wicker laundry basket, and with a little padding our little baby fit perfectly for the short time we had left at Fort Leavenworth. It was that caring couple who became her godparents.

Roi would call the hospital in the morning before class; they would give us her weight gain during the past twenty-four hours, and we'd mark it on the graph the hospital had provided. He would call again in the afternoon when he arrived home. We visited the NICU together on weekends, but Roi didn't accompany me during the week. My anxiety level kept me feeling like I was in the tropics and uncomfortably hot, wishing I could wear a sundress, even though it was March and bitter cold with harsh winter winds.

Luckily, we passed the state inspection, and our baby was doing well enough at six weeks—weighing in at four and a half pounds—to transport her, in the incubator, to the hospital at Fort Leavenworth. Our first attempt to drive to Kansas City was canceled due to threats of high winds across the flat land, so another week passed. I rode with the EMTs (emergency medical technicians) to the University of Kansas so as to be with the baby on the return trip. Our son and his dad were waiting for us as the ambulance arrived. Because our baby was put in a room by herself, we were able to let her brother hold her for a short time while he made sure she had ten toes and ten fingers. It was a crazy week running between our quarters and the hospital every two hours. I was operating at full speed, even managing, in a spare moment, to put a dinner together for Roi's study group. In my rattled state I dished it out, even broke the biscuits apart and buttered them as if I were serving a bunch of Cub Scouts. On the drive to the hospital I couldn't help wondering if they all thought I was crazy.

Our little baby was like a five-pound sack of sugar with arms and legs and really nothing to hold on to. We put her in a bunting to keep her warm for the ride home, but she kept sliding to the bottom. Baby carriers hadn't been invented, but she fit perfectly in that wicker laundry basket.

So, back to the attorney's question: "How did I handle the premature birth and did it put pressure on the marriage?" I answered, "I think we handled an extremely stressful and frightening time exceptionally well."

The opposing counsel wasn't through, however, with his vain attempt to make Roi look good, and his next line of questioning dealt with money. "It's true, isn't it, that your husband made most of the money and he paid for schools, colleges, studies abroad, horses, and sailing classes, etc...?"

I agreed that Roi had made a nice living and the family had benefited from his income. *But what has that have to do with philandering, or are you just grasping for straws?*

Just before they called the next witness, I was given the opportunity to relate how I viewed our marriage. I launched into a litany of all my accomplishments. I had lived in Europe and then experienced the Vietnam War, and stood by Roi during his recovery from the injuries he'd sustained. We then moved to Fort Sill, Oklahoma, and thence to Springfield, Missouri. When our son turned two, Roi volunteered for an unaccompanied thirteen-month tour in South Korea, so Gary and I spent that year near family in Seattle. We then found ourselves in Northern Virginia, and I accepted a career opportunity with an interior design firm in Washington, D.C., only to have to leave it for our move to Fort Leavenworth.

With a new baby, we returned to Virginia where I developed a home-based business. I'd been active in Army Officers Wives Clubs from coast to coast and beyond, and was president of the Saint Stephens Episcopal Boy's School mother's club. I'd spent countless hours carpooling to sport activities, Boy Scouts, and Girl Scouts; my least favorite activity, however, was being a chaperone on the West Springfield High School bus to the Occoquan Reservoir three days a week for six weeks, so my daughter and her classmates could participate in crew. Since I didn't work outside the home, I became the designated mother to ride the damn bus, though in my spare time I served meals, paid bills, cleaned house, and did the thousand other things that make a family run smoothly.

I've had time to reevaluate the futility of giving a summation of my contribution to the marriage. At the moment I was given the opportunity, I was eager to give my version of our forty-five-year marriage; more accurately, I just wanted to defend myself. I had done my best to be supportive of Roi's military career, a life that's not always easy. I kept a stiff upper lip during his endless job losses, and was proud of being a mother to two successful and honest young adults. I lived those years as honestly, lovingly, loyally, and with as much commitment as I could, but in light of Roi's true character I could see that he hadn't given a damn for all my efforts. I was definitely not prepared to tolerate Roi's attorney's attempt to paint me as a wife who hadn't contributed a monthly paycheck and had shunned intimacy, but I'll just let God be responsible for righting those wrongs.

I lived those years as honestly, lovingly, loyally, and with as much commitment as I could, but in light of Roi's true character I could see that he hadn't given a damn for all my efforts.

Nicole was having a difficult time pulling herself together emotionally. She was, after all, going to face her dad who, on the night he told her mother "I'm divorcing you," said cruelly to his daughter, "I haven't been happy for many years, dating back to the day you were born."

And that was justification for his affair? It was just inconceivable that when her dad witnessed her tears he wasn't man enough to tell his attorney to dispense with her testimony, but that didn't happen. I was present for the questioning, my eyes again riveted on Roi and his cold, calculated responses to his daughter. He didn't acknowledge her when she entered the conference room, not even the courtesy of standing, and neither did he make eye contact with her during the questioning. She was there, after all, to tout his generosity as a financial provider. The questions for her focused entirely on her dad's ability to provide for the family. She was asked to confirm that he had provided for her summers at a camp in the San Juan Islands in Washington State; her experience as a full-fledged crewmember on the *Statsraad Lehmkuhl,* the three-masted training ship of the Norwegian Navy; college, her junior year in Paris, and on and on. *So what's the point? Does Roi really think he's Daddy Warbucks?* Once again, we were there because he's an adulterer, not that he wasn't a good provider.

Gary was just plain angry about being subpoenaed to testify in his parents' divorce case; he arrived at the opposing counsel's office with an admittedly bad attitude and a chip on his shoulder the size of a giant sequoia tree. His lawyer was there to represent him, but primarily to ensure that his client kept his composure. When he saw that his sister was visibly upset after questioning, their attorney came to the rescue with reassuring words, reminding Gary that the deposition had nothing to do with him and that he needed to keep as calm as possible for his mother. He had just told me that I looked strong and pleasant, considering the circumstances, and reassured me that all would go well and he would remain calm, though from day one he's been on high alert and in overprotective mode. Gary's composure didn't last long when he met his dad's attorney, whom he describes as "a short gnome-like fellow with long hair and an unkempt beard, looking more like a used-car salesman than a lawyer."

To say that my son was on edge as he entered the conference room would be no exaggeration. He glared at his dad, who didn't acknowledge him but rather glared at the floor. It was like watching two outlaws circling, their hands on their pistols, waiting to be the first to draw and fire. The proceedings at the "not so O.K. Corral" (it was almost exactly 128 years to the day that the gunfight at the O.K. Corral had taken place in Tombstone, Arizona) weren't about to improve. Everyone at the table was scowling and I could see my son's hand was shaking while he took the oath.

With pistol drawn, the attorney's leading question was, "Are you the natural son of Roi and Nancy?"

Sarcastically, my son answered, "As far as I know."

The attorney was visibly annoyed with his response. Dem and I exchanged a glance, as we didn't understand the relevance of the question. A leading question is one that suggests a desired answer or puts words in the mouth of the witness. Oh, to have been able to cross-examine the source of that question, but truth does have a way of coming out sooner or later.

Having survived the first shot, my son responded to the remaining questions, which mostly dealt with what his dad had provided time-wise and monetarily. Roi had been the Scoutmaster of the Boy Scout troop, and had been supportive of his riding, sailing, study abroad, travel, and the many other things that parents do for their children. The attorney then asked, "What did you learn during your time as a Boy Scout?" Hindsight being so clear, my son has told me that he'd have liked to have said, "The Boy Scouts taught me to be trustworthy, loyal, helpful, friendly, courteous, kind, obedient, cheerful, thrifty, brave, clean, and reverent— qualities I now know I didn't learn from my father."

In the end, we all walked away from the corral physically intact but emotionally wounded.

Chapter Thirteen Take-Aways

- ◉ Opposing council will likely use any trick they can, down to deposing your children (depending on their age).

- ◉ Adult children are just as negatively affected by divorce as little children. My daughter has expressed that the divorce would have been easier to have handled had she and my son been much younger; at age 32, she knew right from wrong and her entire world was suddenly destroyed. Little children are more able to recover and adjust to a new normal.

- ◉ You cannot prepare for a deposition.

- ◉ Tell the truth!

Unprepared to Divvy Up My Life

When I became a client of the law firm, Dem discussed the merits of going to court versus mediation. He gave me a list of mediators that the firm recommended, and among them were two retired judges. At that point they could have been retired dogcatchers for all I cared, as I was pretty sure that the ramifications of being dumped like garbage in a careless and hurried way by a husband of forty-five years was not going to be cut and dried.

I wanted to go to court because I wanted Roi charged with adultery and abandonment. Choosing between court and mediation was very difficult, as neither option truly offered an outcome that was going to satisfy me. I discovered that he had extensively been using Internet pornography and online dating sites, including one whose slogan is "Life is short. Have an affair." Going to court would be the most expensive option, and mediation just slightly less. It seemed impossible that the judge wouldn't find Roi guilty of adultery, but what I had to weigh out was that I could be spending more of my money with no guarantee of Roi walking around with a large letter "A" around his neck for the rest of his life, and was it worth it? In the end it was agreed that we would meet at the opposing counsel's firm and the two lawyers would duke it. We met on November 21, 2009, exactly fourteen months from the day that Bunny had called to inform me of their affair and their engagement.

Choosing between court and mediation was very difficult, as neither option truly offered an outcome that was going to satisfy me.

Dem and I arrived at 9:00 a.m. for a grueling day that came to an end about 7:00 p.m. The two attorneys were cross-town rivals, as one had graduated from Washington and Lee University and the other from Virginia Military Institute, both in Lexington, Virginia. Dem had his W&L tie on for good luck and possibly an "in-your-face" impact/ moment, while doing his best to negotiate an equitable settlement in the opposing attorney's office, which looked more like a VMI gift shop.

We were divided into enemy camps, leaving the opposing counsel's office as the command center. That office was configured like the interior of a spaceship, with at least five computers placed in a semicircle at one end of the room, with large overstuffed leather swivel chairs so the attorneys could be comfortable while carving up people's lives. I was totally unprepared for divvying up my life, and no one could have prepared me for what was going to happen that day. Meeting on the enemy's turf was extremely uncomfortable, because it gave them home-team advantage and one of the team members wanted the divorce. Knowing that the term "equitable distribution" does not mean equal or fair is a threatening concept. While my life was being negotiated in the command center, I was stuck alone in a shabby, unused office at the end of a corridor. Dem would pop in with either an offer or a rejection of an offer, then we'd discuss a strategy, and off he'd go back to the command center. It's so artificially civilized, when two adults who can no longer work it out on the playground need two grown men to run back and forth to try to negotiate who gets the most toys, and that in the end no one is happy. The goal was to formalize a marital agreement that would specify how our marital property would be divided. Each of us was asked to prepare a list of negotiable and non-negotiable items, and then the attorneys would negotiate the rules of the game.

When the toys include a family home, family heirlooms, money, and hundreds of other things, some significant, others just favorites, it becomes another emotional crisis. People who in all probability wouldn't agree with the rules when it came to their own toys established the rules for distribution. In any event, it boils down to "Who owned what?" When did it become a family possession? Who inherited it? Was it a wedding gift? And whose family owned it? In the end it didn't matter who polished the silver or dusted the cherished furniture pieces over the years. There are people who are fond of saying "possessions are just things" and can be replaced, but I want to be the one who makes the decision as to the "replacing" of any of my things. The thought of those family heirlooms being given to a woman with no knowledge of their history and perhaps no real appreciation for them was repugnant. Those things should be given to our children as a part of their heritage, but Roi evidently wanted to shower his lover with nice things. He did agree to modify his will thirty days after the divorce became final, stipulating that if he preceded Bunny in death she would return the furniture and silver to his children. Anyone who believes those things would ever be returned to our children would also believe that the 14,410-foot snow-covered Mount Rainier is located in the Mojave—and, of course, Roi's will was never modified.

The Seattle home was a far more complicated emotional issue for my kids and me, and Roi's attorney made the settlement as difficult as possible. There were about ten pages out of forty-nine in the marital agreement devoted exclusively to refinancing and the removal of Roi's name from the mortgage. The wording was so convoluted that it read like the twists and turns of a pretzel, but eating a pretzel made more sense. The time frame for refinancing gave me just five months to have it completed and that was one of the issues we argued over, as Roi's attorney wanted the refinance completed in two months.

This made it obvious to me that Roi's attorney hadn't refinanced a home in years as the wording he insisted on severely limited the time it would take to complete the refinancing process; I had to wonder if it was designed for me to fail. If I failed to refinance the home, Roi would be able to reenter the picture, and according to the agreement, I'd have to sell the home just to get his name off the mortgage.

He wouldn't have benefited from any proceeds from the sale because I was ordered to pay him $142,000 from my investments, which represented his portion of the home after factoring in my inheritance. To me, the most important matter was the removal of his name from the mortgage, and believe me, I wanted him out of my life.

> *To me, the most important matter*
> *was the removal of his name from*
> *the mortgage, and believe me,*
> *I wanted him out of my life.*

The final issue was a $250,000 life insurance policy that we had paid premiums on for years. Roi's attorney awarded the policy to him as its sole owner, but I was ordered to pay the premiums for five years. Just a minute, let me understand this: Roi has sole ownership of the policy, and I pay the premiums, and he gives me his word that I'll remain the beneficiary just in case he kicks the bucket in five years? To accept the word of a lying, cheating weasel who'd given my dental policy to his "partner" would make me an utter fool. One wouldn't have to be a rocket scientist to know that Bunny had already been named as beneficiary. Oh, "Mr. Murph", you little devil, you tried to put one over on me, but your client is going to have to continue paying the premiums on his own insurance policy.

Finally, after ten stressful hours, copies of the forty-nine-page marital agreement specifying how our marital property would be divided, the date for the refinancing of the Seattle home, the stipulation that alimony payments would be paid on the first of each month for the next three plus years and, last but not least, the date for the removal of his personal property from the Seattle home, were retching out of the computer and landing on the floor like a puddle of vomit. He and I sat side by side, watching our forty-six-year marriage, if you count the year it took to get this far, unemotional and silently watching the forty-six years reduced to forty-nine pages. Roi couldn't look at me and couldn't or wouldn't say anything, so I sat there, sizing up the contrast between our two attorneys, which was glaring: mine acted like a pit bull in a tux, and his like a mutt in sweats, both trying to make their clients reasonably satisfied while keeping in mind that no one wins.

He and I sat side by side, watching our forty-six-year marriage, if you count the year it took to get this far, unemotional and silently watching the forty-six years reduced to forty-nine pages.

His attorney poured us each a shot of bourbon. I'd never drunk straight bourbon; it burned all the way down—perhaps the most civilized way to end a marriage. As my "Sisty Ugler" said, "You always do things with such flair." Without thinking, I approached Roi, gave him a hug, said, "Be happy," and walked out. Safely in my car, I called Nicole to tell her I was on my way. Then the stress of the wretched day turned into tears and I cried all the way home.

Without thinking, I approached Roi, gave him a hug, said, "Be happy," and walked out.

How ironic: we met in November 1960, and in November 2009, forty-nine years later, we were divorced and Roi walked away with a $250,000 life insurance policy and $142,000 from me. All that the marital agreement required of him was to pay me alimony on the first of each month for the next five years, and arrange to move his belongings from the Seattle home by February 15, 2010.

I allowed myself a day or two to cry and relive the hostile day that produced the roadmap we were to follow for the demolition of our marriage. My understanding of the agreement had me doing all the heavy lifting and all the mopping up. With Thanksgiving just four days off and Christmas not far behind, I needed to get my act together. It would be our third holiday season without Roi, and I knew we were going to have a wonderful time, as he wouldn't be there to sabotage our holiday meals. I ordered Dungeness crab to be flown in from Seattle, my brother and his wife sent a beautiful salmon for Christmas dinner, and Santa Claus was his jolly-old self in a peaceful setting.

*I knew we were going to have a
wonderful time, as he wouldn't be
there to sabotage our holiday meals.*

Chapter Fourteen Take-Aways

- Understand the difference between going to court and mediation.

- Mediation is less costly and less risky. Should you go with mediation, be very sure that you keep your wits about you. It can be an emotionally draining experience and if you are not fully aware at all times, you could sign away property that you had never intended to.

- You will find that many of your decisions come down to how much it will cost you.

- The marital agreement will be the road map for how to distribute one's things, dates to do so, rules for alimony, and dates for alimony to arrive.

- It is a hostile day whether you're in court or mediating and there is no true way to prepare, just be very much on your "A" game.

Headwinds Make Flying Solo Difficult

New Year's Eve 2010 had come and gone, and I was ready to try out my new single status. I started with the easiest chore on my list and contacted the United States Automobile Association (USAA) to have them put the insurance policies in my name. They couldn't have been more helpful, and didn't require me to present legal papers proving anything. I soon learned that changing the name on an insurance policy would be the easiest step in spreading my wings.

Obtaining a new military (ID) card would be on hold until the final divorce decree was issued, which also held up my being able to apply for a copy of Roi's Discharge from Active Duty (DD 214) form. Simply put, a (DD 214) is a form signed by the service member upon retirement from active duty, containing the history of the member's assignments, awards, and benefits. As Roi's wife of well over twenty years, I qualified under the 20/20/20 rule to receive all benefits. Additionally, I would need our marriage certificate, or at least a copy, to complete the ID process.

We had stored all of our important papers, including our marriage certificate, in a safe deposit box with the Army and Air Force Mutual Aid Association (AAFMAA), which provides a variety of financial services, including survivor's assistance to the member's family. When I called to request the certificate, they told me they'd contact the service member for permission to give it to me. Whoa! I must have misunderstood the reason for our placing important papers, like wills and marriage certificates, with that organization for safekeeping. My understanding was that it was similar to putting things in a safe deposit box at a bank.

AAFMAA responded by letter, stating that Roi would not authorize them to give me a copy of the marriage certificate. Adding more billable hours to my tab, my attorney wrote a letter attaching a copy of the AAFMAA letter to Roi's attorney, and several weeks later I had a copy of the certificate. Maybe my husband just wanted to keep the original for his memory book!

Moving on didn't get off to a smooth start, but having never been in this position, I had no reason to think it wouldn't. I was learning on the job, so to speak, and being naïve was no longer an option. I had no idea how incredibly difficult and time consuming it would be, and I'm convinced that moving on completely is a myth, a fantasy. It could have been much easier if Roi had said, "I want a divorce, I'll help you get the military forms you'll need, and divide everything equitably. I'll also pay alimony on the first of every month, and I'll maintain a relationship with the kids." I'd have been a little surprised, as his mother taught me to say. That approach to divorce would have been a gift but like I said a fantasy. If you expect the worse, you'll never be disappointed.

I was learning on the job,
so to speak, and being naïve was
no longer an option.

Before the court had processed all the final paperwork for a new identification card (ID), I was shopping at the Fort Lewis Commissary, Fort Lewis, Washington, using my authorized ID card with Roi's Social Security number. (Military dependents are identified by the service member's Social Security number.) All my purchases had been checked, and I handed the clerk a personal check, but after trying to process it she leaned toward me and whispered that the check had been refused for lack of funds in my account. Knowing there must be a mistake, I asked her to run it again, and again it was refused. The line of customers behind me was growing, and the clerk was clearly embarrassed for me. As I swiped my credit card, I had every intention of calling the bank as soon as I returned home. Sure enough, there was more than enough in my account.

I didn't give the incident much thought until about four weeks later when shopping at another commissary in the Seattle area. I had completely forgotten the Fort Lewis Commissary episode. I wrote a check for the items, and again the clerk whispered that my account didn't have enough funds and my check had been refused. Once again, I used my credit card. Instead of being embarrassed I was royally pissed, because in forty-six years of shopping at commissaries all across the U.S. and Europe I'd never had a check refused. My built-in radar was telling me that Roi was somehow responsible for this inconvenient and embarrassing fiasco, and I was not about to leave that commissary without asking for an explanation from the manager. With all the changes taking place in my new life, I was at least positive it had nothing to do with my personal finances and everything to do with Roi.

The commissary manager checked her computer and with an understanding smile, handed me the phone number for the Defense Finance and Accounting Services (DFAS). I drove home as fast as possible, but unlike the Washington D.C. area where going over the speed limit is the norm, the Washington State Patrol lurk around every corner to make sure that all drivers stick to the 60 mph limit. When I'm in the Seattle area I constantly have to remind myself that going 80 mph in a 60 zone could ruin my driving record, and I just keep pace with all the other lemmings who are afraid to speed.

My conversation with the DFAS was very interesting; I was told that someone by the name of "Bunny" had tried to pay for groceries at the Fort Belvoir, Virginia commissary and had used someone's Social Security number without a government-issued ID. The representative gave me the date of the check and the amount, and then told me that the woman was not authorized to use military facilities. When I heard that she (his mistress) had used Roi's Social Security number, I remembered the day at the private investigator's office when he said, "She's not a nice woman. Her profile shows that she's used three Social Security numbers, and one of them is not in her name."

That brazen hussy thought she could get away with using Roi's Social Security number, thus causing Roi and me to lose check-cashing privileges for forty-five days at every military installation worldwide. I love Judge Judy's saying: "Beauty fades, stupid is forever."

The Circuit Court of Fairfax County, Fairfax, Virginia, granted the divorce on January 29, 2010. I didn't expect the day to be out of the ordinary; indeed it was anticlimactic, considering it was the official end of a forty-six-year marriage. I could only hope that Roi would move forward with his new life and abide by the court-ordered sanctions, such as monthly alimony payments and the removal of his belongings from the Seattle home. I wanted to be free of the drama and move forward myself.

> *I wanted to be free of the drama*
> *and move forward myself.*

At last, I had a copy of his discharge papers (DD214), the divorce decree, and a copy of the marriage certificate, and could obtain a new ID. With all the necessary paperwork in hand I made an appointment at the Coast Guard Station Seattle. The army, air force, and navy facilities all have access to the Defense Enrollment Eligibility Reporting System (DEERS), and in no time I had a new ID. The computer-generated photo made me look like I had bags under my eyes the size of small Chanel clutches. With so many ups and downs in my life, all I needed was to be depressed over a plastic card with my photo on it. (I now have a new ID, the photo a slight upgrade from the old mug shot—progress!)

My attorney handled the application for my half of Roi's army retirement pay, a process that was scheduled to take about four months. In the interim my ex was to make direct deposits to my bank through May 2010, and when that didn't happen I opened a bank account closer to his apartment. I wasn't really surprised, however, that the problem wasn't the bank's location.

Roi's a big boy, making big-boy decisions like betrayal of a relationship, and it was about time he knew when the first of the month rolled around—after all, it's when his paycheck arrived. It was absolutely clear, however, that he'd never learned financial accountability, and neither was he the least bit interested in being legally answerable for the court orders. The court can render a ruling in your favor, but in my case it was just a bunch of costly words on paper. I'm positive that I could fill a stadium with ex-wives who've had an ex give the finger to the court ruling and laugh like a hyena while riding off into the sunset.

> *I'm positive that I could fill a stadium with ex-wives who've had an ex give the finger to the court ruling and laugh like a hyena while riding off into the sunset.*

Eventually my portion of the retirement pay came directly to me. I was also awarded half of Roi's Social Security, which I applied for on my own. What a horrifying thought to face the possibility of physically going to a Social Security office to obtain the forms, though with one quick call they were mailed to me. The Social Security payments would come to me for life with one exception: if I renounced my American citizenship. I don't worry about where to spend the windfall, though, because the government withholds federal tax before the payment reaches the bank, and what's left won't cover the cost of a well-deserved vacation.

When my attorney informed me that I'd be paying income tax on the alimony while Roi would be able to write off the payments on his taxes, all I could say was, "You're kidding, aren't you?" Alimony is considered income, and the ex is the payer. It's a wake-up call if you've never made quarterly payments to the IRS or, for that matter, paid any federal and state taxes. In my world, the betrayer would be responsible for the alimony and all taxes, assuming he paid the alimony. On the other hand, I'm thankful my ex isn't responsible for my IRS obligation—it would just be one more occasion to be screwed!

By April 2010, just two months after the divorce was final, I had successfully obtained a new ID and overcome the probation period at military facilities, but Roi's stuff was still in Seattle, and the alimony and my portion of his army retirement allotment was of course missing in action. As a novice to the court process, I naively believed that an order by the court meant that a person would obey that order, as Roi had obeyed orders as an army officer. Disregarding an order in the army could have one before a court-martial. Rather than constantly have to re-file for a noncompliant jackass and run up costly attorney fees, I wanted Roi's wages garnished from the beginning, but his attorney rejected that option as it would be embarrassing and could cause him to lose his government security clearance. I suppose the loss could cost him his employment, but his employment and paycheck were no guarantee of his paying alimony, and I don't remember him ever being embarrassed.

> *As a novice to the court process, I naively believed that an order by the court meant that a person would obey that order, as Roi had obeyed orders as an army officer.*

Chapter Fifteen Take-Aways

- Once your divorce is official, per the courts, then it is time to make changes to appropriate documents such as: insurance policies, mortgage, bank accounts, etc.

- The marital agreement is no guarantee that your ex will follow the letter of the law.

- Be prepared to owe taxes on the alimony you receive while your ex-spouse gets to actually write the alimony off.

- Even though you are legally divorced, the story does not always end there.

Showing Respect to His New Wife

The most challenging requirement stipulated in the marital agreement was refinancing my childhood home, which turned the process into an eight-month nightmare. I started it without a thought to the possibility that I might not qualify for refinancing. My investments didn't count for anything, as my eligibility was based solely on the amount of alimony I'd receive as stated in the agreement. I was most concerned that I wouldn't be able to complete the process in the time stated in the agreement, and feared that Roi might get involved as ordered.

> *I started it without a thought to the possibility that I might not qualify for refinancing. My investments didn't count for anything, as my eligibility was based solely on the amount of alimony I'd receive as stated in the agreement.*

I contacted USAA, and they sent me a boatload of forms to fill out and a request for additional personal information. That process took about six weeks, and there were so many people involved that I had to have my daughter's help to identify the players. They finally turned me down for refinancing because I wasn't going to receive enough monthly income to qualify. The monthly income or alimony was stipulated in the marital agreement and determined by the attorneys and Roi's age and earnings. It was another emotional setback for me.

Down but not out, I applied at a bank where my father had been vice president and where I'd been a customer for fifty years. Again, I filled out a multitude of forms, but this time I had copies of the personal information, and not having to collate that stuff was a time and energy saver. The bank, however, requested an appraisal, and wouldn't accept either of the two previous appraisals because they were over six months old and not considered current. In addition, they requested that Roi sign a quitclaim deed, a legal document used to transfer a person's rights to real estate to another person. At that point, he dug in his heels and wouldn't sign till I handed over the $142,000 stipulated in the marital agreement.

I had tried to force "good behavior" by putting that money into an escrow account in hopes that I could force Roi to start making the retirement and alimony payments, but it became apparent that I was going to be held to a higher standard. I needed him to sign the quitclaim deed, and he was using the signing as leverage to force me to release the money. Is there no one holding him accountable for the court-ordered removal of his stuff from Seattle that had been taking up space for six months? And how about those retirement and alimony payments? It seemed I was going to be in a Mexican standoff with the Defense Finance Accounting Systems (DFAS) till they got around to sending my portion of the retirement directly.

My attorney and I had a "come to Jesus moment" via email; he reminded me that I needed to stay on the high road, as my reputation before the court was impeccable and I didn't want to go to court with unclean hands. Clean hands is a funny legal term, but it makes sense in a simple way: As the good guy in the divorce, I do have clean hands, and Roi, as the cheater who ignores court orders, has very dirty hands. At that very moment, however, I couldn't have cared less. I was the one who'd been unceremoniously dumped, and I just wanted to be able to call the shots about something.

My attorney and I had a "come to Jesus moment" via email; he reminded me that I needed to stay on the high road, as my reputation before the court was impeccable and I didn't want to go to court with unclean hands.

In a follow-up email Dem said, "I apologize if the tone of my email is somewhat strong. I know your ex-husband's trustworthiness is worth about as much as a bucket of warm spit, words of former Vice President John ("Cactus Jack") Garner of Texas, but let him be the one held accountable before the court for his actions, not you. You have nothing to lose by being compliant before the law." Reluctantly, I had the money transferred to Roi's account, and he then signed the quitclaim deed.

It was May 1, 2010, and time was flying by toward the refinancing deadline. It was an arbitrary date set by attorneys who know the law but perhaps nothing about the pitfalls of refinancing. I needed to have my attorney intervene on my behalf with the lenders in an attempt to explain my monthly income. The underwriters from both banks took only three years of alimony into consideration instead of the five and a half years clearly ordered in the marital agreement. Reading and understanding seemed to be a problem for the mortgage lenders—or were they clairvoyant, able to perceive a situation involving an unethical person for future nonpayment of alimony?

Out of the blue, King County (Seattle), Washington meddled with the quitclaim deed assuming (and you know what happens when you assume) that the quitclaim deed was for the sale of real estate, and the city wanted me to fill out forms so they could assess taxes. Roi was merely transferring his rights to the property back to me, and no sale of real estate was involved, but King County was on a fishing expedition for revenue. The second bank also turned down my application for a mortgage; however, they did manage to sic the City of Seattle on me.

With time and options running out, I talked to my Merrill Lynch advisor and again filled out a mountain of application forms and supplied them with a growing stack of personal information. Had I known from the start of the refinancing process that I'd be going through lenders like water down the drain, I'd have made six copies of bank statements, marital agreements, divorce decrees, social security information, and heaven knows what else. I have plastic containers under beds and in closets filled with every word of the divorce and refinancing, and it still appeared I was nowhere near putting a period after divorce.

One evening, Nicole was having dinner with a friend, Joe, who was a financial advisor with Bank of America. She was unaware that B of A and Merrill Lynch had merged and was now Bank of America Merrill Lynch; neither did she know that Joe was a colleague of my wealth management advisor. Their conversation led to the fact that I was going through a marathon refinancing exercise and was now in the early application process with Merrill Lynch. Joe became integral to the step-by-step process of refinancing, despite the hurdles—and there were many. There were several that he had no control over, but with his guidance, Gary became a cosigner on the mortgage. We thought that would be the end of it, but wait, that would make too much sense, be too reasonable, too easy to understand.

The lenders were requesting a title search, something I hadn't experienced. I needed to find a title company immediately. With the fourth appraisal and a boatload of paperwork in hand, I headed to a title company in the area. Fortunately, with each new appraisal, the value of the home had increased, as it could have easily gone down in value with the uncertain market. I was beginning to feel more confident that the refinancing would be approved. I hadn't gone this far with the first two lenders, and the title search would make sure there were no liens against the property.

Before the title company could go any further, they requested that I hire a real estate attorney to do a property search to make sure the title to the property was legal. Ever mindful of the time constraints, Dem found the name of an attorney ten minutes from my home, and lo and behold, I could meet with him in a matter of hours. I could hardly believe my luck—finally something I didn't have to wait weeks for.

Upon arrival I had a sense that the firm wasn't going to be as exciting as my family law firm. The office was large and gray and quiet; even the receptionist whispered, "Take a seat." As the only person in the large room, I had my choice. I knew I was in the right location, but it felt like a funeral parlor. A series of closed doors circled the reception area, and I wondered if the bodies were behind those doors. The attorney I was meeting with didn't come out of one of those doors, and as we walked down the hall to a room past more closed doors, I felt very uneasy.

I filled out some paperwork, answered a few questions relevant to my property, and left as soon as possible. The attorney and his receptionist had the personality of asphalt, and to this day the approximately thirty minutes I was there still gives me the creeps, but three weeks and $500 later, I was able to give the results of the title search to the title company.

August 2010 was nipping at my heels; fortunately, I hadn't heard from Roi or his attorney wanting to know if I'd completed the refinancing according to the July deadline. The marital agreement stated that if Roi's name was not removed from the mortgage, he could come to Seattle to see if I'd maintained the house in satisfactory condition in order to sell it. Believe me, that was the last thing I needed; he could have taken responsibility for his stuff, which was still taking up space in my carriage house. I just wanted to be free of him and his property as was the promise he'd made in court six months earlier.

At 4:30 p.m. on a Friday afternoon, the title company called to inform me that they had just received information of Roi's recent marriage. And I needed to know that for what reason? As I mentioned, it was Friday and it was 4:30 pm Pacific Time and they wanted to inform me that they would require the "new bride" to sign a quitclaim deed before they could sign off on the title. Shit! "What in the hell are you saying? What in the hell does Roi's wife have to do with my family home?"

Perhaps I should have hung up and dialed 911, because I was about to go into cardiac arrest. The poor representative from the title company calmly tried to explain that it was for my protection to have the new bride sign a quitclaim deed, though, the term "new bride" was about to make me throw up. I needed to breathe deeply so I could perhaps calm down; then maybe it wouldn't sound so outrageous. Let me get this straight, Bunny (aka "New Bride") was now married to my ex-husband and when the refinancing was complete Roi would no longer have any claim to my home, so the title company was informing me that since

Bunny and Roi were now married, that Bunny could somehow pop up in the future to put a claim on my home unless she signed a quitclaim deed. Unbelievable! But in all honesty, I was positive that she was capable of doing anything for money.

The weekend loomed ahead; I wouldn't be able to talk to my attorney until Monday, and believe me, it's no wonder attorneys don't give out their home phone numbers. I called every member of my support group to bitch, and then my son called to tell me where I could find a photo of the newlyweds on the Internet. Congratulations to the American High School sweethearts, who married exactly two years to the day after they'd met at the high school reunion in 2008. They were photographed standing in front of the Fort Belvoir Officers Club in their wedding finery. Bunny was falling out of her long white strapless wedding dress, and Roi was wearing a new dress blue uniform. He may have retired in 1983 with the rank of lieutenant colonel but the eagle, the insignia of a colonel, was embroidered on the sleeve of his uniform.

Nothing Roi has done since meeting Bunny has surprised the kids or me, though we find it pathetic. It's not against the law for a lieutenant colonel to pretend to be a colonel, but it sure poses an ethical question. Bunny's gown was purchased with marital money in June 2009, shortly before Roi bought the $21,000 diamond necklace that sparkled from around her neck in the wedding photo. I wonder if any of their American High School classmates were there waving pompoms in the school colors and yelling, "Hey-hey! Ho-ho!"

Monday morning, I was out of bed before anyone on the East Coast had even thought about getting up, wearing jammies and no makeup (not that we were going to Skype), but serious issues require serious attire. While waiting for the clock to chime 6:00 a.m. Pacific Time, I hoped that he would not be in court that day. I'd waited all weekend to hear Lenora say, "The Law Firm." She then said, "He isn't in yet," but assured me that as soon as Dem walked in she'd give him my desperate message. Knowing your attorney isn't just sitting in his office waiting for your call so he can solve the newest disaster is like being a teenager waiting for "him" to call. The good news at that hour of the morning was that I could remember Vikki Carr singing, "Let it please be him, oh dear God, It must be him."

When Dem called soon after he'd arrived at his office, I told him about the title company's request for a signed quitclaim deed from the "new wife." He too explained that in the end it was for my protection: in case Roi should precede her in death, his wife would be his benefactor, and if the title on my house wasn't completely clean, she could make my life hell. What a bone-chilling thought!

Dem emailed Roi's attorney and explained the title company's request while also stressing the urgency of the quitclaim deed, since the refinance was complete and we had a deadline to sign in three days. I kept checking my email, hoping to have their response to Dem, but instead I had an email from Roi. *He's probably writing to congratulate me on the refinance and to tell me when he'd be moving his stuff.* But no, that was just a figment of my imagination. He was angry and of course, arrogant. He stated that he'd already signed a quitclaim deed and not only didn't he have to sign one but wouldn't. *Hey, fella, you're not being asked to sign one, your wife is!* Roi then wrote, "If you want Bunny to sign a quitclaim deed, you'll have to send her a respectful note requesting her to do you the favor of signing one, and send it to my email address."

Dem wrote the respectful note, loaded with legalese and no slobbering, and after sending it to me I copied and pasted and pressed FORWARD. The computer is such an amazing invention!

The chutzpa the new wife demonstrated in demanding that her new husband ask for a respectful note from his former wife is absolutely contemptible, and it doesn't say much for him, either. When they moved to Texas she must have insisted that he get a nose ring just like all the bulls on the ranch, to make him compliant and easily led. The consensus of my "support group" was that Bunny should have respectfully requested the favor of letting her have my husband and the father of my kids.

Eight months and three lenders later, the deed arrived at the eleventh hour; my son and I signed a ream of paperwork, and the refinance was complete. What a relief to be able to cross that off my list, but instead of celebrating the refinancing marathon at a cocktail lounge, my son and I went to lunch. I could tell he was excited, but certainly not about the mortgage. He wanted to tell me about his girlfriend who lived in Bogotá, Colombia. She would be joining us for Thanksgiving and would stay in

Virginia until he and his fellow soldiers from the 29th Infantry Division of the Virginia Army National Guard deployed to Afghanistan for a year. We didn't dwell on his deployment, as he knew I was already emotional about his leaving. I had said goodbye to his dad in 1966 when he left for Vietnam, having no idea what having experienced war on a personal basis would mean upon his return. This time it was my son, and I was no longer naïve about the effects of war.

Gary had taken on the role of protector for his sister and me when his dad made the decision to betray the family. In preparing for his year out of the country, he sent his dad an email as cosigner on the mortgage, requesting that Roi make arrangements to remove his property from the carriage house in Seattle within two weeks. Roi had told the court he would have his stuff removed on February 15, and as of September 15 it was still taking up space. Free storage, anyone? In the email Gary intentionally did not mention his deployment or his promotion to lieutenant colonel.

Gary had taken on the role of protector for his sister and me when his dad made the decision to betray the family.

Gary's email to his dad was evidently considered disrespectful, as the reply indicated that Roi had become totally unglued and was in desperate need of an industrial-strength adhesive to hold him together. He sent each attorney, my son, and me a four-page email, backed up with a copy by registered mail just in case our computers were down. When the mailman came to the door and asked me to sign for an envelope, I knew whom it was from. Since Roi was in arrears again for the September 2010 alimony I reluctantly signed, suspecting that if the envelope had contained the missing check Roi would have told his attorney that he'd tried to give me the money and I wouldn't accept it. Knowing how differently Roi and I viewed money, from day one of the divorce I feared that money and Roi would be the bane of my existence. I have a theory that spitefulness became his *modus operandi* in order to maintain control and power over the alimony check; his withholding payment was like being screwed over again and again. As each month passed I gained power as I vowed to hound him legally and hoped that he would take the court orders seriously, but maybe I was hoping for something that was not going to be winnable.

Since traveling through the divorce jungle, I've learned that an immoral person is like a leopard—his spots never change. Two months after the last promise to send the alimony, and nine months after the divorce was final, my attorney was yet again emailing Roi's attorney about yet another missed payment. About the middle of the following month, he was in his attorney's office with a cockamamie story to cover his *derriere* claiming he'd sent a check, all the while knowing damn well that he never had. The attorney had him write a new check, supposedly an exact copy of the phantom check, then faxed a facsimile of that check to Dem with NOT NEGOTIABLE written on it. In the accompanying message, Roi's attorney continued to bluster about seeking legal fees from me for involving Roi in a court case over a missed payment. Perhaps the bullying lawyer didn't understand the difference between missed payments and no payment!

> *Since traveling through the divorce jungle, I've learned that an immoral person is like a leopard—his spots never change.*

Just seven days later, Roi was still claiming he'd mailed a check one Sunday, but couldn't remember where he had sent it. He supposedly stopped payment on that check, claiming that his bank (a rather large institution) was not serving his needs and that he was no longer able to trust them. He found a cashier's check somewhere and gave it to his attorney, who FedEx-ed it to my attorney's office. I can only surmise what that stupidity cost him. Dem's legal phrase for the fiasco was "dumb shrewd." Unfortunately for him, Roi's attorney was "dumb screwed" by his client, and of course no apologies for suggesting that the whole episode was my fault.

Chapter Sixteen Take-Aways

- If you need to refinance your home, know ahead of time that removing your ex-spouse from the mortgage could be a challenging experience. (I never imagined that my son would have to co-sign the refinance, though in essence, I could purchase the home with my investments.)

- Be prepared to feel like you're under the microscope during the refinance process. You might be asked to do outrageous things like asking the "new bride" to sign a quitclaim deed.

- Even though you have been awarded alimony, your ex-spouse might not pay it. Be prepared to continue taking him to court. You will need to decide if you want to continue fighting for what is legally owed you.

- Your marital agreement outlines when certain things need to be accomplished; your ex-spouse might not follow-through. Decide if you wish to open the proverbial "Pandora's box" or wait.

- Maintain all information related to every aspect of the divorce as it's impossible to remember all details.

17

My Son's Deployment

I needed to put the issues of alimony and removal of Roi's belongings aside, as Thanksgiving 2010 was approaching at breakneck speed and with it my son's departure for Afghanistan. Nicole and I were looking forward to meeting his girlfriend, who we suspected was a little more than a girlfriend. She arrived from Bogotá, Colombia for her first American Thanksgiving, and we were happy to welcome her into our little group. The day could not have been more perfect, with great food and lots of laughter and no mention of the next day's departure.

Gary has always been funny and often the life of the party, though as a fourth grader at Saint Stephens Episcopal Boys' School the funny episodes caused him to spend many Wednesdays in demerit hall, a school tactic that put parents in rush hour on Interstate 395 South. Today he's far more mature but just as funny. I suspect all the comedy on Thanksgiving Day was to relieve the anxiety of leaving for a war zone early the next morning. We all welcomed the comedy, but we did take a moment to discuss plans for all of us to meet in Europe for his R&R and the countries we would visit; however, without a definite date we didn't know when we'd be meeting.

I suspect all the comedy on Thanksgiving Day was to relieve the anxiety of leaving for a war zone early the next morning.

Very early the next morning we dropped his girlfriend off at Reagan National Airport for her return to Colombia, and we three then drove in silence to the Fort Belvoir, Virginia headquarters of the 29th Infantry Division of the Virginia Army National Guard. The buses were lined up and the soldiers were loading their gear for the 6:00 a.m. departure. There must be a regulation in some military manual stating that departures must take place somewhere between midnight and 6:00 a.m. I'm familiar with that drill, but when it's your son leaving for a war zone it's a whole different drill. We were going to wait for the busses to pull out, but when one of my son's best buddies gave his sister and me a hug and said, "I'll take care of him," I managed to maintain my composure long enough to hug both of them and say, "I love you, be safe."

In the privacy of our car we let the tears flow, very reminiscent of the day we'd arrived at Valley Forge Military College, Valley Forge, Pennsylvania in 1986. We had just parked the car in the designated lot when an upper classman descended upon us to welcome us to VF and hand us the schedule for the day. The first item on it was for him to take control of my son and his trunk. I thought I was military savvy, but letting go of Gary so abruptly was gut wrenching. I was aware, however, that we wouldn't be able to communicate for six weeks. Somehow I made it through the day without drowning in tears, but as soon as we were back on I-95 south heading home to Virginia, my tears were uncontrollable. His dad suggested we stop somewhere along the route for a drink, which sounded like a perfect idea. I'm positive that the hostess, seeing my red nose and puffy eyes and my teetering on the verge of another outbreak, thought someone had just died.

"Be safe"—what else does one say to a soldier going to a war zone? With forty-four years between my first deployment experience and my son's, I'm no closer to the perfect encouraging words; just saying those two words to my son was agonizing, and no easier for the parents and wives of any soldiers.

Twenty years ago, when my son was a freshman at Valley Forge Military College, his dad encouraged him to join the ROTC (Reserve Officers' Training Corps) program. I was not in attendance that day, and wasn't onboard with that decision even even though I was a proud military wife. I didn't want to experience the day my son would leave for war. While, I had just experienced what I'd feared most, that decision made years ago has enhanced every phase of his life.

Six years after his deployment, Gary has just made the decision to hang up his uniform after twenty-seven years, and for his wife, his sister and me (not to mention our beloved soldier) our emotions are fragile.

Due to the fact that Roi had made the decision to abandon his children for his new life, he had no idea what was going on in their lives. Perhaps if he'd maintained a relationship with his kids, he would have been present for his son's promotion to lieutenant colonel—the same rank he himself had attained—and for his departure to Afghanistan. Roi lived only nine miles from Fort Belvoir, but history has a way of repeating itself. Roi's parents, despite the family's long line of military officers, were present only for his promotion to second lieutenant, and didn't make the eighty-mile drive from Pebble Beach, California to the Oakland Army Terminal to hug him goodbye as he left for Vietnam. My parents and one brother had flown to San Francisco to see him off and help me drive north along the beautiful Pacific Coast Highway to Seattle, where I would stay for that year.

Military families traditionally circle the wagons when a fellow military family member is in need of support, and especially in time of a deployment. Nicole and I reorganized and pulled up our bootstraps in order to become caretakers of his house and yard. We called ourselves *Mow, Blow, Go, and Some Pruning.* Thank goodness my daughter's townhouse association maintained the lawn, as one rather large yard was more than enough. I enjoy gardening, but mowing the lawn and pulling weeds on the hazy, hot and humid days of a Virginia summer is dreadful. Nicole was also tasked with trying to keep his car running, but keeping the battery alive proved to be a losing battle. She did jump it from time to time, and I give her credit for knowing about cables and terminals and where they should be attached—as Martha Stewart often says, "That's a good thing."

*Military families traditionally circle
the wagons when a fellow military
family member is in need of support,
and especially in time of a deployment.*

We spent Christmas 2010 in Seattle. Despite my son not being home, Santa was his jolly old self; we had a lovely day topped off with a family dinner with our neighbors. The downside of our holiday came the day after Christmas. Before Gary left for Afghanistan, he'd tried to motivate his dad to remove his belongings from the carriage house. When that didn't happen, however, he arranged and paid for the delivery and pickup of a commercial storage container, insurance, and one month's rent. All we needed to do was pack it with the offending stuff. Since announcing he wanted a divorce, Roi had had a little over two years to remove his things, but as with everything else he agreed to comply with, he gave the finger to doing that as well. Once again, my daughter and I would do the heavy lifting and take responsibility for Roi's mess. Thank goodness we had moved everything from his man cave in the basement of the house to the carriage house sixteen months prior. It was filled to the rafters with his furniture and books and hundreds of tools, some small, some large, some electrical, and some almost too heavy to move. There were metal footlockers that we had to unload so as to move them into the shipping container, and then repack them. We cursed every tool and personal item we touched.

*Once again, my daughter and I
would do the heavy lifting and take
responsibility for Roi's mess.*

We worked like dogs, as we had only two days to load the container. Having made over fifteen moves, I've marveled at the precision with which a professional would load a moving van, but my daughter and I not only lacked the talent to load it efficiently but didn't want to do it in the first place. In Roi's response to Gary's email several months earlier requesting him to remove his stuff, he blustered about suing if anything was damaged, so we photographed before, during, and after the packing. *If you're worried about the condition of your stuff, then come and pack it yourself—and forget suing, you can't afford to!*

> *In Roi's response to Gary's email several months earlier requesting him to remove his stuff, he blustered about suing if anything was damaged, so we photographed before, during, and after the packing. If you're worried about the condition of your stuff, then come and pack it yourself.*

When we received notice that the container was safely stored in a warehouse, Gary sent his dad an email to inform him that his belongings were no longer freeloading at the Seattle house. Roi was given all the information he'd need to take responsibility for the container. My son's email address would also inform his dad of his promotion and his deployment to Afghanistan. I wanted to think that as a former soldier having experienced war, he would at minimum say, "Keep your head down." A tragic missed opportunity by a so-called father!

Having cleared my carriage house, I returned to Virginia in February 2011 with a sense of accomplishment and filled with excitement about our vacation in Europe for Gary's R&R, but my euphoria didn't last long. Knock-knock! It was the mailman, and he was again handing me a large envelope that I needed to sign for. I could just tell that whatever was inside was smoking, and I knew in an instant it wasn't from Saint Nick. Surprise, surprise! It contained a three-page letter from Roi, complete with letterhead, looking like a terribly important business deal. It began with the all too familiar salutations: I'm a little surprised about his promotion and deployment. *Now whose fault might that be?* The bulk of the letter was a diatribe about Roi's belongings and the nerve of my placing them in storage without his permission, and on and on. Oh, but wait! When I finally read through the crap, I noticed that the signature looked different, and his name was spelled wrong. Having forged his name for the forty-five years we were married, primarily because he was either out of the country or on a business trip, I knew it had to have been signed by someone other than Roi. Surely the new wife didn't expect me to respond to a letter written and signed by her on his behalf?

Chapter Seventeen Take-Aways

- It's so important to keep Thanksgiving, Christmas and all family traditions alive.

- Find the humor in all things.

- Divorce will seem like it goes on forever, and sometimes it truly does; you may even have to keep up the fight after you're legally divorced.

- Be prepared to feel as if you are the only one following the marital agreement, giving your ex-spouse everything he wants and never getting what is owed to you.

18

War, Love, and R&R

It was time to be excited about our European vacation and our rendez-vous with our soldier. I'd been to Germany many times, but hadn't visited Austria or Italy since we lived there. According to our plans, my son's girlfriend would fly to Washington, D.C, from Colombia and join us on our flight to Munich, but her flight from Miami was canceled, and the next flight to D.C. would arrive too late for our flight to Germany. With quick maneuvering and scheduling skills, my daughter was able to help her book a flight from Miami to Richmond, Virginia. Richmond is a four-hour round-trip drive from Northern Virginia, but at midnight traffic is manageable. Starting off with a little drama was no guarantee that it would be the last in an otherwise perfectly planned vacation.

> *Starting off with a little drama*
> *was no guarantee that it would be*
> *the last in an otherwise perfectly*
> *planned vacation.*

My daughter and I are drama experts when it comes to family travel, especially if it involved a car driven by Roi. His tirades have erupted worldwide;

we just never knew what would trigger them. In Germany, early one morning on the Autobahn, the windshield-washer fluid in the BMW we were driving had frozen, and the windshield was clouded by road spray, so he hung out of the driver's-side window splashing bottled water on the windshield as we sped to Munich Airport. Fortunately for my daughter and me, our lips were frozen shut and we didn't make a peep. A roundabout in France is another drama just waiting to happen. If you're not familiar with the roundabout and the signs in French, it often requires a second or third trip around the circle as you try to translate the EXIT sign while dodging crazy drivers who know where to exit. Those were the times to keep one's French skills under wraps.

Though perhaps less exciting than Europe, drama can happen in Des Moines, Iowa, at the Hampton Inn on Interstate 80 West during a drive to Seattle in 2007. We had driven about 600 miles that day when, out of nowhere, Roi started verbally attacking me. His normally laughable drama had changed to rage; it was no longer funny, and I became afraid of him. We had checked in at the Hampton Des Moines-West and were on our way to find dinner, though at that moment, instead of food, I was thinking about how to get out of a moving car. I regret that I called my daughter while it was going on, but I thought that Roi might not want her to hear him and just give it up. Fortunately for me, that was the last cross-country drive we made together, but it was one I'll never forget—and, as usual, Roi didn't apologize.

A sandstorm in Kuwait kept the flight to Germany grounded, so the three of us picked up our rental car at the airport and drove south to Garmisch to the Edelweiss Hotel and Spa. The Edelweiss is the Armed Forces Recreation Center in Europe. It had been about ten years since Nicole and I had been to Garmisch, and the Edelweiss was only in the planning stage at that time. My first visit to the charming resort village was in 1963, and forty-eight years later it's still a magical place—a fabulous new hotel sitting at the base of the Zugspitze, Germany's highest mountain. The snow-covered mountains were so close I could almost reach out and touch them, and suddenly the drama of the last two and a half years was lifted from my shoulders, at least for a little while.

We returned to Munich Airport the next morning to pick up our soldier. It was such a relief for us all to be together that we graciously let him drive to Garmisch, which was to be our home base. We would drive south to Verona, Italy, where Gary and his girlfriend would catch the train to Rome; meanwhile, Nicole and I would take the train to Venice and spend two days there. We'd return to Verona, pick up our car, and drive to Assisi for an overnight, then finally rendezvous with Gary and his girlfriend in Florence to continue our vacation together. It's a few hours' drive from Garmisch to Verona, where the four of us had a leisurely lunch on the Piazza Bra near the Roman Arena, and afterwards had a quick look at Juliet's balcony. From here they caught the train to Rome.

My son's plan was to propose to his girlfriend in Rome but he needed stateside assistance, so Nicole and I packed the requested suit, tie and cufflinks that he wanted to wear for the special occasion (all he had in Afghanistan were ACUs or "fatigues" as they were called years ago). My daughter was in charge of the engagement ring, and to keep it safe she slid it onto a necklace that she wore on the flight. Gary was, however, going to have to pull off the proposal on his own.

We loved our day and a half in Venice, which we spent simply walking with an occasional stop for a glass of wine and some gelato. We took the return train trip to Verona for another night before having our car delivered to the hotel for the drive to the walled city of Assisi, perched on the slopes of Mount Subasio in Umbria. We became mountain goats as it was necessary to park close to the top of the mountain above the city; fortunately from there the walk was downhill. We had reservations at the Hotel Umbria, which we finally found nestled down a medieval back street. We hadn't been in the charming hotel ten minutes before my daughter got locked in the bathroom. I went off to search for the owner, and after a little game of charades, she was liberated. As the game played out, we were advised not to close the door tightly.

We climbed back up through the portico that led to the main street and headed farther down the hill to the Basilica of Saint Francis, a magnificent structure clinging to the side of that hill in the medieval town. I had hoped to find a statue of Saint Francis for my garden, as Saint Francis is the patron saint of animals and the environment. Frankly, it was fortunate that I didn't find the right one, as I didn't hear any offers to help carry it. The next morning we hiked back up the steep cobblestone street to the garage to retrieve our car for the drive to Florence, thankful with every step for the inventor of luggage on wheels.

Our drive to the outskirts of Florence was flawless, but for some unknown reason we lost the GPS signal when we really needed it. Our hotel was located on the Piazza Duomo; we could see the dome in the distance, but which narrow one-way dead-end street should we drive down? After several futile attempts to reconnect the GPS, we experienced a miracle, and by chance arrived at the Piazza only to be stopped by two carabinieri waving like crazies for us to halt. Speaking Italian and using hand signals, they told us that no cars were allowed on the piazza. Our reservations, however, were for a hotel on the piazza across from the Duomo. Nicole was pretty rattled by then, and I was desperately trying to stay calm as we tried another approach that took us right back to the piazza, where we decided to park the damn car. Since we couldn't read the street signs and didn't know if it was legal to park there, we determined—after having executed a perfect parallel park job—that it would be wiser to try driving the two blocks back to the piazza before the car was towed or stolen. Two more carabinieri appeared out of nowhere, and in English said, "We've been watching you." How did they know we spoke English, as we were driving a car with a little "D" for Deutschland on the license plate? Oh, goodie! I'd never pictured myself in an Italian jail, but then, it would have made a great story. I'm glad that my daughter regained her composure; she remembered that the hotel reservations were at her fingertips, and was able to show them to the police. Following their explicit instructions, we turned left on the piazza, and she brought that car to such an abrupt stop at the hotel's entrance that I nearly got whiplash. At that moment we were so thankful to be out of the car, no longer going in circles and being watched by the carabinieri, that we really didn't care where the hotel parked it.

Speaking Italian and using hand signals, they told us that no cars were allowed on the piazza.

We couldn't wait to share in the engaged couple's excitement. We hit the streets to look for a place to celebrate their engagement with a little champagne. They told us that our soldier had executed his proposal with perfect military precision, and to the delight of the crowd at the Trevi Fountain, she accepted. As the saying goes, "When in Rome, do as the Romans do"—a little romance, some wine and cheese, and everybody's happy. We spent the next three days doing what all tourists do: shopping, eating, visiting museums, and just enjoying the sights.

> *As the saying goes, "When in Rome,*
> *do as the Romans do"—a little*
> *romance, some wine and cheese,*
> *and everybody's happy.*

Roi and I had visited Florence in 1965, and I was eager to retrace our steps to the places we had visited. Nothing had changed noticeably except the crowds. I have a favorite photo of myself taken at the Piazza Michelangelo, and wanted to recreate the same setting, obviously a little older and a whole lot wiser. The girls had tickets to the Uffizi Gallery, so my son and I took a cab to the piazza where, after wading through the crowd and the tourist junk, I positioned myself for the photo. The piazza, located on a hill across the Arno River from Florence, offers a panoramic view of the city. Despite the crowds, nothing can change that view.

As we started our descent down the hill, across the river, and back to the Duomo, I found a bench to sit on while my son took photos of a beautiful tulip garden. I heard someone who was sharing the bench speak to me. He was an older gentleman, and I didn't understand what he had said, so I said, "I speak English."

In English, he replied, "I told you that you are more beautiful than the tulips."

I gasped and said, "Thank you." Who'd have guessed that I'd have to travel all the way to Italy to have a charming man seated on a bench with me enjoying the tulips and the panoramic view of Florence to hear such lovely words? I would've gone to Italy years before if I'd only known that sitting on a bench in a garden could be so reassuring. I'd have loved to share with my Italian admirer that I had visited the Piazza forty-six years earlier as a young bride and was there to recreate the memory. I don't know why I became so rattled; to this day I'm sorry I didn't try to communicate, as I usually strike up a conversation with someone wherever I go.

> *I would've gone to Italy years*
> *before if I'd only known that sitting*
> *on a bench in a garden could be*
> *so reassuring.*

We were brave enough to have the car delivered to the hotel the next day for a drive to see the Leaning Tower of Pisa, which, by the way, is still leaning. I swear, while we were away from Florence, that in a matter of hours the Italians dug up the very street we needed in order to return to our hotel, and they failed to put up signs saying, STREET CLOSED. Luckily, my daughter-in-law spoke Italian, so when we found ourselves on a closed one-way street with a perfectly good place to turn around, she was able to calm the Italian men who came running out of somewhere waving their arms and yelling no! We backed out, as it had been explained that we had to go out the way we'd come in. It still doesn't make sense, but when in Florence, do as the Florentines. My daughter and I hurried to the market the next morning for a last-minute purchase before leaving. I'd been disappointed about not finding Saint Francis, but without him taking up space in the car there was room for several handbags. Hardly set up for the day, the vendors gave us the "can't pass it up deal" as their first customers. I hope we brought them luck and a profitable day.

It was time to say *arrivederci* to Italy and head to Innsbruck, Austria, though not before we made a detour to Maranello, Italy, home of the Ferrari factory and museum. Gary is a Formula 1 racing fanatic, and that experience was definitely the icing on his cake. We were all excited to view the collection of former racing cars and the bevy of icons who'd driven them, but to see the excitement on my son's face was worth everything. With a few items from the gift shop, and after lunch in the little village, listening to the distinct sound of Ferraris shifting gears on the track that surrounds it, we left happy.

Having had the Ferrari experience, my daughter was ready to drive the steep, winding mountain roads through the Brenner Pass to Austria. Our German Ford couldn't compete with the unique sound of a Ferrari, so we just drove along quietly, changing gears and accelerating without calling attention to ourselves. Leaving the maze of Italian roads far behind, we welcomed the more orderly Austrian roads and drove to our hotel, The Goldener Adler in Innsbruck, like we knew where we were going. The family-run hotel, located in the heart of old Innsbruck, perfect for walking and enjoying charming little shops, was built in 1360, but don't worry, it's had many lovely upgrades. Some famous people have also enjoyed the hotel, like Wolfgang Amadeus Mozart, John Glenn, and hundreds of others. We left with a pledge to visit again soon.

We returned to our home base in Garmisch, with just two days left of my son's R&R. The early spring weather in Bavaria was just perfect for touring King Ludwig's two castles, nestled amongst the glistening snow-covered Alps. With a few Euros burning holes in our pockets, we went shopping and then indulged in more Weiner Schnitzel before saying *Auf Wiedersehen* to our wonderful vacation. Sometimes it's difficult to arrange just a dinner with one's kids, so to have spent sixteen days filled with fun and laughter in Europe with them was a great privilege.

I'm sad to say I've just learned that due to a Status of Forces Agreement between the United States and Germany, as of July 2015 military retirees and some active-duty service members traveling in Europe will not be eligible to stay at the Edelweiss. Don't panic, though, there are many lovely chalets to choose from in Garmisch.

Chapter Eighteen Take-Aways

◉ Life must continue even though the divorce drags along.

19

Where, Oh Where is the Alimony?

We'd been home from Europe for several days, suffering from post-vacation blues, when the news announced that a trusted Afghan soldier had held a number of Allied soldiers hostage and then murdered them in Kabul. We knew our soldier was back in Kabul, the capital of Afghanistan. By the time we heard the news, the incident had occurred over nine hours earlier, and finally we received a simple email that said, "We're okay." The tragedy had occurred within fifty yards of his office, and put the entire compound on lockdown for hours, so those two words were the answer to our prayers.

A friend gave me an article that covered the incident in Kabul, and I sent it to Roi. I had no way of knowing whether he'd heard the news of the murders, but he wouldn't know of his son's proximity to the tragedy. I had hoped that Roi, as a severely wounded Vietnam veteran who had personally experienced the ravages of war, would have concern for his son and reach out to him. I'd like to think that the article and the note didn't reach him, rather than think that he chose not to respond. It was the one and only time I tried to contact Roi with news of any kind.

Communications from a war zone today can be a blessing, with the opportunity to email, Skype, or use a stateside cell phone. It's a communication marvel, as "on the spot" reporting can leave a family in a state of panic, wondering if their loved one was in the area the media had just reported on. During Vietnam, if there were any embedded journalists out roaming the jungles of South East Asia, their instant-news capability wasn't that instant. Sometimes I would wait days for a letter; more often than not they came in bundles of two or three. Talk about a slow boat to China. I was notified by postcard from the Red Cross in the Philippines that my husband had been injured in Vietnam and would call me within a week.

Communications from a war zone today can be a blessing, with the opportunity to email, Skype, or use a stateside cell phone.

Ironically, I hadn't yet received the Red Cross notification, so when the Military Auxiliary Radio System (MARS) operator called, I thought it was just an opportunity for Roi to call me. The amateur radio operator explained that we would take turns speaking, rather like "over and out," and then I heard my husband say, "I'm in the hospital in the Philippines, I'm okay, but I don't look good, over." The word "hospital" and visions of "I don't look good" rendered me speechless. Without a heads-up from the Red Cross, I was caught by surprise. I told the operator that I didn't know what to say, and he said, "Tell him about the weather," so in the midst of a call from my hospitalized husband I said, "It's raining." And then I said, "Daddy just returned from the bakery with fresh hot bread and I'm eating a piece." Oh, jeez, that went well! I think Roi might've said that he didn't know when he'd be back in the U.S., but I don't remember any more of the conversation. I do remember that it was a Wednesday, it was definitely raining, and I was eating a piece of hot buttered raisin bread while looking out the window at the lake. Oddly enough, I was standing in the same location when that same husband said, "I'm divorcing you"—forty-one years later and I was once again speechless.

Today, if at all possible, the service member will call; if not, an official military member calls with as many details as available. It's a call no one wants to receive, though a little more personal than a postcard.

Roi's attorney suddenly canceled our court date for April 2011, placing the alimony issue on hold once again. Another word for alimony is "maintenance," and technically it means preserving someone's living expenses. I'm thankful that term was never used, as it sounds more like keeping the old car running. There's just something about saying, "I'm pursuing the maintenance man for living expenses" that could really give someone the wrong impression.

> *Another word for alimony is "maintenance," and technically it means preserving someone's living expenses.*

Court may have been canceled, but it was April, and the IRS was waiting to hear from me. It would by my first year to pay taxes on the elusive alimony payments, as the army retirement and Social Security benefit taxes are deducted at the source. The IRS recommends that a taxpayer file estimated quarterly taxes if the tax owed is more than $1,000. To avoid penalties or a large payment on April 15th, one can pay the predetermined payment schedule established by the IRS. My income was changing due to the fluctuation in alimony payments, but that was no excuse for my not paying what the IRS claimed I owed based on the previous year. The truth is, those three letters scared me to death. For the first filing after a divorce has been officially sanctioned by the court, and with one's new life still in disarray, it might be a good time to dump the whole mess in the lap of a professional tax preparer.

June 1, 2011 was the new court date for the second Rule to Show Cause against my ex for willfully violating the final order of divorce entered at the end of January 2010 and for bad faith in compliance with the terms of that order. Two and a half years had passed, and we were still doing the "hurry up and wait": wait for the attorney to file, wait for the court to set a date, wait for alimony, and wait for the stress, which is always the first to show up.

Two and a half years had passed,
and we were still doing the "hurry up
and wait": wait for the attorney to file,
wait for the court to set a date, wait
for alimony, and wait for the stress,
which is always the first to show up.

Perhaps the third court ruling would be the charm, as the *pendente lite* and the first Rule to Show Cause hadn't made Roi drop the alimony in the mailbox. Nicole and I were headed out the door in our finest going-to-court outfits when my cell phone rang. Dem had called to say that we'd be meeting at the opposing counsel's office instead of court. They must have figured they can't win in court, so perhaps with a "come-to-Jesus" meeting they might be able to work out the alimony issue, pay legal fees and no court costs, and above all avoid garnishment of Roi's wages.

I had requested his wages be garnished in the two previous lawsuits, but the request was blocked each time, due, I believe, to Roi's security clearance. To obtain a security clearance or retain one, very personal information is required, such as employment records and financial history such as bankruptcy, wage garnishments, tax liens, and unpaid judgments. The process is intended to select only people who exhibit high standards of honesty and integrity. Perhaps when Roi obtained it, he qualified.

Once again my legal team and I had spent weeks preparing for court, collecting bank statements for the last two years along with copies of checks returned for insufficient funds, and a copy of the now-famous bogus check. I was reminded that making copies of anything I might be asked to provide was a time saver and a stress reducer. Preparing to present a solid case takes time and is expensive. Dem gave me a printout of a few questions that he'd be asking while I was on the witness stand, and I read over them several times to refresh my memory. The few times I've been under oath, my memory has disappointed me. Despite the coaching, however, I've never come off as rehearsed.

We looked fabulous and capable of taking on the opposing counsel and his nasty, lying, scowling client. I was pleasantly surprised to see that the opposing counsel's office had been remodeled since that dreadful day in November 2009, when two well-paid attorneys attempted to create a legally binding marital agreement that ultimately became unenforceable.

The reception was cordial and civilized until Roi's attorney said, "Congratulations on your marriage" in front of Nicole, Dem, and me. What a disrespectful and insensitive thing to say in our presence, which simply validated our opinion of him. The meeting didn't take long, as we'd been endlessly charging Roi with noncompliance of alimony payments for two and a half years.

The opposing counsel's wife is a notary, and when she entered the conference room to notarize the new/old marital agreement she said, "I haven't seen you in a long time and you still can't look me in the eye." Whoa! She must have Roi's number. With that comment, his scowl worsened. The "come to Jesus" left him holding the bag for my attorneys' fees of over $2,000 and once again declaring he would pay on time. Each time Roi agrees to be punctual with payment, I notice that his nose grows longer and more bulbous, just like Pinocchio's. Dr. Phil often says, "Past behavior is a predictor of future behavior." I'm positive we'll continue to be involved with Roi and the alimony dilemma. It was time to make a speedy retreat from the intimate meeting, when the opposing counsel asked if there was anything else to discuss. With that, Roi launched a verbal attack. He'd just been waiting for that moment, and his attorney gave it to him. He accused me of packing his property, which had been in my carriage house for almost two years, without his permission. He claimed that my placing it in a storage facility under my name had made it impossible for him to take possession of the container. Anticipating the need to keep one step ahead and outsmarting him concerning the storage issue, I'd called the facility the day before this meeting to make sure he'd received the paperwork and had been paying the fees. They told me that he could have the "stuff" shipped anywhere, any time. He, however, wanted to continue attacking me, until eventually his attorney said, "She's answered your complaint."

I'll never know if his attorney was set up to ask whether there was anything else to discuss so Roi could launch into accusations about his stuff or whether his attorney was giving him the opportunity to divulge the fact that he was moving to Texas. Roi is one angry newlywed!

On our way home, Nicole told me that when she'd come face to face with her dad, whom she hadn't seen for a little over two and a half years, his greeting was "icy," but he did tell her that she was beautiful. They tried to make small talk; he failed to ask about his son's deployment, but he did say, "When the divorce is settled perhaps we can meet for coffee."

I thought the divorce had been officially settled for over a year and a half, but in his mind he kept it going. I can't say whether Nicole would agree to meet with him at some point, but I'm almost certain Gary would not be open to a meeting. I do believe that time heals some wounds, and changing circumstances and a little maturity might make a wound more tolerable, but I'm positive that neither of them would meet their dad in the company of his wife, and my instincts tell me that she wouldn't allow Roi to meet with them alone.

I could be crazy, and believe me that divorce will do that to you, but I walked away from the opposing counsel's office that day appreciative of the courteous way we'd been treated in light of the emotional drama that my daughter and I were experiencing. My intuition, or my antennae, as I refer to simply getting the vibe, gave me the feeling that the attorney/client relationship Roi had enjoyed was frayed or had unraveled altogether. For several days I pondered calling the office to thank the attorney's wife for their hospitality; again, I know it sounds crazy, but I had a sense that she had respect for me and I had nothing to lose by being polite. Just staying on the high road!

By George, the June 1, 2011 alimony payment was deposited in my account the very day of our "come-to-Jesus meeting"! I didn't hold my breath, because by July the old payment schedule was back in place, and the attorney's fees ordered the month before were not included. The brazen SOB was back!

Chapter Nineteen Take-Aways

- 👁 Going to court is the only way to address a non-compliance issue. You may end up having to keep going back to court. There really is no way for the courts to enforce payment of alimony.

- 👁 Be prepared to wait.

- 👁 Keep accurate notes and dates and stay on the high road; there's less traffic up there.

- 👁 Going over and over this crap is exhausting but good notes are a must.

A True Brats' Love Story

After a face-to-face with Roi I was once again headed to Seattle, loaded down with a suitcase-full of court documents, Microsoft Word 2012, an external hard drive, and various sundry other information.

I was becoming quite adept at jumping over and through hurdles and hoops, only to be faced with another roadblock set up by Roi. I felt inspired to share the nitty-gritty details of divorce, but where in the world did the idea to write a book come from? Oh, that's right—divorce made me do it. I hated English class. I wrote papers in school as a requirement, and I wrote thank-you notes because it was polite. If, however, I couldn't find a book that explained what really takes place in a divorce, perhaps I wasn't the only one.

> *I felt inspired to share the nitty-gritty details of divorce, but where in the world did the idea to write a book come from?*

With my limited email and Google skills, I clicked on the Microsoft Word icon, but I didn't know the term "icon." When I clicked on the "W," up popped something that looked like a sheet of paper, so I began to type. I was quite pleased with the first few pages, filled with my most brilliant words, when those pages suddenly vanished. It was horrifying! I couldn't remember one word I'd written, and I wasn't sure how it had happened, but the DELETE button may have been involved. That reminds me, I know how to type only because my mother enrolled me in a typing school in downtown Seattle the summer before my senior year in high school, and I very reluctantly went. The next Christmas I received a portable typewriter to use in college; years later, with the purchase of a family computer, that typewriter became a yard-sale item. Deleting something on a typewriter was either done with an eraser or Wite-Out, which made it darn hard to get rid of brilliant words quickly.

It was August in D.C., and my daughter was ready to escape the humidity for the cooler weather in the Pacific Northwest. With our family "computer guy" still deployed in Afghanistan, I needed Nicole's help to overcome my fear of mistakenly touching a wrong key. I wanted to be self-confident, have fun with the computer, and perhaps then be able to graduate to whatever new gadget might come along.

With her own version of the dummy manual, my daughter helped me create an icon for my book; then she had me click on the icon, and with that accomplished she instructed me to click on the word "File" and then on the word "Save." With several other newly learned tricks, I did my best to remain calm rather than in a perpetual state of panic. I know it's not easy giving your mother instructions, but having been a camp counselor for several summers, herding elementary-school girls around for eight weeks, she was able to be very patient while trying to bring my skills to a kindergarten level. I've come a long way since August 2011, and I learn something new every day or, for that matter, I learn what not to do but with confidence.

I hadn't been paying attention to what Nicole was doing with my so-called manuscript when I heard her say, "Oh, no!" She had entered Bunny's name and instantly several titles appeared, but the one that really caught her attention as well as mine was Voice America, featuring Roi and his wife telling their story on a live Internet program called Bratcon. Sons and daughters of military men and women are referred to as brats, and the two of them qualify for that distinction. With one click of the mouse, we became embroiled in a live Web program recorded on May 26, 2011.

Oh, no!

Bizarre hardly describes the experience. We had the volume on our listening ears as high as it would go so as not to miss a word. The host opened the program with a tribute to honor Memorial Day. Then he welcomed Roi and his wife who as members of the military brats group were there to share their "true love story" with the interviewer, the only reason they were on the program.

Nicole and I and I were utterly speechless, and we'd heard only the opening of a fifty-five-minute program. A quick synopsis of their brat lives indicated that both their fathers had been air force colonels and both teens had attended American High School, though their paths hadn't crossed in high school, as Roi had graduated twelve years ahead of his wife, who'd graduated from high school in the States.

The host said, "You were married thirteen months ago after meeting in Orlando at the American High School Reunion?" They responded yes. The host then went on to ask about children. Bunny said, "I have three daughters and five grandchildren," but Roi wasn't asked if he had children; neither did he mention that he did, and his wife remained silent. She then said, "I moved to Northern Virginia to sightsee for two years." Roi explained that he had come from a family with a long line of military service dating back to the Civil War and that he was a fifth-generation West Pointer. That could have been an opening to say, "My son is a lieutenant colonel serving in Afghanistan," but since he'd passed up the opportunity to say that he had children, why bother?

Roi did attend West Point, but he didn't graduate from there. The host then asked, "When you retired from the army twenty-three years ago, you stayed in Northern Virginia?" He gave a weak yes, and went on to say, "I've worked for several beltway contractors—it's my way of repaying my soldiers." By then, Nicole and I were just about ready to puke, but we soldiered on through the amazing tale. Asked to describe their meeting in Orlando, in unison they said, "We hit it off immediately." While under oath at her deposition, she'd stated they had met at the registration desk.

Roi went on to tell how he had been sitting at the pool waiting for Bunny, and as she approached he realized she was wearing the most amazing bikini. That made her giggle on air. Roi explained how he couldn't keep his eyes off her for the next four hours while the sun burned him to a crisp. He then said, "In spite of the sunburn, I was a rock star doing the twist that evening at the gala while wearing tennis shoes." He sounded like a certifiable goofball in his attempt to sound like a teenager in love.

When they'd exchanged addresses and phone numbers, they were thrilled to find out that they lived about ten miles from each other, and started dating immediately upon their return to Virginia. In the thrill of the moment of being interviewed on a live talk show, Roi not only forgot to mention his kids but also forgot to mention that *he was living with his wife* just ten miles from Bunny's apartment. Immediately before the program took a break, the host congratulated them for being the first brat couple to tell their love story on the show. Since we were listening to a tape, we didn't have to wait for the break to end; we fast-forwarded into the rest of the story.

The host asked Bunny to tell the audience about the wedding and she said, "Before I tell about the wedding, I want to tell you about flying out to Nevada to visit the cemetery where my father is buried, so Roi could ask my father for permission to marry me."

The host then said, "You knew right then that he was an officer and a gentleman."

More giggles, and she said yes. An officer and a gentleman—what a load of crap! Something tells me that the interviewer wouldn't have given them air time had he known about Roi's philandering, adultery, abandonment, and lying.

Bunny described the wedding as one of red, white, and blue. OMG, she's giggling again. She said, "It was a wonderful day. My three daughters were bridesmaids and all of my family including my mother, was there. When I entered the sanctuary all I could see was Roi wearing his beautiful, blue uniform with all his shiny medals waiting for me to walk down the aisle. The wedding was unbelievable."

Roi then said, "It was a perfect day, and our perfect days haven't stopped yet."

The host asked Bunny to describe her wedding flowers and how she gifted them to the Vietnam Memorial. She explained the sadness that her family had endured over the loss of her brother, an air force officer missing in action in Vietnam, and how she wanted to remember him by taking the French tulips that had decorated the church and lay them at the base of the memorial from one end to the other. She said, "The French tulips signify our Paris connection." (At about that time I remembered an old camp song: Hasten, Jason, fetch the basin. Oops! Slop, fetch the mop.) Roi waited in the car near the memorial while his wife made repeated trips with buckets of tulips until they were all distributed, and then she left her red-rose bouquet at the base of the panel that contains the name of her brother.

Roi was then asked to describe an event that took place in Laos on April 14, 1968. The host asked, "It was a Central Intelligence Agency (CIA) mission?"

Roi sighed and whispered, "Yes, but as you know, we were not in Laos," giving the impression that the mission was highly classified. At that point the host said, "Uh-huh."

What in the hell did he just say? We lived at Fort Sill, Oklahoma and I was seven months pregnant, exactly two months and five days before our son's birth. We couldn't wait to hear the rest of the story, though nothing could have prepared us for what we were about to hear.

> *We couldn't wait to hear the rest of the story, though nothing could have prepared us for what we were about to hear.*

Roi was filled with emotion as he said, "I was flying in support of a night incursion into enemy territory to pick up five guys. I don't know how long they had been in the area, but we successfully picked them up, but then I took a round in the hydraulic of my chopper and we crashed." He started to sob but pulled himself together and continued, "The five guys were killed, and my crew chief and I became guests of the Pathet Lao for the next three and a half months." Roi then told about the monsoon season, when he and his crew chief, Dave, lost so much weight that they were able to squeeze out between the bamboo poles that kept them imprisoned. Free from captivity, they ran, swam, fell down, got up, ran, and swam till they were rescued and medevaced to Brook Army Hospital in San Antonio, Texas.

OMG! Is this ever going to end?

Roi explained that he'd been unable to talk about the classified mission and had kept his emotions bottled up for forty-one years. Bunny had encouraged him to attend a group that she had sought comfort from in her past. Roi said, "I agreed to go, even though I thought it was hocus-pocus and gobbledygook." The forum was a weekend event and the first night's topic was personal and family loss. The group was asked to close their eyes and imagine an event in their lives, when Roi said, "Evidently I was acting out or having a panic attack when the forum leader came off the stage to see if I needed help." Roi then said, "I told him about the five guys who died in the crash that night and how I felt responsible." The facilitator told him to go home and write down the details of the Laos mission.

The next evening, Roi said, "I spent forty-five minutes pouring out the details of that event in a letter, and after writing it all down and letting it go, I felt so calm." He was asked to read his letter to the 150 participants, and with convincing passion he said, "Now I can honestly say it wasn't my fault. I didn't put that bullet through my aircraft."

The host asked if there was anyone he'd like to thank, and Roi said, "Yes, I give credit to my wife for helping me shed the weight of grief that I've been carrying for so many years."

The host lamented that it was a huge burden to carry all of those years, and then asked, "Have you been in touch with your crew chief, Dave?" Once again Roi was boo-hooing and told the host, "I frequently talk to Dave, who lives in Orlando, and I wanted him to come to the wedding but he has cancer and couldn't make it."

In wrapping up, the lovebirds are asked to describe their memories of being brats. Roi said, "I'm honored and very fortunate to have served with so many soldiers and officers with tremendous skills. Because of my dad and his career I lived out of a suitcase for years, and went everywhere in the world along with my dogs. I'm blessed to have survived and met this beautiful woman, and it's my hope to spend many years with her and the happiness that she gives to me every day."

The host said, "In closing, it's very clear you have a unique love story, based in your culture and your brat roots, and I know how tough it must have been for you to talk about Laos. Our honor and pleasure, it's a true brat love story."

My daughter and I were in a state of disbelief, but she was still capable of pressing the SEND key, and the whole sordid conversation was off to Afghanistan for her brother to critique. Should we laugh or should we cry or should we use a few four-letter words to express our complete incredulity over what we'd heard come out of Roi's mouth and in his voice? It was sickening. Not only a cheater, he lied by omission, telling a cock-and-bull story. Only his voice remained the same. Did we find that Web program taped on May 26, 2011 by chance, or were we meant to hear it?

> *Not only a cheater,*
> *he lied by omission, telling a*
> *cock-and-bull story.*

When you've been officially married to someone for forty-six years you know all the important events in your shared life. The story Roi had told about his life, other than his new life, was untrue. I was present from the beginning; I pinned on his second lieutenant's bars before he reported to the US Army Field Artillery School, Fort Sill, Oklahoma and upon completion of the course reported to the US Army Airborne School, Fort Benning, Georgia widely known as Jump School. He didn't complete the course at Jump School, having been diagnosed with colorblindness, a condition that disqualified him from Jump School and the Army Aviation School. There was no way he could have flown anything but a kite.

In the forty-two years since his return from Vietnam I had never heard the lie about being an enemy combatant or being tortured with needles much less anything about a CIA mission in Laos, simply because it never happened. His whereabouts at the time can be substantiated.

My son's explanation for the lie is that Roi fabricated the story when he met Bunny to make himself appear more important and successful, as he gives her credit for encouraging him to tell the really big lie to a really big group.

Within hours of Gary receiving the email with the link to the broadcast, we had his reply to the host of the VoiceAmerica Bratcon program. My son's email reads:

I am afraid you have been duped. It has recently come to my attention that you ran a program on 26 May 2011 in which you hosted two individuals, Roi and Bunny. I am the son of Roi. I am writing you from the NATO ISAF Joint Command in Kabul, Afghanistan, where I have been deployed since December 2010 in support of Operation Enduring Freedom. I felt it was necessary to make you aware of the true facts, as I am sure you intended your program to be a somber reminder of those who have died serving our country, and not a forum for someone to make outlandish claims.

Roi retired from the army in 1983 after twenty-two years in service. This much is true; however, he didn't graduate from the United States Military Academy. He moved to Seattle where his father and mother lived at the time. He met my mother in 1960 at Seattle University, and they were married for forty-six years. His current wife was his most recent mistress until my mother divorced him in 2010. It is unfortunate that my father would use your show to degrade the military and the memory of those who have served and died protecting it. It is true he served in Vietnam, but for less than one tour, as he was wounded in 1967 while commanding a field artillery battery in Pleiku Central Highlands. He was by no means involved in any way in classified operations flying around in Laos in April 1968, nor was he held captive by the Pathet Lao as he claims. Instead he was attending the Field Artillery Advanced Officers course at Fort Sill, Oklahoma, and in June of that year I was born. My father was at Comanche County Hospital in Lawton, Oklahoma, in June 1968, and not swimming out of some monsoon-soaked jungle in Laos. He has fabricated this incredible story of clandestine operations to impress his new wife.

I apologize that he chose to make a mockery of your show to perpetrate his fantasies. I write only because those stories have hurt my mother and sister and me, who stood by him for over forty years through his recovery from wounds sustained in Vietnam, numerous failed jobs, and of course a few adulterous affairs. I recommend that you withdraw this recorded program from your archives out of respect for the great number of veterans and comrades in arms you paid respect to at the end of your program.

It was a matter of hours until my son received an email from the show host expressing his shock and the need to evaluate the information he had been given. The host, who just happened to be a retired army criminal investigator, said, "My initial reaction is to obtain corroborating evidence. In no way do I mean to dismiss what you have told me, but I don't want to act prematurely or without a clear understanding of the facts, as our broadcast is interested in the truth."

> *The host, who just happened to be a retired army criminal investigator, said, "My initial reaction is to obtain corroborating evidence. In no way do I mean to dismiss what you have told me, but I don't want to act prematurely or without a clear understanding of the facts, as our broadcast is interested in the truth."*

Gary was asked to provide the program host with several names of people who would know the truth about Roi's career. My son gave him several names of long-time military friends who had served with Roi, along with my name and our contact information. Knowing that I as the divorced wife was undoubtedly thought to be a raging bitch, I didn't expect to talk to the host; but about a week later he called. We had all become embroiled in Roi's unimaginable lies. The host had a nationally broadcast program to protect and I wanted to expose those lies.

The program host called former colleagues of his at the Army Criminal Investigation Command (CID), who sent a member stationed in

Afghanistan to visit Gary in Kabul to verify that he was who he said he was (Fool me once, shame on you; fool me twice, shame on me). With his identity confirmed, the program proceeded to get in touch with Roi, giving him the opportunity to explain his participation in the hoax before they printed a retraction of the May broadcast.

The email to Roi from the host of Bratcon said:

> Our program has been contacted by a person alleging that certain comments made by you were a misrepresentation of the facts. We were naturally caught by surprise and felt the obligation to verify the source of those claims. We therefore reached out to my former colleagues in the Army Criminal Investigation Command to assist us in sorting out the facts. The person who contacted us is the Lieutenant Colonel Gary, whom we have now confirmed as your son and a bona fide active-duty army officer stationed in Kabul, Afghanistan.
>
> It was asserted that you had not participated or piloted a clandestine mission in Laos and had not been shot down or held as a POW and subsequently escaped. Our investigative sources have confirmed that you were severely wounded in the spring of 1967 in Vietnam and spent the better part of twelve months recovering, including surgeries that would have precluded you from such a mission in 1968 as you represented. Furthermore, we have determined through the Defense Intelligence Agency records on Laos that your name and the mission you recounted were not found in any records relating to Laos missions. We are confident that our source on the matter is accurate. We will air an editorial correction, and we welcome you to explain your representation of the Laos mission. We did honor your fine military service record on the program when we were honoring the "fallen" on Memorial Day.

Only a contemptible person would become so caught up in his lie about being a captive in Laos that he would repeat that lie to his mistress, strangers, and his attorney when he was interviewing as a client. Roi's attorney found that the date of his captivity in April 1968 and my son's birth in June 1968 implied that I must have had an affair; therefore all of the offensive questions during the deposition were about where and with whom I lived during Roi's tour in Vietnam, and then questioning my son about his paternity. Roi's callous lies caused my son and me to endure ugly questions, while Roi sat there knowing the real truth. The most pathetic aspect was that he didn't give a damn. It would be two and a half years before we would know the rationale behind the distasteful questions asked during our depositions; thanks to the online broadcast, we finally had an answer.

It has taken me almost eight years to come up with a theory about why Bunny believed I had been dead for five and a half years, and according to the Bratcon interview, she must have believed Roi's POW story, as she'd encouraged him to seek professional help.

Roi states that he spent one evening writing a letter outlining all the details of the clandestine foray into Laos, including the chopper crash, the five lives lost, being held captive, his escape, and his rescue—and poof—he was cured of guilt. It's a miracle!

My theory is that he and Bunny met online prior to the American High School Reunion in April 2008. His profile undoubtedly listed him as a widower and likely a former POW. He convincingly told everyone his fabricated story about Laos. I'm positive that in his wildest imagination he never anticipated that his ex-wife and children would hear the broadcast and end up being investigated by the Army Criminal Investigation Command and that the story would be eventually expunded from the Bratcon radio show. Life becomes so complicated when people lie.

It's a small world, even in the National Capital Region with its population of over 9 million. Surprisingly, there were others who hadn't heard the live broadcast; instead they heard it straight from the horse's mouth. Poolside seating was limited that Sunday at the Alexandria, Virginia apartments where Roi and Bunny lived, when they asked a couple if they might join them. The woman at the table thought she recognized the man, though until they made introductions she wasn't certain that it was Nicole's dad, whom she'd met at a function they had both attended. I'm sure she and her husband had gone to the pool for an enjoyable afternoon; instead they were going to hear what they'd missed on the broadcast. Upon excusing themselves and walking away, the husband said, "That guy is full of shit." You just never know whom you're talking to, much less whom they know. The gracious lady who'd shared her table at the pool that afternoon was my daughter's boss.

It had been a little over a year since we listened to the VoiceAmerica Bratcon broadcast, which is no longer on the air when the Supreme Court overturned the original Stolen Valor Act of 2005 backed by The American Legion. The act was passed to address the issue of those who deliberately lie about military service; wear medals they did not earn or make claims of combat heroism they did not achieve. The Supreme Court deemed the act unconstitutional because in the justice's opinion it was too broad in scope and violated the right to free speech. The Court held that one's First Amendment right to be ordinary garden-variety pond scum, while contemptible, was protected by the First Amendment.

The amended Stolen Valor Act of 2013 "makes it a Federal crime for an individual to fraudulently hold oneself out to be a recipient of any of several specified military decorations or medals with the intention to obtain money, property, or other tangible benefits." The new law was the government's latest attempt to protect real military heroes from the phonies. Roi is a retired army officer who served for twenty-three years, but he has falsely claimed a rank he did not earn and a bogus CIA mission. How very sad to believe, as my children do, that he sacrificed his integrity for a woman.

Chapter Twenty Take-Aways

- ◎ You may surprise yourself and learn new skills such as using the computer for more than email and surfing the internet. I became inspired to share my story.

- ◎ The journey may continue even after you're legally divorced.

- ◎ You may need to continue your investigative process.

- ◎ There's no doubt that your ex-spouse will continue to shock you and you will find out you really no longer know who he is.

- Stay on the high road and keep dates and notes. It takes over your life, but you deserve to live a comparable life to what you had before he made the decision to divorce you.

21
The 29th Returns

I returned to Virginia the middle of September 2011 so my daughter and I could spit shine my son's home and garden for his return from Afghanistan at the end of October. Nicole had done her best to keep the lawn mowed, but the weeds had thrived in the hot humid weather and some were the size of small trees. It was evident that we needed reinforcements to help polish the place. The cobwebs and dust had taken over inside but that too shined when we were through. Just three more days until he would be back on United States soil and his fiancée had arrived from Colombia. The two ladies were busy painting a huge WELCOME HOME sign to hang across the front of his house, when my cell phone rang. Nicole grabbed it and answered, and as I looked at her I realized her expression was that of a deer caught in the headlights, but I had no clue as to who was calling.

Nicole grabbed it and answered, and as I looked at her I realized her expression was that of a deer caught in the headlights, but I had no clue as to who was calling.

Whispering, she said, "It's dad."

In a questioning voice, I asked, "Who?"

"It's dad!" She handed me the phone and I answered with the usual niceties and then he explained that he and the wife had moved to San Antonio, Texas. In a confrontational tone he told me that the storage container we had packed ten months earlier had arrived from Seattle. He then said, "I haven't completely unloaded it, but I noticed some items are missing."

I knew immediately which items he was referring to; however, I didn't take the bait. He had caught me completely off guard, as the last time I was on the phone with him was the night, four years before, when he said, "I'm divorcing you." I was desperately trying to shift gears from having fun preparing for my son's return to responding to a jackass on the phone who was insinuating I hadn't included all the stuff he wanted from Seattle. In response to his arrogance, I said, "I considered those items abandoned, just like you abandoned your children, darlin." That was undoubtedly a poor choice of words, even with a Southern twist. The veiled endearment did not turn him into Mr. Nice Guy, and he didn't disappoint me, as he immediately turned into his arrogant whoop-de-do persona, threatening to sue me for the missing items. I'm thankful I was able to gain control of my mouth, as I really wanted to say, "Hey fella, you're mighty lucky to have any of your stuff without ever lifting a finger or reimbursing our son."

After we'd been legally divorced for twenty-one months, just how long was I supposed to offer free storage?

Roi then told me that he'd lost his job and wouldn't be making alimony payments starting immediately. He claimed that the marital agreement contained a provision for the loss of employment and forgiveness of alimony payments. There are only forty-nine pages in that agreement, and nowhere does it mention a "get out of alimony payments free card." I wanted to say, "We'll just see about that," but, eager to end the conversation, I simply said, "You lie, but thank you for callin'," and I hung up. What a pompous ass, continuing to ignore the fact that a marital agreement is a legal contract that cannot arbitrarily be breached by a guy who, for whatever reason, finds it inconvenient.

> *Roi then told me that he'd lost his*
> *job and wouldn't be making alimony*
> *payments starting immediately.*
> *He claimed that the marital agreement*
> *contained a provision for the loss*
> *of employment and forgiveness*
> *of alimony payments.*

The girls had their eyes glued on me while I was on the phone, and when I hung up the three of us simply looked at each other until I was able to process what Roi had said. My son's fiancé was new to our family drama, and I didn't know how much Gary had told her, but I've tried to be careful about the details. I'm positive that she'll never hear Roi's side of the sordid affair, and we know that the pancake does have two sides, though the side with the butter and syrup is the best.

I had my attorney's office phone on speed dial, and thank goodness he was available as I was eager to report the latest from Roi. Dem told me that we'd have to wait about two months before we could once again file with the court to make sure Roi was telling the truth. Divorce is all about waiting and due process, and so the wait began.

Our soldier's return was the most important event, and all other issues would be handled in time. It was a day filled with emotion, as he and his fellow soldiers of the 29th Infantry Division returned safely, though sadly not to a parade or a band or a blizzard of confetti. We all knew that they deserved a ticker-tape welcome but having him home would have to do. Adjusting to having him back in the States was so much easier than letting him go the year before. Juli returned to Colombia while her paperwork was processed for her new life in the U.S. In the meantime, Thanksgiving and Christmas had come and gone, and I returned to Seattle.

There comes a time when you go to the mailbox and wish you were staring at a snake that some little jerk put there, instead of an envelope with IRS in the upper left-hand corner. Those three letters are far more frightening than a serpent, especially when you know it's not a refund. The letter suggested that I might have failed to file a 1099 form for capital-gains interest in 2010 on some jointly owned savings bonds. Just a minute, now! I'm quite sure that I fall into the ultra-organized-person category, and would never knowingly ignore the mighty IRS.

When Roi was a second lieutenant, he signed up to purchase savings bonds out of his monthly pay, and did so from 1963 to 1974. In January 2010, in compliance with the marital agreement, while suffering from naiveté and doing the right thing, I cashed the bonds at my Seattle bank and dutifully wrote Roi a check for half of the amount. The bank never mentioned that there would be an obligation to pay interest on the income from the bonds during the cashing-out process, and the thought of taxes had never occurred to me—just another of those occasions for a "happy pill" and deep breathing!

I sought the advice of my mother's accountant, who had handled all of Mother's financial needs, including her federal income taxes, for years. Within seconds of reading the IRS letter, he said, "Just pay the $3,000." I suddenly recalled he'd taken the same approach with my mother's money. He then advised that I wouldn't want to mess with the IRS, and believe me: I was savvy enough to know that. The tax bill needed to be shared, however, and I knew that involving attorneys guaranteed that I'd be paying the attorneys' fees while still holding the bag for the whole tax bill. It was imperative that I find another solution; I just needed to research my options. I'm reminded of the old days, back in the 1960s, when you had to drive to the library to do research, find a parking space, remember to keep track of the time on the meter, and then spend what little time you had searching for the information. Whoops! The meter's up, and you'll have to return another time. I love Google: no car, no parking, no meters, no ticket, and no library memories. By the way, the accountant didn't charge me for the free advice, and I didn't become a client.

Chapter Twenty-One Take-Aways

⚬ You may need to chase your ex-spouse to a new state. Be prepared to find a family law attorney in another state to enforce the marital agreement.

- In my case it always felt like I was filing another motion; I was either taking him back to court, or waiting for his due process, or waiting for a court date and waiting, waiting and waiting.

- Should you have to work with the IRS, do so calmly and you will typically find them to be helpful. They may have resources to help you identify who really is responsible for paying them.

- Be tenacious and don't give up.

Contempt of Court – and Stalking

Three months had passed since Roi had discontinued his alimony payments and had been given time for due process, so on January 23, 2012 we filed with the Fairfax County Court for the fourth time due to his inability to follow court orders. My son was busy keeping tabs on the address we were given for the San Antonio residence; he found the deed of trust and all the paperwork connected with the Veterans Home Loan (VA) purchase of the home on the Internet, and printed copies. That information gave us the ability to modify the court order from renter to owner. It's frightening to realize just how much of our personal information is public knowledge and available to anyone; but in this case it was to my benefit, as owning a home showed that Roi was able to qualify for a home purchase and knowingly chose to ignore alimony obligations.

> *It's frightening to realize just how much of our personal information is public knowledge and available to anyone; but in this case it was to my benefit, as owning a home showed that Roi was able to qualify for a home purchase and knowingly chose to ignore alimony obligations.*

The home is a two-story with four bedrooms, four baths, a three-car garage, and an in-ground pool and hot tub surrounded by an outdoor kitchen. It's a lot of house for seventy-year-olds, but plenty of room for Bunny's daughters and a pool for her grandchildren. Obviously, my alimony payment was needed to maintain the lifestyle. A nice Texas lawman served Roi with the Fairfax County Court summons in February informing him that a Rule to Show Cause, requesting a judge to make a decision about a case, was filed in January and that there'd be a court hearing on March 9, 2012.

I'd been in Seattle for a few weeks intending to stay through March, but my attorney strongly encouraged me to be in Virginia for the court date. I immediately rescheduled my return flight (at cost, of course), allowing me time for a visit to the hair salon and coaching for questions that I'd be asked under oath.

While I was at Dem's law firm, an email arrived for my attorney from Roi. It stated that his Virginia employer had terminated him due to his voluntary relocation to Texas. He further stated that he had contacted his Virginia divorce attorney to represent him, as he couldn't afford to travel to Virginia. The attorney had informed him that his workload would not permit him to represent Roi; instead he'd refer him to a colleague. It would take several days to retain the new attorney, as Roi would have to sign the client agreement and arrange for money to pay the retainer. Something tells me that after four years of defending the indefensible, the attorney realized his client was nothing but a repeat offender.

My attorney agreed to postpone the court hearing for no longer than one week, and informed Roi that if he wanted to avoid court we would accept $30,000 in certified funds by close of business Thursday, March 8, 2012, which represented the alimony arrearages up to that time. He told Roi that he would ask the court to continue the hearing to July 13, 2013 for a dismissal conditioned upon his timely payments of the full amount of spousal support per the June 1, 2011 agreement. "You stated that your credit cards were maxed out and that you are on limited Social Security and military retirement income. It is not my place to state where the funds come from, but if you have any available private sources of funding, perhaps through your spouse, that would be perfectly acceptable."

My impression of Roi's spouse is of a woman on a mission to entrap a gullible dolt who undoubtedly boasted that he could offer her a lavish lifestyle, and just because the two engaged in collective incompetence with his money, she was not going to be dumb enough to share her good fortune with his ex-wife.

Going home confident that my hair looked great and my outfit was ready, I would review the questions just in case I might be called to the witness stand. The questions mostly concerned dates. Having reviewed my deposition transcript from October 2009 in which I repeatedly said some event took place (for example in 1997 when it had actually occurred in 2007); I was determined to be more precise at the next hearing. Roi always claimed that I could remember our first argument in 1963, so I'll attest to having an excellent memory— but evidently not under oath.

My son accompanied me to court on March 16, 2012, though the alimony check, Roi, and his new attorney were no-shows. No surprise! We were assigned to a courtroom filled with people, when Dem suddenly said, "Follow me" and we found ourselves in a room with a court recorder, a sheriff, and the three of us until the judge arrived. She came swishing into the room just like Judge Judy, though in Judy's court she'd have had some very choice words for the delinquent Roi, but that's the difference between TV and real life.

Dem presented exhibits numbering about 150 pages including copies of the deed of trust for the Texas property, copies of the Virginia employer's letters, and Roi's current correspondence. Without his appearance, I again didn't have the opportunity to prove that I could be compelling on the witness stand. The whole proceeding took about thirty minutes, and we left not knowing how the judge would rule. In four days the verdict was returned, and on Monday morning Dem's chuckling paralegal called with the news that the charge was "contempt of court," and then we were both laughing.

So, what does that mean? The ruling gave Roi thirty days to pay the arrears, and if at the end of ninety days he had not had his attorney set a court date to vacate, the contempt of court would be permanent and he would still owe me $30,000. Going to court to vacate a contempt of court order could cost him several thousand on top of the $30,000 he owed me, so the best advice for Roi would be to just pay up and stay away from Virginia.

With the most recent court case in my rearview mirror, it was time to deal with the IRS and their monthly reminders of the "need" to pay. In fact, the exact wording was "The income and payment information that we have on file does not match entries on your 2010 Form 1040." It went on to inform me that if I didn't respond by March 22, 2012 the interest would increase along with penalties.

I was exhausted from dealing with the ongoing divorce but I couldn't take my eyes off either issue. It was time, however, for my yearly visit to the eye clinic at Walter Reed (now known as Walter Reed National Medical Center), to make sure I would continue to see everything clearly. When I arrived at the clinic, I told the receptionist my name and handed her my ID card. She returned the card along with several forms for me to give to the doctor, but to my horror the name on the forms was that of Roi's new wife. I gasped and said, "The name on these forms is my ex-husband's new wife," and with that the receptionist grabbed the forms out of my hand to the amusement of other patients, as I hadn't exactly whispered my indignation.

> *I was exhausted from dealing with the ongoing divorce but I couldn't take my eyes off either issue.*

Roi and I had been patients of chief of ophthalmology services at Walter Reed for many years. The doctor strongly suggested that before I left the hospital I should visit the personnel office as the fiasco had everything to do with the ex's Social Security number; one number and two wives was once again the problem. I'd been running around with my new ID for almost two years, oblivious of any problem and assuming (and we know what that means) that when, after the divorce, I renewed the card with all the required forms, that the correct information would have been entered on it. A cute navy corpsman corrected the error, ensuring that I would never again be identified as Bunny.

Seeing clearly and with a cup of coffee in hand, I phoned the number on the IRS notice; after holding for an hour, I spoke with a very nice agent who gave me the information I'd need to navigate the IRS's own ruling on savings bonds. The IRS has a whole brochure, Publication 550, explaining who is responsible for paying the tax owed on United States Savings Bond Interest, and I could download all the information from the Web for "free," one of my favorite words, and follow the instructions. It suggested that I write a letter explaining whose income had purchased the savings bonds, enclose copies of each bond, and forward everything to the address on the notice. Of course I had to pay the bank for copies of the bonds, but having learned the hard way I made extra copies just in case. I sent that packet off by registered mail, return receipt, and within a week I received the confirmation that it had reached the IRS.

In the meantime, the visa papers were approved for my son's fiancée, and it was time to help plan a wedding. They were married in Virginia at Great Falls Park, overlooking the Potomac on a perfectly beautiful day in early May of 2012. Good friends and family attended, and later enjoyed a beautiful luncheon reception for the newlyweds. It was hard to believe that it had been a year since the four of us had been in Europe for my son's R&R, and that it was now time to add a new chapter to our family history.

An arrogant person knows no bounds, so you never know when or where he will choose to treat you to his offensive air of superiority. About two months after Roi had thumbed his nose at the Virginia Court I was in church one Sunday in May and there he was, seated across the aisle from me. Evidently, he'd lied to my attorney and the court when he said he couldn't afford to come to the D.C. area for court, because the person across the aisle sure looked like my ex. The moment I saw him glaring at me, I experienced a jolt of fear that ran from the bottoms of my feet to the top of my head. I became so overheated I thought I might faint. I hung on to the cool edge of the pew until I'd calmed down and felt somewhat in control. I hadn't seen Roi in almost a year because he'd, of course, ignored the court summons, so what in hell was he doing in church?

> *The moment I saw him glaring at me, I experienced a jolt of fear that ran from the bottoms of my feet to the top of my head.*

I began to question, "Is that really him?" But I made eye contact with him on two occasions, and recognized the anger and hatred in those eyes. I managed to make all the appropriate devotional moves, but instead of listening and participating fully, I was planning how to get safely to my car. I probably shouldn't waste prayers asking for a parking place near the church, though considering that it's located on one of D.C.'s busiest streets, I did that morning. Who am I to question how it happened but one spot was available right in front of the church just waiting for me, and I took it. At the end of the service, I remained seated long enough for the other parishioners to exit, and before leaving the steps I made sure I couldn't see Roi anywhere near my car. Truthfully, I was embarrassed to ask for help and I acted irresponsibly by going to my car alone, even though it was parked within sight of the church doors.

When I told my attorney about the incident he immediately called it stalking, as did everyone I talked to including the rector of the church. We developed a plan just in case Roi pulled that stunt again. With the unpredictability of divorce, anything can happen. I firmly believe that had my duaghter been in church that day she would have had no doubts about his identity, and I'm certain she'd have had him respectfully escorted out. Her father may be a member of that church, but certainly not one in good standing.

> *With the unpredictability of divorce, anything can happen.*

While juggling court cases and a stalking ex-husband, I continued to receive IRS notices suggesting I might want to pay the taxes. Having sent copies of the bonds and an accompanying letter as I'd been instructed to do by an agent six weeks earlier, and having received proof that the information had been received, I expected a letter saying MATTER CLOSED. Quite evidently, I don't understand the IRS!

It was once again time to head to Seattle for the summer, and I arrived simply wanting to relish all the things I love about having a home there. Before I could enjoy anything, however, I needed to visit an IRS office. Meeting face to face with an agent might make understanding the problem easier, and perhaps it could be solved on the spot. It was absolutely the last thing I wanted to do, so I arrived early to get it over with. I was the only one standing at the door when they opened, which caused me to wonder why I'd thought it would be a lousy experience; when I left an hour later every chair was taken. My guess is that most everyone filing IRS forms needed a little 'splainin.'

The agent walked me through the process and gave me the proper forms for the year the taxes were to be filed. I left with a few extra forms just in case I made a mistake. For some reason, I'm always nervous about errors when I fill out a form. Later that day still believing I had conquered the IRS, I sent the 1099 INT forms by registered mail with return receipt to the location on my paperwork and kept a set of copies for my growing pile of IRS correspondence. With that behind me, I could move on to the fun stuff. Needless to say, the IRS didn't resolve the issue on the spot.

Chapter Twenty-Two Take-Aways

- Do your research. The Internet can be amazing at helping you to find information (also scary how much information is out there). Keep track to the best of your ability as to what your ex is doing; it will be beneficial if you have to continue pursuing them for alimony, child support or something else.

- Keep your wits about you; you never know when your ex-spouse will show up. Be safe at all times.

23

Texas, Here I Come

By July 2012 it became evident that Roi had no intention of complying with the contempt of court order. Since he suffered from a grandiose sense of self-importance, he must have been under the impression that since his move to Texas he was out of the reach of the Fairfax County court and his tenacious former wife.

I had discussed the possibility of retaining a family law firm in Texas with Mr. McGarry, but I was agonizing over spending more money. With the help of my attorney, my kids, and faith—though none of them offered to write the check—I made the decision to go forward. I really wasn't ready to give up. There'd been so many twists and turns in this case, why not spice it up a bit and move the proceedings from one state to another and make travel a challenge? Besides, I hadn't been to Texas in years.

> *With the help of my attorney, my kids, and faith—though none of them offered to write the check—I made the decision to go forward.*

Mr. McGarry recommended a firm in San Antonio and after a very pleasant interview with Ms. Vance I knew that as costly as signing a new retainer would be that she was going to be amazing in court. Ms. Vance didn't say in so many words "We eat men for breakfast and still have room for oatmeal," but I had the feeling that Roi was going to experience a Texas-sized whupping by a woman. I couldn't wait to meet her and witness her taking him on. The court date was set for November 8, 2012, in San Antonio, but before the hearing could go forward, Roi would have to be served and given enough time to hire an attorney. Jermaine was the courier assigned to deliver the court summons, and for over a week I considered him my new best friend. He would call each day to give me a blow-by-blow account of the trials and tribulations of serving Roi. His first call was to introduce himself and ask if I had the code to the gated community Roi called home. I was unaware that he was living such a lavish lifestyle, but why was I really surprised by anything?

Jermaine told me that he was a retired policeman, so I had no doubt that he would find a way to get through that gate. When he called the next day he told me that he had been to Roi's home but no one had answered the door; it appeared that they might be out of town as newspapers were piled up on the driveway. I just had to ask, "How did you get through the gate?" Jermaine told me that when a car came out, he'd driven in via the out lane. I knew he would figure it out, but the paperwork had to be served by a certain date or the hearing would have to be rescheduled. I sure didn't want that to happen, as I didn't want to reschedule my son's and my airline and hotel reservations. Each time Jermaine called, my anxiety level would kick up a notch—probably time for a calming pill. Fortunately, after eight days of trying, he found them home and successfully served the papers. Also, he told me there was a new SUV parked in the driveway. I wondered if the vanity plates said ALIMONY.

I arrived in San Antonio ahead of the court date to give myself a day to meet with Ms. Vance. I was looking forward to meeting her based on our conversation prior to my retaining her firm. Traveling to San Antonio and taking Roi to court in his new home state was turning into an adventure, almost like going to a theme park called Divorce Land. My son would be arriving the next evening so we could go to court together.

I treated us to the Hilton Palacio del Rio, with a balcony overlooking the Riverwalk, as the whole episode was going to be stressful enough without staying at Motel Not So Hot.

I took a cab driven by a very chatty driver to the law firm on Mistletoe Avenue. On the way I mentioned that I had lived in Oklahoma, just over the border with Texas. Unimpressed, the driver said, "Oh, those Oklahomans want to be Texans, and they dress like we do."

We know that being Texan is more than an address, but I had no idea there was a border distinction. How ironic, for a family law firm that deals with separation, child custody, and divorce to be located on Mistletoe Avenue. When I think of mistletoe, I immediately think about the Christmas tradition of hanging it and kissing under it, though mistletoe is described as a mysterious plant, considered a parasite, and one that can shorten the life of the tree it attaches itself to. Some cultures consider it magical, mysterious, and sacred, with miraculous healing powers. I hoped those miraculous powers would work to my advantage in court. I'm sure the firm was not located on Mistletoe Avenue for any other reason than location, but upon arriving at my destination I was immediately charmed by the Victorian-style house in the heart of San Antonio. It was surrounded by a picket fence, and an arched gate led into an unexpected English garden. The interior of the house lived up to my expectation of vintage charm, but with a Texas twist. While I waited to meet Ms. Vance, I relaxed in a Victorian chair and felt transported to another era. The high ceilings of the original parlor reminded me of photos of my grandparents' home in Butte, Montana, in the early 1900s. Pictures covered the two-story walls, with the symbolic Lone Star of Texas hanging proudly in the middle. My grandparents had pictures covering the walls of their home, but no grizzly bear, the symbol of Montana. The décor of the new firm was the polar opposite of the Virginia firm; the statement being made by the décor in this setting was more about the sincerity of the legal team and your ability to put your trust in them to represent your case to the best of their ability (keeping in mind that there are no guarantees that the outcome will be perfect or that the law won't let you down).

Ms. Vance and her paralegal welcomed me to their charming office, and my impression of them from our phone interview was immediately confirmed. I knew from Ms. Vance's website that she had reddish hair; I just didn't know she was petite. I was about to take part in my fourth rodeo in Texas, no less, once again trying to legally straighten out Roi, and Ms. Vance would be formidable in her effort to do just that.

We sat down to strategize around a table made from an old doorframe with a glass insert showcasing vintage cards and photos. Just before leaving the hotel that morning, I'd watched an HGTV program filmed in Texas featuring two hosts who'd created something very similar. Time is money, which meant we had to get down to business instead of looking at each Victorian card or photo.

Ms. Vance handed me a set of spreadsheets that Roi and his wife had created for his new attorney. The financial information was comprehensive and the numbers were staggering, making their spending look like one family's version of America's national debt. The reckless spending included the depletion of Roi's investments, including his IRA. There was a mile-long list of creditors: credit card debt in the thousands, insurance policies covering dental and long-term care, gym membership, lawn care, pool maintenance, home improvements, gifts, clothing, travel, personal grooming, food and entertainment, a Tuscan timeshare, local, state and federal taxes, and my favorite—his wife's new $60,000 car parked in their driveway. Alimony was glaringly missing from the list.

> *The financial information was comprehensive and the numbers were staggering, making their spending look like one family's version of America's national debt.*

The application and down payment for the Tuscan timeshare occurred on our forty-fifth wedding anniversary, May 23, 2008, after the duo had breakfast at the Silver Diner Restaurant in Springfield, Virginia weeks after their affair began. I had no knowledge of the timeshare purchase till I saw the spreadsheets. As diligent as I thought I'd been, it was obvious that a multitude of things had passed under my radar for years. I arrived at the table with a copy of a posting on social media: information that the duo had celebrated Roi's seventy-third birthday in August by traveling to Tahiti, including a stopover at a resort in California, along with proof of their two trips to the D.C. area after the contempt of court ruling in March 2012. One of those visits was the stalking incident at church.

When I returned to the hotel, I called Nicole as I sat on the balcony enjoying the lovely warm November day, as I couldn't wait to share the financial information with her. It was simply too mind-boggling for me to digest on my own. It just blows me away to know full well that the immense debt is a joint debt, but the debts are solely in Roi's name. In our forty-five years of marriage aside from a mortgage and car payments, we were never in debt to one creditor, must less forty-nine of them. Texas is a community property state, and Roi's debts were accumulated after marriage. My understanding of community property is that all assets are shared.

Gary arrived about 9:00 p.m. and we enjoyed a few minutes watching the riverboats in the 80-degree evening before we discussed my meeting with Ms. Vance. He too found the spreadsheets unbelievable, more an affirmation of how low his dad had stooped, while at the same time realizing that the new financial information would give Ms. Vance ammunition for a winning case.

We were up early and dressed in our best goin' to court duds for the 7:00 a.m. rendezvous with Ms. Vance and her paralegal. While we waited to be assigned to a courtroom, we were ensconced in a small room with a table where Ms. Vance could lay out all the information for him to look over while she and the paralegal filled him in on the strategy for the case and asked whether he had anything to contribute. The room had a window in the door, through which he could see his dad sitting alone, though I'd been tipped off that his new wife would be there. After several changes of courtroom, we eventually arrived at the room we'd spend the next six and a half hours in. When Roi saw our son, his scowl turned into anger; he was beyond "a little surprised," and at that moment the day couldn't have gotten any worse for him.

*When Roi saw our son, his scowl
turned into anger; he was beyond
"a little surprised," and at that
moment the day couldn't have
gotten any worse for him.*

The attorneys for each side left the room to confer with the judge in his chambers, giving him an overview of what the case was about. Roi's attorney evidently laid out the sob story of her client's inability to pay, as well as his claim of double jeopardy in that he was being recharged for contempt of court, a charge that had already been rendered in Virginia. All legal wrangling! That's when Ms. Vance dropped the bomb about the couple's Tahiti vacation and their repeated trips to the D.C. area. I watched Roi's attorney come flying out of the judge's chamber and summon Roi into the hall. Whoops! Since he suffered from convenient memory loss, that most recent vacation must have simply been an oversight when he was claiming poverty. *Just tell the truth, the whole truth and nothing but the truth; it saves time.*

Gary and I were then asked to join Ms. Vance in the judge's chamber, as Roi and his attorney were prepared to make a small monetary concession in order to resolve the case out of court and avoid the possibility of incarceration. I didn't have to ponder for one second; I refused the offer immediately, and we headed back to the courtroom. The proceedings were about to get underway when Ms. Vance made the announcement that my son would not be testifying on my behalf, obviously a courtroom trick to confuse the defendant. I was then called to the witness stand and sworn in, but the judge ruled that my testimony was not necessary. At that point he glanced at the large wall clock and said, "It's ten to twelve and there won't be time for questions before our lunch break, so we will resume at 1:30 p.m. with the defendant taking the stand.

Everyone but my legal team left for lunch, and my team enlisted Gary to help crunch the numbers on the duo's spreadsheets. What they really needed was a calculator capable of performing rapid calculations of large sums of money. Excessive overspending had started on the weekend the two met, over four and a half years before, and the numbers indicated that their debt was still rising. The inability to honor his alimony obligations had everything to do with *la vida loca,* or living way beyond their means. Watching my team masterfully hone the strategy for the questioning gave me confidence about the outcome of the hearing and, to be truthful, a feeling of superiority. There was no doubt that Ms. Vance gave a feminine twist to tough; she'd come to court to win, and she was going to call the arrogant SOB's bluff and show him how Texas ladies dealt with lying, cheating adulterers. Roi may have been able to get away with his loathsome disrespect for the law with the Southern gentleman lawyers of Virginia, but we were in Texas and there was goin' to be a showdown! I could hear the Texas Longhorn bulls pawing the ground and snorting in the bullpen just outside the courthouse, and everyone was ready to ride.

The case continued to be the only one pending in that courtroom. Gary resumed sitting in the gunfighter's seat, which gave him a panoramic view of the courtroom and anyone coming in or leaving. When court resumed, Roi approached the stand as erect and sure of himself as if he were reporting for a plush assignment as an aide-de-camp to a four-star general. I'm surprised he didn't salute the judge just before swearing, in a strong assertive voice, to tell the truth. Oh, my God, there's that elusive word "truth" again.

Just about the time the questions became more difficult, which was right after Roi stated his name and verified his rank at the time he'd retired from the army, Bunny showed up. It was obvious that she'd come directly to court from her dance class and hadn't taken time to change out of her Texas hoedown outfit, complete with fringed boots. At one point, Ms. Vance leaned over and asked, "What was he thinking?" I reminded her that the decision to engage in adultery hadn't taken place in the body part sitting on his shoulders, and while his wife's style was inappropriate for her age, it was a sign of the new dude.

The legal teams sat at adjoining tables, the attorneys facing the judge, while Bunny and I sat at the ends of our respective tables, facing one another. I'm not known for having a poker face, and cognizant of that fact, I did my best to keep a pleasant, nonjudgmental look on my face. It was very uncomfortable to face the woman who still demonstrated the same patronizing superior attitude as the first time I'd had the displeasure of meeting her in 2009. It was interesting to watch her nod in agreement with Ms. Vance each time she asked Roi about not complying with his obligations to pay me, as if Bunny had been an innocent bystander, tirelessly trying to get her husband to do the right thing. As the afternoon wore on, it became more difficult to maintain a phony detached look; frankly, my facial muscles needed a break. My chair had casters, so each time Bunny looked at Roi struggling to answer the unanswerable; I'd push the chair backwards ever so slightly, till I was out of her line of sight

Ms. Vance's questioning was direct and hard hitting, but the answers wouldn't have required Roi to stay up all night studying, as he himself had created the issues he was being grilled about. Ms. Vance presented him with exhibits that required his acknowledgment, such as the spreadsheets he and his wife had prepared, the Virginia contempt of court ruling, and the trips to Tahiti and D.C., all of which gave Ms. Vance hours of grilling material. When you're not accustomed to telling the truth, especially under oath, answering questions about epistemology would be like a walk in the park. (Epistemology, the study of knowledge, by the way, was a required subject as a student at Seattle University.)

When it came time to explain how he could afford a vacation in Tahiti with a stopover at a resort in Marina del Rey, California, Roi hmm-ed and hawed and finally said, "I don't know. My wife made the reservations and paid with her inheritance." That response was absolutely bizarre, as he claimed he couldn't remember how many days they'd spent in Tahiti or what they'd done while there or how long they'd been away from home. It's hard to believe that one couldn't remember what he did in a tropical paradise just three months earlier. Ms. Vance was quick to pick up on the mention of the wife's inheritance, and Roi claimed he didn't know much about it, but faking cluelessness wouldn't incriminate his wife.

Ms. Vance then asked him if he couldn't mow his lawn and clean his pool rather than pay someone to do those chores while he looked for a job that paid as well as the one he'd left in Virginia. He claimed that he had injured his back in a fall. He also claimed that he'd submitted a list of job searches to his attorney, but none of them had responded to his résumé. Right on cue, Ms. Vance asked, "Have you thought about being a greeter at Walmart?"

> *Right on cue, Ms. Vance asked,*
> *"Have you thought about being*
> *a greeter at Walmart?"*

That remark was priceless, and Roi more than deserved to be reduced to the little man that he'd become. I couldn't help laughing, as the hilarious question had been delivered with such perfect timing—just one of those special moments you couldn't choreograph. Knowing Roi as I do, he was seething with rage to think a little redheaded lady attorney would have the gall to question him with such disrespect. It was a beautiful moment for my son and me.

Luckily for me, my experience with courtroom drama is very limited, though I've come to the conclusion that a really good attorney knows the law inside out and upside down; at the same time, I've also observed that there's a theatrical side to presenting and winning a case, and Ms. Vance is a master.

When a short break was called, I walked out to the hallway for a change of scenery, and came face to face with Roi's new wife. That wasn't the scenery I was looking for, so I returned to the courtroom. When questioning resumed, Ms. Vance once again bored in with more questions regarding Roi's cutting off alimony payments, and after each response to a question, Ms. Vance would say, "Your Honor, Roi needs to go to jail to learn respect for the law." She repeated that over and over for four hours, and by the way, she never addressed Roi as "Lieutenant Colonel."

Ms. Vance said, "Your Honor, I have no further questions for Roi, but I'd like to call his wife to the witness stand." Wow! I had no idea that she was going to be called, and I couldn't wait! Bunny demonstrated that she too had a problem telling the truth and that her lack of empathy was a trait she shared with her husband. Though not the brightest bulb in the pack, she is cunning. With the questioning going nowhere, Ms. Vance said, "I rest my case" and the judge retired to his chambers to make his decision.

I wanted Roi to go to jail for his repeated willful disregard of court orders for punctual payment of alimony and for his termination of those payments, not to mention what it's cost me to sue him repeatedly. I also wanted him to go to jail for emotionally wounding our kids by his abandonment of them, and for his total disrespect for me. I'd been faithfully married to him for forty-five years, and believe me, I deserved better! Still, getting that close to putting your ex-husband in jail is a difficult concept, but one I was quite sure I could get over.

While the judge was out forming his ruling, the courtroom was eerily quiet. My team remained seated, while Roi and his wife milled around on the far side of the room. With the possibility of jail hanging over his head, I truthfully wanted Roi to just say, "I will honor my alimony obligations." Then the judge returned to render his verdict. I wanted to leave believing that, finally, the drama of the past four years had ended, but then asked myself "How stupid can you get?"

We all stood as the judge, a big Texas dude, ascended to the bench. His expressions throughout the day had reflected his incredulity with Roi's responses, though the judge came across more like a softie than someone who relishes putting anyone behind bars. It was 4:58 p.m. when he began to read his verdict, and by 5:01 p.m. it was over. The ruling of the court was as follows:

> The order from Virginia dated March 16, 2012 with regard to the $30,000 is to be paid in amounts of $2,000 per month beginning January 1, 2013, until said amount is paid. Roi is found in contempt for not making payments on April 5, 2012 of $6,000 on May 5, 2012 of $6,000 on June 5, 2012 of $6,000 on July 5, 2012 of $6,000, on August 5, 2012 of $6,000 on September 5, 2012 of $6,000, on October 5, 2012 of $6,000, and on November 5, 2012 of $6,000.
>
> He is held in contempt and sentenced to six months in jail for each violation, to run concurrently for a total of four years. Said commitment is suspended on the following terms: $15,000 is to be paid to his ex-wife by 5:00 p.m. on December 14, 2012, until said amount for the violations is paid. Attorneys' fees in the amount of $12,000 are awarded. And just so it's clear with regard to the amounts, the six months, those are to run concurrent, and same

is suspended under the terms set forth. The court will have a compliance hearing with regard to the payment of the $15,000 on December 18, 2012. Will the attorneys be available?"

Both responded that they'd be available and that I'd be available by phone.

OMG! I thought I'd heard the judge say "jail" and something about $2,000, but what else had he said? Thank goodness, my son would be able to explain it to me later, as I was stuck on the word "jail." Ms. Vance and her paralegal came to court to win—and they had. They gave me a hug and asked if I was pleased. I think I said, "Absolutely," but it's not every day your ex-husband is facing jail with your legal team's assistance, and it was going to take a few days for me to digest the whole event.

> *OMG! I thought I'd heard the judge say "jail" and something about $2,000, but what else had he said?*

Suddenly, chaos took over the quiet courtroom as the legal teams began to pack up their volumes of paperwork. We stood around wondering what to do next, rather like what do you do with your hands when you don't have pockets? About that time Roi's attorney told him to speak to his son. As he approached his son, I walked to the other side of the room. Bunny was not in sight, and I figured she'd left. I just waited and watched the body language of the dad and his son, when the bailiff approached me to make small talk. The conversation was very brief, but he managed to say, "Thank you for taking care of your mother." When Roi walked past me to exit the courtroom, he scowled at me with the hate-filled eyes he'd displayed at every legal meeting we'd had over the four years. *I can imagine that seeing your ex-wife whom you dumped would be very uncomfortable, so simply lay the blame and guilt for your infidelity on her—after all, she made you do it.*

As we all exited the room, my son saw Roi and his wife standing in the hall, and said, "Wait just a minute." He approached Bunny, extending a hand to introduce himself. She was visibly taken aback; it reminded me of the day she was deposed in October 2009, when she'd had the nerve to want to shake my hand at my attorney's office.

Chapter Twenty-Three Take-Aways

- Alimony is a domestic obligation as defined by US code 71; alimony is never discharged.

- While you may always be the winner in court, that doesn't prevent your ex-spouse from thumbing his nose at the courts and not paying you. Sadly, there are no cops to show up and make your ex pay up.

- You will likely continue to be amazed at the extreme and outrageous behavior of your ex-spouse. In my case, a man I had known for 49 years was beyond a stranger to me. The real loser in all of this is my ex-husband, for he walked away from his children. As Dr. Phil often says, "You need to resolve one relationship before you enter another." He's never done that so I'm pretty positive Bunny is experiencing the same challenges I did. Hope they're having great fun!

- Your trust will be put to the test and likely damaged. You will need to work on ensuring it doesn't negatively impact every aspect of your life. Like Dr. Phil says, though; work on resolving your issues stemming from your broken relationship before thinking of entering a new one.

24

Cocktail Napkins Say the Darnedest Things

Once we got back to the hotel, I was physically and emotionally drained; it was cocktail time. We sat on the balcony in the early evening warmth, and enjoyed the Riverwalk from ten stories up; but why waste the perfectly lovely November evening in San Antonio without a walk along the winding river and a stop for dinner and a margarita or two? My son and I hadn't been on a trip together since he was about four, and neither of us wanted to ruin the few remaining hours to dwell on our courtroom experience. We've laughed about aspects of the day, but have never shared our feelings about watching my ex-husband, my son's dad, stand before the judge, portraying confidence, but within hours hear the judge rule that he'd pay a stiff penalty for his failure to comply with previous court orders. I don't believe for one moment that Roi is solely responsible for those actions, but he's the one being charged with the consequences. I can just hear Flip Wilson say, "The devil made me do it." Flip was a laugh a minute, but I can't say the same for my ex.

We left the hotel very early the next morning to catch our flight to D.C., and by the time I finally got home I was beyond exhausted. I changed into something comfortable and was waiting for Nicole to arrive from work when my phone rang. It was Dem, who said, "I couldn't wait all weekend without knowing how the hearing went."

If I could've hugged him through the phone I would have, as he was the one person I wanted to share the whole experience with, and I'd thought I would have to wait till Monday. The events of the Texas round-up were so poignant that I was going to have to come to terms with my feelings before I could share them with friends. Dem knew every she-nanigan that Roi and his attorney had pulled over the past four years, and I needed to discuss the possibility of jail with him. I told him about the disastrous financial situation the two had created, and about Bunny's claim to some inheritance. Dem was pleased with the sentencing and felt that after every opportunity Roi had been given, that the verdict was fair, just, and well-deserved.

December 14, when Roi would have to make the first payment to me or go to jail, was slightly over a month away. Truthfully, I hoped for a check for several reasons. Unless he had hidden assets, I wasn't expect-ing a good outcome. I wondered what the duo might have been thinking as they walked out of that courtroom; could it possibly have been "How do we dodge this one?" Knowing my ex's past behavior, I was suspicious of his next move.

Just before Thanksgiving, my daughter-in-law and I attended a Christmas bazaar in the picturesque village of Middleburg, Virginia, a city established in 1787. Today, many of the original buildings along its tree-lined streets have been turned into quaint shops and inns, making it a wonderful destination for a quiet lunch or just window shopping. We, however, were there to shop, and while we browsed through one of the stores, my daughter-in-law handed me a package of cocktail napkins. In bold black lettering on a yellow background, the caption was "Can You Fix My Husband? He says He's Broke." Obviously, I'm not the only one with a jackass for a husband, or with an ex, for that matter. The timing of the find was like a comic setup, but that's what made it so delightful.

Back in Seattle, Christmas music filled the air, and it put me in the mood to start decorating for the holidays. It would be my daughter-in-law's first visit to our family home and Washington State, and I wanted it to be spe-cial. One of my favorite tools is a Little Giant ladder that extends to heights that I couldn't reach otherwise. I can drape garlands, hang wreaths, and decorate trees to my heart's delight. Time raced toward Christmas; it was suddenly December 14, 2012, and Roi had till 5:00 p.m. Central time to deposit the $15,000 he'd been ordered to pay me. I checked my bank account online just to see if he might have deposited the payment ahead of time, but the balance hadn't increased; the day was still young.

For most of the day, the consequences of Roi's not complying with the court order played over and over in my mind like a broken record, despite *Jingle Bell Rock* and "fa-la-la-la-la." By mid-afternoon I'd gotten myself worked up, but then the phone rang. Ms. Vance informed me that they had just received information from the United States Bankruptcy Court that the debtor had filed a voluntary petition for relief under Chapter 13. "What in the hell does that mean?" Well, Ms. Vance said, "We believe he filed on December 14, 2012 to avoid paying the partial down payment of $15,000 and to avoid jail time."

> *By mid-afternoon I'd gotten myself worked up, but then the phone rang. Ms. Vance informed me that they had just received information from the United States Bankruptcy Court that the debtor had filed a voluntary petition for relief under Chapter 13.*

In other words, we were now involved in a legal version of cat-and-mouse. With Christmas and my kids' arrival just days away, I'd do my best to be jolly and not involve them in their dad's latest attempt to thwart the justice system. And to think I'd questioned the jail option.

I checked my calendar, as I was scheduled to call the IRS for the umpteenth time on December 18, 2012. Having kept in touch with that agency for the past nine months, I knew what time to call in order to speak with an agent in Fresno, California. He had a year's worth of my letters, forms, and information necessary to relieve me of the tax burden. I've found the agents courteous and helpful, though I was asked to write yet another letter explaining the savings bond issue from 1963 to 2010, and to please have it in their office by December 31. I was thoroughly sick of the tax issue, and the last thing I wanted to do at Christmas was take time to write another letter. I wondered what had happened to all the correspondence and copies of the bonds I'd been sending for nine months; were they trying to wear me down, IRS style? Figuratively speaking, I saluted and got busy so I could fax the darn thing by December 31.

We had a wonderful family Christmas, despite one or two more rainy days than we'd have liked; we acted like true Seattleites and didn't let the rain dampen our tourist activities. We went to the top of the Space Needle, saw the fish-throwing at Pike Place Market, and took a ferry ride across Puget Sound to Bainbridge Island for lunch. The season passed in a flash as good times always do, and with Nicole's help all the decorations were stored away by New Year's Day; I awaited the appearance of the first Forsythia blossom announcing spring.

Chapter Twenty-Four Take-Aways

- Find the humor in all things.

- Be prepared for your ex to pull a fast one. Bankruptcy was the farthest thing from my mind!

- Stay on top of your notes and dates and keep detailed copies.

- Learn the different types of bankruptcy and what they mean for you.

25

His Net Worth

Many of us start the New Year with a resolution to accomplish something worthwhile, like lose some weight. I could perhaps lose several pounds but I'd convinced myself that as I matured, being slightly overweight was healthy and I'm stickin' to that resolution. I would, however, be thrilled to divest myself of my ex-husband, whom I'd had to drag around for over four years and counting.

I received official notice from the United States Bankruptcy Court in the Western District of Texas that Roi had indeed filed for protection from creditors and jail time. Dem explained that alimony is a domestic support obligation as defined by a U.S. Code and such debts or obligations are not dischargeable in the case of bankruptcy. I don't know why legal wording is so difficult to understand; the bottom line is, you might get out of paying some creditors and jail, but your ex-wife is like an albatross hung around your neck.

I don't know why legal wording is so difficult to understand; the bottom line is, you might get out of paying some creditors and jail, but your ex-wife is like an albatross hung around your neck.

With the knowledge that I was entitled to the alimony, I was once again faced with the decision to retain an attorney; this time, one who specialized in bankruptcy issues. Never in my wildest imagination would I have thought I'd be collecting law firms while my friends were busy collecting handbags and shoes.

If I'd read the information from the bankruptcy court correctly, I would need to have a representative for a court hearing on January 23, 2013, just ten days away. Not knowing where to begin, I called the bankruptcy court attorney listed on the official papers and got in touch with a Mr. Chance McGhee. I'd already worn out the possibilities for using chance, but what a great name for a Texan, and one involved with law and money. His information led to a dead end and to what I consider my biggest mistake in the divorce. I regret not contacting Ms. Vance for a referral to a firm that specialized in bankruptcy and creditors' rights, as I am sure she'd have put me in touch with an attorney far more qualified than the one I retained. The outcome would more than likely have been the same as it involved Roi, for heaven's sake.

I contacted a firm in San Antonio and spoke with the senior partner who just happened to answer my call. I explained that I'd been put in the position of needing representation in the bankruptcy court by my ex-husband who, ordered by a Texas court to begin making settlement payments for alimony arrears or go to jail, had chosen to file for Chapter 13 protection, as he apparently hadn't liked the selections from columns A or B, and those were the only options. The gentleman was sympathetic and understanding, and explained that his firm represented corporate issues, but he would talk to a few of the younger lawyers to see if anyone would be interested in taking my case.

A few days later I received a call from the firm with an attorney willing to take on my case. In my rush to sign the engagement letter and include a check for the retainer fee and run it to the post office before closing, I forgot to sign the check. When the attorney called to inform me of that, I just chalked it up to one of those crazy divorce moments. It was absolutely clear that I needed to educate myself as quickly as possible about bankruptcy. Subjects like debt, credit, and bankruptcy just never came up over coffee with friends, but of course we'd all just charged our coffee at the local Starbucks, and now each of us had an unsecured debt. Truthfully, I didn't want to spend any time learning about bankruptcy; I just wanted the divorce nightmare to be nothing more than four large bins full of paper that my kids could shred one day and use as packing material when they moved on. Then I thought about the thousands-plus that Roi owed me, and the United States code that held him responsible for it. The saying "Knowledge is power" motivated me to start learning just enough to get by.

> *Truthfully, I didn't want to spend any time learning about bankruptcy; I just wanted the divorce nightmare to be nothing more than four large bins full of paper that my kids could shred one day and use as packing material when they moved on.*

Googling *bankruptcy* gave me more information than I needed, but it answered my questions about creditor categories, the Meeting of Creditors, and creditor's rights, which are determined by both federal and state laws. The federal bankruptcy code provides a uniform way of filing, and state bankruptcy laws generally determine property rights. In other words, it's all designed to provide the honest debtor a shot at a fresh start, with the opportunity to pay down his or her debts with court protection from the harassment of constant calls from bill collectors. I had a real problem describing Roi as an "honest debtor"—perhaps I just had a problem with the word "honest."

Within weeks of filing for Chapter 13 protection, a debtor is required to attend the first Meeting of the Creditors, commonly called a 341 Meeting, where all debtors are thoroughly briefed about the rules of filing and what they need to present to the court. The instructions are very specific, and the debtor must be able to present a feasible creditor repayment schedule called "the Plan," and proof of having paid taxes. If the court agrees to a debtor's repayment plan and the debtor has an income source, then the debtor could take up to five years to repay the debt, while other creditors would never receive a dime. I had no idea how complex bankruptcy was or that I would need to become a participant in Roi's bankruptcy.

After the debtor has complied with the federal bankruptcy rules, he then looks to the state for its bankruptcy-protection laws. The state of Texas offers many great reasons to move there, such as a strong economy, fine weather, and no state income taxes. Something they don't advertise, however, is that Texas is known as a "debtors' haven," based on the number of exemptions the state allows. It exempts the home, the cars, and everything inside the home and the garage, though my favorite allowable exemption is for the horses, the mules, and the donkey, plus a saddle, blanket, and bridle for each. Roi was in deep doo-doo of his own making, to the detriment of the forty-nine creditors he's used and abused in a matter of five years because he's the domestic ass.

While I was consumed with bankruptcy education, good news finally arrived from the IRS. The letter stated that I owed the federal government no interest on the bonds. Hallelujah, great news for a change! Tenacity and perseverance and cogency can pay off. If by chance I'd been a candidate for a PhD, those three qualities would be what a professor would be looking for, but winning an issue with the IRS without a lawyer was far more beneficial to me than a PhD. Talk about timing: while I was receiving the good news from the IRS, the bad news was on its way to San Antonio; it arrived two days before the first bankruptcy hearing and just in time to be added to Roi's list of creditors. Now the IRS could dog him for the taxes—and believe me, they love to pester.

I had a burning desire to confront the lazy accountant who'd suggested I just pay the $3,000 rather than mess with the IRS on my own; but in another brilliant decision, I chose not to be a bitch.

My new bankruptcy attorney attended the first Meeting of Creditors on January 23, 2013. I was told that Roi and his wife were "a little surprised" that I had an attorney present. Looks like the IRS aren't the only ones that can show up when you least expect them. That meeting stipulated that Roi was to prepare the "Plan" for repayment of creditors, along with proof of having paid his federal taxes for 2011, and present that information at the second Meeting of Creditors in February. The court papers for February, however, state that he arrived at that meeting unprepared, and the trustee moved to dismiss the bankruptcy case due to his failure to present a workable repayment plan and failure to file his

1040 tax return for 2011. A dismissal of the case removes the protection from creditors that the bankruptcy process allows. Whoops!

The United States Bankruptcy Court for the Western District of Texas, San Antonio, states that the following facts demonstrate that the debtor filed his Chapter 13 petition in bad faith to avoid having to pay the unpaid spousal support and to attempt to thwart the state court order by filing for protection on the same day that the state court order required him to make the down payment or report to jail. The court also found that the debtor used unsecured credit prior to bankruptcy to finance the excessively comfortable lifestyle that he enjoyed with his new wife. They'd purchased custom-made furniture, took lavish vacations, and bought a new luxury SUV and assorted pieces of expensive jewelry for his wife, to mention just a few.

Roi told the court that he provided complete or near-complete financial support for his wife, declaring her income as zero, despite her claim that she owened an LLC (with no clients). He claimed their monthly expenses included a mortgage, two cars, lawn and pool maintenance, utilities, food, recreation, cable bundling, and cell phones that totaled in excess of $7,000. It sounded like Roi was pleading with the court to understand that he just couldn't afford alimony, as it would leave him shortchanged and with a dirty pool and an overgrown lawn.

The trustee further stated that the debtor had undertaken no appropriate steps to adequately value his list of property and had altogether omitted valuable luxury property from the list. The debtor stated that in 2010 he'd received $142,000 from his ex-wife as a result of disposition of certain property; however, the debtor could not account for how those funds were spent, other than to say they might have gone toward living expenses and attorney fees.

In the ensuing weeks after that 341 Meeting, the Chapter 13 trustee and the two attorneys submitted endless court filings. In early March, the court, once again stated that the debtor had not filed in good faith as required, and that the repayment plan was not feasible. The debtor would not be able to make all the payments required to be paid under his domestic support obligations, as he had not filed all applicable federal, state, and local tax returns in a timely manner. The trustee was again prepared to file a Motion to Dismiss based on Roi's failure to file his tax return for 2011, which was holding my support payments hostage. He and his attorney objected and asked the court to continue with the case; with my attorney's coaxing I reluctantly agreed. March and April came and went, and by mid-May the trustee's Motion to Dismiss was set for August 1, 2013—over eight months of delayed action by the court, the debtor, and his attorney.

The Memorial Day celebration was over, but I was still caught up in the patriotic music when I checked my email. One message was from my attorney and I immediately snapped out of the reverie as the email explained that when Roi had filed for bankruptcy he was asked to establish his net worth. In establishing his net worth he claimed that some of his valuable items were in Seattle. Oh, you have got to be kidding! I'm going to spend my fourth summer in Seattle, three of those years legally divorced, dealing with an arrogant little man in his latest attempt to out-maneuver the law?

> *In establishing his net worth*
> *he claimed that some of his*
> *valuable items were in Seattle.*
> *Oh, you have got to be kidding!*

Only six months since the trial in San Antonio, I became aware that I was not the only one looking for a check on the first of each month. I thought I was suing Roi for the payments stipulated in our marital agreement, only to find out that I'd been thrown in with the bunch the duo had stiffed. I was right in there with the new wife's SUV, the custom black-leather furniture, the marriage counselor, the Tuscan timeshare, and forty-some others. When my ex filed for Chapter 13, I became embroiled in his drama, which kept me in a perpetual state of anxiety. I was disgusted by the court order, which obliged me to participate in his biggest farce to date.

My new attorney had a slight disadvantage coming into a divorce that had been in and out of court for over four years, the ensuing drama, and the fact that I was not happy to have another attorney in my life. Her email said that I was about to be compelled to comply with a request by the bankruptcy court for access to the items Roi claimed were inside my home, further stating that he wanted certain items that he hadn't stipulated in the 2009 marital agreement moved to Texas.

It was exhausting to deal with one issue after another for over four years, making me wonder if I'd have enough summers left to deal with that contemptible obnoxious couple. I was anxious to find out what Roi was claiming as his property. I should have been asking, "Just what does he think he's entitled to?"

The unequal deal had begun with "I'm divorcing you," no discussion; Roi also abandoned his kids, canceled the lease on our apartment, drained our marital money, and gave my dental plan to his mistress. I then give him a huge court-ordered buyout, but he ignored the court order to remove his belongings from Seattle, so my daughter and I had to pack his junk, and my son paid for moving it. Roi did not make alimony payments, didn't show up for court, stalked me in church, and when a judge ordered him to pay alimony arrears or report for jail, he filed for bankruptcy, jail dismissed and again no alimony payments. Oh, wait! He now claimed that some of his net worth was in my home, and the court was coming to evaluate it and give it to him. I thought I'd been spared experiencing Roi's Napoleon complex when the divorce was final. (Napoleon was actually a bit taller than the average Frenchman of his day, and the complex might be questionable today, but I know Roi.)

In order to establish Roi's net worth_my attorney—with my reluctant help—was going to readdress the belongings listed in the divorce agreement of 2009. I saw no reason why she couldn't print out a copy of the original list of items on file with the Fairfax County court, check off those items that were in Texas, and add the items that he'd forgotten to list four years earlier and was claiming were still in Seattle. But we made a costly new copy. My solution was so simple, but it would only save me money.

The attorney informed me that an appraiser of Roi's choice would call and make an appointment, come to my home, and appraise selected family pieces. The value of those items would then be subtracted from what he owed me. Oh, why not? I was given the list of items that the appraiser was to assess, and of course I had to put out the crystal and silver and then put it away. At least the chandelier and carved chests were in plain sight. There must be a statute of limitations on property not claimed after three years; otherwise Roi could show up in ten years and demand something else he'd forgotten.

It was threatening to be told that I would just have to accept an appraiser and a moving disruption in my home and be gracious, having already made fifteen major moves in my lifetime and each with some form of drama and inevitable damage. The court was requesting the appraisal and Roi was taking the opportunity to request items he hadn't cared enough about to retrieve in the past three years; but with the backing of his new attorney he was emboldened and felt entitled to special privileges. I felt I had every right to request that the appraisal and the packing and moving take place the week of June 10, 2013. I asked that one of the nationally known moving companies be responsible for packing the breakables and antiques, remove the chandelier from over a stairway, and move them all safely out of my home. I didn't want to spend my entire summer in a home invasion, and Roi's attorney agreed to the timing.

My attorney's next email informed me that Roi had a "trusted friend" in Seattle who would make arrangements with me to come and remove the items. Whoa—wait a minute! It had been just days since I'd requested professional movers in my home and Roi's attorney had agreed to that and to my requests concerning the dates, and now they're sending whom? Immediately, I was suspicious of the "trusted friend." My reaction was like waving a red flag in front of a bull. I didn't know that Roi had friends in Seattle, but then I supposed it could have been one of the "aging brats" from American High School. My attorney sent me a photo ID of the trusted friend, which identified him as a theater rigger; it was apparent that he wasn't an aging brat. I'd had a sailboat during my high school and college years and knew how to rig it, but not being a theater aficionado, I frankly had to Google the meaning of *theater rigger*. Desperately trying to remain open-minded, however, I was also beginning to smell a rat, so once again I had to resort to a Web search. What in the world did we do before Google?

Yep! The rat turned out to be none other than Roi's stepson-in-law, and as I scrolled down the page there was the smoking gun. Of course, I hadn't recognized the guy's last name, and wouldn't have known he was the new wife's son-in-law except that I recognized the maiden name of the person listed as co-owner of a home in Seattle as one of her daughters. I find it chilling that Roi and his wife would have the gall to conceal the identity of the trusted friend, but I recalled the day the private investigator called her a predator, a con artist, and not a nice woman. They had to be delusional if they thought that Roi's stepson in-law, and perhaps his wife's daughter—as we were never given the name of the rigger's assistant—would be welcome in my home!

I'd never thought about describing Roi as a con artist, though that was exactly the terminology the private investigator had used to describe Bunny. A simple description of a con artist is a cheater, an ordinary person adept at lying, one who violates court rules and takes no responsibility for paying alimony, and as a result is facing a four-year sentence in an orange jumpsuit.

Somehow from day one of this relentless divorce, I knew I needed to be proactive; this was not something I wanted to do or was particularly comfortable doing, but the information I'd gathered had been invaluable for establishing the facts. By doing the searches I had reduced my legal fees a teensy bit, making it well worth the time.

Somehow from day one of this relentless divorce, I knew I needed to be proactive; this was not something I wanted to do or was particularly comfortable doing, but the information I'd gathered had been invaluable for establishing the facts.

I took for granted that my attorney would be loyal to me (after all, I'd paid her retainer) and protect me under the Bankruptcy Code as a priority creditor. I did not retain her to be a spokesperson for the plaintiff's attorney. Instead of supporting my request for professional movers, she suggested that I was being uncooperative by insisting that a professional be responsible for the move. She found nothing offensive about the stepson-in-law coming into my home, since she'd been told that Roi couldn't afford a mover. Our client/attorney relationship hit rock bottom and would never recover. I met my obligation to the bankruptcy case by allowing the appraiser in my home; enabling the bankruptcy trustee to establish Roi's net worth which would reduce what he owed me by a few thousand dollars, but resolving the moving of his stuff had been an issue since February 2010 and in June 2012 it was still an issue.

The two attorneys had become moving expeditors for the "new" stuff Roi had decided he wanted. Their strategies for moving were similar, and both plans had me doing the heavy lifting. My attorney suggested that to avoid just anyone entering my home, I arrange for my brothers to help move the items to an area in the yard or to the street where the stuff could be picked up. She would request that Roi pay them for their time. She has got to be joking! First of all, they weren't actors in my drama; neither were they stupid enough to think Roi would pay them ahead of me, and furthermore how did she know I had brothers? Even though I live in an upscale neighborhood, or perhaps *because* I do, the vultures case the area on a regular schedule, and Roi's belongings would have been picked over in fewer than twelve hours; in fact, at street level, in broad daylight, it might have stayed there an hour or two.

I emailed photos to my attorney of those items going to Texas, so she could understand that it wasn't a matter of grabbing a few boxes on the fly. My home sits on the side of a hill, similar to the homes in San Francisco, forty steps up from street level with no yard in which to place the items safely. The chandelier removal would require two people, a two-story ladder, and a foray into the attic; and the stacked Chinese chests would be too big and heavy for one person to move. If Roi had been the slightest bit cooperative and had followed the court orders, I'd have packed the small items, but Nicole and I had already packed a garage full for him (without reimbursement) and I would no longer accommodate him under any circumstances.

His attorney's plan was for me to move the items near to an outside door, as Roi had advised him that nothing was heavy. The small breakable items in the home could be moved to create a pathway that would make it possible for the stepson-in-law and his helper to be in my home for only a matter of minutes. That comment left me with the vision of

TLC's program *Hoarding; Buried Alive*. The legal wrangling was turning into "can't we make a deal?" It was a move, for heaven's sake!

I was through being exploited by a devious, insufferable manipulator. The attorneys considered my request that professionals handle the move as my inflexibility, but Roi was manipulating them, too. He had taken victimization to a new level by suggesting that he couldn't afford a professional mover and that I wouldn't allow his stepson-in-law in my home. Too bad his attorney didn't just say, "Stop screwing around and wasting time and fees; just arrange to get your beloved stuff and move on." Oh, I nearly forgot—wasted hours are billable hours!

I've received hundreds of emails from my attorneys, but only one has made me see red. The bankruptcy attorney definitely had a burr under her saddle, and her message was uncalled for as well as unprofessional. It read: "The Chapter 13 Plan on file with the bankruptcy court proposes to pay the alimony in full, plus attorney's fees, however if you do not want to go through with it, the other option is litigation, and you are free to choose that at any time." What did she say—if I don't want to go through with it? Good grief, after six months of time and fees, she's frustrated? Try walking in my flip-flops! I decided not to respond to her email and instead stay on the high road and just wait. I've learned to wait, though not always patiently!

Chapter Twenty-Five Take-Aways

- A person who files for bankruptcy does so by filing a Chapter 7 or 13. Learn how each will affect you.

- Bankruptcy is very complicated, even if you are not the one with the debt.

- Should your ex file bankruptcy, you will need to hire a lawyer who specializes in this particular field of law.

- In a bankruptcy, be prepared for your ex to claim that some of the contents remaining in your home make up a portion of his wealth. For example, my ex-spouse still hadn't come to pick up some of the items he was "supposed" to get per the marital agreement. Even though it was nearly two years after the deadline to retrieve personal belongings, per the marital agreement, he was still allowed to claim that property as part of his wealth. It was shocking to me that there was not a statute of limitations!

- Over and over you may find yourself dismayed at how unfair the courts really are. My ex left and walked away without much thought, and yet he was now going to be permitted to claim ownership over things he had left in my home, a home he no longer was entitled to.

- As I have said previously, you do need to remain on the high road. Easier said than done! Therefore, I was willing to allow him to have the things he, in essence, abandoned at my home. Yet, I was not willing to allow just anyone to come in my home to pick up those items. Stand firm on this front! Do your due-diligence about who your ex wants to come into your personal space. Turns out my ex wants Bunny's son-in-law to come and get the items. I think not! You want the items badly enough, then you will pay for a commercial mover who is licensed and bonded.

26

The Battalion Commander

While the attorneys and the bankruptcy trustee frittered away time and money in vain attempts to coax Roi to arrange for moving his stuff and create a workable repayment plan for the court by the August 1, 2013 deadline, I made plans to return to Virginia in July to surprise my son at his change-of-command ceremony at Fort Belvoir.

One Saturday, about a month before the change of command, a mere click of the mouse opened the door to a life-changing event in our family. There had been a family disconnect on Roi's side for a number of years, and when Gary saw his uncle on a social website, he threw caution to the wind and made a connection. The next day they spent about three hours on the phone, filling in the missing years, though they barely touched the tip of the iceberg. My son invited his uncle and his family to his change-of-command ceremony, and they accepted. Divorce undoubtedly divides families more often than not, but the division was really between two brothers. The family needed a hero to open the door and bring both sides together, and the upcoming event was a very fitting incentive for a family reunion.

On one of the hottest and most humid days of the summer of 2013, my son became Battalion Commander of Headquarters and Headquarters

Battalion of the 29th Infantry Division, stationed at Fort Belvoir, Virginia. By the end of the ceremony, my makeup was MIA; however, after my son expressed how proud he was of the 761 soldiers still standing in their ACUs in the stifling humidity, I felt ashamed to have complained while wearing a sleeveless sundress and sitting under the protection of a tent. I've attended many military ceremonies over the years, but when it was my son accepting the responsibility that goes with the achievement of becoming a battalion commander, I suddenly felt a lump in my throat and was about to cry. Patriotism filled the air that afternoon, with marching, formations, and the band. A reception followed, with friends and family and fellow soldiers all gathered to congratulate him. For our immediate family, though, it was a time to toast a new beginning. About a month later Gary and his wife were in New York. Over lunch, plans were made for them to share Thanksgiving with us in Virginia. I dare suggest that the bad apple had been thrown out of the applecart, and it was time to start a new tradition!

I returned to Seattle, a city experiencing an unexpected run of dry weather and no humidity. It was obvious that my garden needed more than rain, though my water bill indicated that I might have filled a large pool. In June, I had purchased dozens of white-flowering plants and several bags of potting soil mixed with the good barnyard stuff from the best nursery in town, and I expected to have a beautiful display of lovely flowers by August. The plants, however, looked more like they belonged in the gigantic yard-waste container provided by the city, so while I awaited news from the bankruptcy court, I said goodbye to the plants, leaving my yard colorless but neat.

Around the first of September 2013 I received a copy of the Order Confirming the Debtors Chapter 13 Repayment Plan. It was rather short, but stated that I would be allowed priority claim of over $100,000 under the "domestic support obligation" as defined by a U.S. code. "In the event the debtor fails to make a plan payment during the plan term and does not correct the violation of the contract within sixty days of the date the missed plan payment was due, it constitutes a default. If the automatic stay is lifted by the court, the trustee shall cease disbursement to the ex-wife on the Priority Claim."

Somehow, I didn't think that sounded too positive, though legalese is not very clear to civilians—but then again, I should be used to winning one day only to lose a week later.

A follow-up to the August 1 court hearing came from my attorney a week later, with my first pre-confirmation payment of $800. The letter informed me that another check for the same amount would follow, and then I would begin to receive payments of over $2,000 a month until the full repayment was satisfied. Imagine: just five years and nine months until I'm fully reimbursed! May my ex live long enough to pay, and may I live long enough to receive. In closing, my attorney wrote, "I am hoping, for your sake, that with the agreement on your claim in place you can finally 'put a period at the end of this sentence.'" She then stated, "Please remit payment in the amount of $6,555."

> *Imagine: just five years and nine months until I'm fully reimbursed! May my ex live long enough to pay, and may I live long enough to receive.*

Boy, easy come easy go!

It seemed impossible that five years could have passed since Roi's mistress called to tell me she was engaged to my husband. The friends who harbored me that evening and I were finally going to dinner to celebrate September 20, 2013. The fact that I was still standing, still pursuing justice, and that my sense of humor remained intact felt comforting. We saluted the fifth anniversary with bourbon and selfies and lots of laughs before pressing EDIT, quickly followed by CANCEL.

By late October, I'd given up looking for another check from the Chapter 13 trustee, and rather than call my attorney, I went directly to the United States Bankruptcy Court. I was informed that Roi had not made any payments for three months; in fact, he'd made a total of only three payments to the court's confirmed repayment plan, so he was considered to be in breach of contract. Surprise, surprise! Maybe he'd just forgotten to put the payments in the mail before he and the wife ran off for another weekend with the military brats group in Daytona Beach, Florida, and a few weeks later to one in Laughlin, Nevada.

It'd been just two months since my attorney had written, "I'm hoping… you can finally put a period at the end of this sentence." Reluctantly, I called her for legal clarification of a dismissal. I seriously doubt she was surprised that Roi hadn't followed through. She advised me that there were several options I could take, and I chose the one that didn't cost a penny; however, I still had his "stuff," having wasted my summer with appraisers, stepson-in-laws, and ridiculous moving suggestions at the cost of over $6,000—and no alimony payments.

I wished her a happy holiday season as a newlywed, ever mindful that I needed to remain diplomatic, though I really wanted to tell her exactly how I felt. Before the Chapter 13 was dismissed, I did receive a whopping $3,900 from the court. I simply redirected the checks to cover legal fees, but I still owed her $3,000. It was a case that I'd been involuntarily sucked into due to Roi's shady attempt to use the legal system for his own benefit.

The Texas bankruptcy trustee filed the Motion to Dismiss on December 3, 2013. A hearing would be held on February 6, 2014 in San Antonio. The document states, the "Debtor has failed to make payments as required by the plan and is in arrears over twelve thousand dollars through December 2013, and to make the plan feasible the Debtor must increase the plan payment by one thousand a month beginning December 2013."

In other words, the court has the power to enforce its rules and also has the power to dismiss the protection the rules allow. With that protection gone, the unsecured creditors would legally be able to start ringing Roi's phone and every number he's ever answered, like my daughter's home.

The United States Bankruptcy Court, Western District of Texas, formally dismissed the case on February 6, 2014, along with the Debtor's Motion to Dismiss filed on February 5, 2014. Roi's attorney requested that the Debtors Motion to Dismiss be dismissed, claiming, "There is no need to file a modification, as the debtor will be current with the plan payments within forty-five days from the hearing date." It further stated that the debtor was expecting a large tax refund, and on and on ad infinitum. But I knew the debtor was a seventy-five-year-old man who must have had to tell himself over and over that he was a truthful, upstanding, person of integrity and strong moral character, who just happens to lie from time to time. Though he might have fooled his new acquaintances in San Antonio and beyond, he has shown nothing but disrespect for the United States Judicial System, and above all he has dishonored himself.

Chapter Twenty-Six Take-Aways

- Unfortunately, while your divorce may be legally terminated, you may still face many legal challenges that will continue to tie you to your ex-spouse.

- Surround yourself with an army of support. You never know, you may end up rekindling lost friendships and relationships with family.

- As part of a Chapter 13 bankruptcy, a repayment plan will be drafted. You will be considered a "primary creditor." How much you receive will be based upon a percentage owed to all primary creditors and how much money is paid in monthly installments. Additionally, you won't receive payment right away. An escrow account is created with the first monthly payments, you will then begin to receive payments from the bankruptcy trustee.

- Should the debtor stop making payments to the trustee, eventually they default on the bankruptcy. After a specified amount of time, typically 3-4 months, you can then file again in family court.

- Every state is different by what is allowable in bankruptcy. Each state will specify how much the debtor may retain of their personal belongings, cars, home, etc.

27

Meltdown with Milou

The year 2014 was off to a good start. I'd been back in Seattle for a month, having escaped the endless snow covering the East Coast. There's nothing as beautiful as a fresh layer of snow that turns a barren winter landscape into something magical; that is, until the first snowplow shows up and the stuff begins to melt and then it can't go away fast enough. If only the snow clouds covering the Cascade Mountains would lift, I could enjoy the beautiful snow-covered peaks from afar without lifting a snow shovel.

Several years ago I rearranged my clothes closet, looking for clothing that either no longer fit or was passé, when I came across a red wool Boy Scout jacket. It was covered with patches from my ex's trek through Norway and his attendance at the World Jamboree in England during his American High School days in the 1950s. I thought I had gathered all his belongings from the house in 2009, but this was one of those "out of sight, out of mind" situations. It was hard to believe that after all he'd put me through I'd question what to do with it. Under civilized circumstances I'd have mailed it to him. I was unable to make a decision at that point, so I just folded it and put it on the floor under the clothing—once again, out of sight out of mind. A week after the bankruptcy was dismissed, I wadded up the jacket and put it in a plastic bag on my way to the trashcan. Without jumping too high, I slam-dunked that sucker right into one of those cans cluttering the alley on garbage day. I had hoped to feel liberated, especially having wasted time agonizing over what to do with it—a reminder of what divorce does to one's good sense.

Unfortunately, the San Antonio judge's ruling did not end the saga. The ruling hadn't inspired Roi to pay the alimony arrearages; neither had it inspired him to follow the bankruptcy rules that he'd chosen as a way out, so with the court protection dismissed, that judge's ruling to pay or go to jail was restored. The dismissal did give Roi a fourteen-day grace period in which he could appeal the dismissal or file for another Chapter 13, but he chose neither. Could it be possible that the "pay or jail" case won by Ms. Vance in November 2012 had been nothing more than a dress rehearsal?

> *Unfortunately, the San Antonio judge's ruling did not end the saga.*

Shortly after the bankruptcy-court dismissal, Ms. Vance was notified that my ex had retained a new attorney to put together an offer for payment of the arrearages that he admitted he owed. Frankly, I was "offered out" and looking for action, though if—and I do mean if—Roi was really going to receive a rather large tax refund, as his bankruptcy attorney had declared, I would not have refused it. The new attorney wasn't the first one to be convinced that I'm a greedy bitch, so why disappoint her?

Still in limbo, I boarded an Alaska Airlines flight to Washington, D.C., for Nicole's birthday. I've made this round trip so many times that I'm occasionally recognized by a flight attendant, although the airline has never offered me a first class upgrade for my dedication.

Once a lawsuit is filed it takes on a life of its own; it becomes a legal contest that lasts for months, even years. During the endless weeks of waiting for Roi's new attorney to send me his large tax refund, which had to have been another pipedream, I felt emotionally drained and ready to be admitted to an intensive care unit. As I drove home from the military commissary, my anger flared when I discovered that my left turn signal wasn't working, though I'd had the bulb replaced just the day before.

Fortunately, my good judgment was unimpaired, and I vowed to deal with the turn signal on a day when I wouldn't embarrass myself. I remembered the rule according to Dem: stay on the high road. Who knew a little taillight could unleash such anger?

When I got home, I ranted and raved for several hours, leaving no topic untouched. I made good use of my rant time, however, by cleaning the refrigerator while my daughter's poor cat, Milou, cowered under a chair and watched me. I suggest that if you're observed while going through a meltdown, it's probably best to do it the company of the family pet. They'll steer clear of you for a short while, but with a little lovin' and food, you'll be back in their good graces in no time. There was not one topic whose details I didn't recall vividly, including one of the most insulting, which involved a refrigerator.

I suggest that if you're observed while going through a meltdown, it's probably best to do it the company of the family pet. They'll steer clear of you for a short while, but with a little lovin' and food, you'll be back in their good graces in no time.

Those of us who've lived in government quarters anywhere in the world are familiar with the housing inspector or post engineer, who checks you in to your set of quarters and at the same time hands you a detailed list of rules for moving out. The checkout list requires that the quarters be returned to "brand-new" condition—whether you've been there one day or three years—even if your quarters are former German barracks built in the early 1930s during the Nazi regime. That was where we lived in the 1960s. Housing inspectors have the snooping ability of the National Security Agency, but we'd successfully passed every inspection over ten years and seven moves since Germany. Now stationed at Fort Leavenworth, an eager college kid and recent grad of the housing inspectors' school arrived to check off each item on the vacate chart. My son and four-month-old daughter and I sat on the grass and waited for the inspection to be completed, as we had a flight to catch, when Roi bounded out of our quarters and asked for paper towels and the spray bottle of household cleaner. The inspector had found microscopic residue in the refrigerator's eggcups. I'd never heard of eggcup residue, but if that was the only infraction and a spritz of the cleaner could clear us from the post, we wouldn't have to pay for a cleaning team. Oh, how I'd have loved to check that twit's refrigerator.

Completely recovered from the meltdown and back in Milou's good graces, I came up with a proposal to offer my ex, a possible way to end the deadlock. Ms. Vance liked the proposal; though skeptical, she tweaked it and sent it off to Roi's attorney. Her letter stated:

> Some weeks ago, you and I discussed your client's plans for payment of the enforcement judgment as well as his ongoing support award to his ex-wife. I understood you to say that your client anticipated recovery monies from the IRS that would be sufficient to cover those obligations. You told me that you would have an offer letter to me shortly after our conversation. I have not received an offer letter, so I assume your client is, once again, continuing to attempt to avoid his court-ordered judgment and support payments.

> My client and I are currently contemplating the next step in this case, which includes moving forward with a Motion for Enforcement by Contempt. If we file that motion, we will seek jail time for your client. I am confident of the outcome.

> My client has a compromise that would allow your client to avoid jail time; this offer is only valid for two weeks and will be retracted by the close of business on May 23, 2014.

> Nancy Stevens will agree to waive the jail-time component of the Motion for Enforcement pending his agreement to and execution of the terms below, as well as prompt payment of all that is due under all the enforcement orders.

> 1. Your client must agree to travel to Northern Virginia no later than June 1, 2014 to meet with a mediator and with Ms. Stevens and his daughter, in a public location of Ms. Steven's choosing. The intent of this meeting is an attempt to find closure in this process;

> 2. Your client must agree in writing that he is in contempt of court and promptly pay the court-directed award of thirty thousand dollars and legal fees as directed by the Fairfax County court

no later than June 1, 2014. Ms. Stevens will retain the right to invoke the jail sanction and continue to pursue all court-ordered settlements and support payments if your client fails to agree to these terms or doesn't fulfill these requirements by June 1, 2014.

Please let me hear from you straightaway. Again, this offer expires May 23, 2014

Sincerely,

L. Vance

We never received a reply from Roi's attorney, so we filed a Motion for Enforcement with the District Court of Bexar County, Texas, in July 2014. The earliest court date would be in October, which allowed enough time to attempt a resolution to the standoff; however, once again, we were in a holding pattern with an unpredictable outcome.

As the October 2014 court date approached, news arrived that Roi had not paid the attorney we were trying to make the deal with. Ms. Vance attempted to email the court summons directly to him, but it bounced back, so on to plan #1,000. We obtained my ex's employer information from LinkedIn, and Googled the company he listed as his employer, located, oddly enough, in Virginia, only to find out that they maintain no office in Texas. With Roi's track record, suspicion was inevitable, so I dug out my private investigator hat and called the company to request employee verification. I learned that he did work for that company, but from home. To try to serve the summons and set a court date before Thanksgiving and Christmas would have taken the fun out of the holidays and a visit to San Antonio. A new trial date was scheduled for January 28, 2015, seven months after filling, and left the holidays free of drama.

I love Christmas, and I start to think about decorations and gifts around July—possibly a little over the top, but I'm following in my mother's footsteps. As we approach our sixth year without Roi, we looked forward to a Christmas of fun and laughter without someone putting a damper on the whole day. No one understands how a parent can justify abandoning his kids, but because my kids were older, the issue of whom they'd spend Christmas Eve or Christmas Day with wasn't a problem I had to face. As a parent, I can't imagine having to deliver my children to an unfamiliar home with their dad's new mistress or new wife and do it with a happy face. My heart aches for every child regardless of age, who has had to accept a parent's betrayal or worse yet, abandonment.

I can speak only of the unfaithful parent in my kids' lives and how it has impacted them. I'm thankful they grew up in a marriage that provided them security until my daughter was in her late teens and a college student, and my son a commissioned army officer. Home for a weekend, my daughter found explicit sexual emails on our home computer exchanged between her dad and another woman. That's when they were put in the position of confidants to an adulterous parent, a disastrous circumstance for a child of any age. My kids protected the marriage and me for over ten years by keeping one of his affairs secret, until their dad's most recent mistress had called to inform me of their affair, which blew the adulterer's secret wide open. With the cat out of the bag, my kids, who'd kept the family from ruin years earlier, were finally able to let go of their dad's hidden deceit.

My simple definition of abandonment is that the parent is here one day and gone the next, as if he or she has fallen of the face of the earth, never to be heard from again. I believe that betrayal and abandonment are the cruelest actions a parent could sentence a child to, and that children are undeserving, innocent victims of divorce and its long-term effects. Today is Nicole's birthday, and as she left for work she said, "There's a bittersweet feeling about my birthday." It marked the seventh year that her dad had ignored the day and another day that made my heart break for her. I'm reminded that he shows no partiality, as he doesn't acknowledge my son's birthday either. That he has intentionally chosen not to recognize his children is deliberate cruelty. I'm sure his excuse would be "Well, they didn't acknowledge mine."

Gary's confidence and self-respect remained strong, in part due to the loyalty of his army buddies and his need to be focused while he prepared for a year's deployment to Afghanistan, and in part, of course, because he'd fallen in love. That's not to say he isn't angry to this day, but perhaps, like me, he lets his ire simmer until something as simple as a taillight malfunction triggers a meltdown. I don't know whether the "Irish temper" is real or mythical, but I've been accused of having one, so I might as well risk perpetuating a myth by blaming my Irish ancestors.

For Nicole, however, the discovery of her dad and his mistress having a slumber party in her parents' apartment was devastating. At midnight, which good friends do you call and say, "I just caught my dad and his mistress in my parents' bed?" You sure as heck can't call your mother! Her dad's adultery instantly destroyed our family unity and overshadowed the excitement and challenge of her new directorship of an association of foreign exchange students, a position that required her to leave for Croatia in a matter of days. Since staying home would have cost her the position, she gathered her strength and held her head high despite the enormity of our crisis. Her few phone calls from Dubrovnik, Croatia reassured her that I was vertical and functional—and still able to pay the enormous phone bill.

The only time I've witnessed my daughter in meltdown mode was upon her return from Croatia, when she called her dad twice to let him have it—a sad waste of her breath! As a young kid, she'd stomp up and down the stairs to let me know she was ticked off, but unlike my son and me, who occasionally explode, she suppresses her anger and disappointment. Eight years later she was still dealing with the pile of devastation left by her dad; the pile had become more manageable, but will never be forgotten. Finally realizing that it was time to unload the years of feeling unjustly treated and soothing that feeling with food, my daughter has moved on and now looks amazing.

Nicole isn't one to give up; she adjusted her plans and moved forward to a new position as Director, National Association of Home Builders (NAHB) Remodelers & CMS Member Services in Washington, D.C.

Chapter Twenty-Seven Take-Aways

- Disrespect of a spouse is not understandable especially after a long term marriage.

- Be prepared to retain attorneys in other locations, it's costly, but if you can afford it, don't give up.

- Your ex-spouse may hire a new family law attorney and they will try to renegotiate an agreement based upon what your ex-spouse tells them of the "story" and not based upon facts.

- You will come to a point in the drama and the journey where you have reached a point where you no longer want to negotiate. You may end up back in court if your ex doesn't accept the offer.

- Determine a limit you would be willing to take in order to end the battle. Have your attorney negotiate with opposing counsel an end to things.

- Find support and humor in as much of the drama as you can. You will be emotionally drained by the days, weeks, months and years of a divorce.

- It's ok to have a meltdown; you may even find yourself incredibly productive.

- An unfaithful parent abandoning children is heartbreaking no matter their age.

- The effects of abandonment never go away. If your ex-spouse has no contact with the children, the effects are exponential.

- Remember the drama will seem endless.

28

Maximilian and Me

Kicking off the New Year of 2015 by going to court was definitely something different. It would be Nicole's first visit to San Antonio, but in truth she wanted to see her dad and hoped to be able to say something to him. In the end she wanted him held accountable and in jail at best, as he had shown only disrespect and had taken no responsibility. I was looking forward to seeing Ms. Vance as a friend, but also as a darn good attorney who was going to do everything in her power to put a crimp in Roi's life. Our flights were beautifully synchronized from opposite coasts arriving in Dallas within minutes of each other, allowing us to fly on to San Antonio together.

My center seatmate on the flight from Seattle to Dallas was the owner of a Chihuahua named Maximilian, whose assigned seat was under the poor person seated in front of his owner. To make sure everyone knew he felt humiliated in such a position, Max barked incessantly before the plane rolled back from the gate. A skilled escape artist, he had no intention of staying confined in the carrier for the duration of the flight. When he wasn't running up and down the aisle, causing me to get out of my aisle seat repeatedly so his owner could corral him, he wanted to be wrapped in a baby blanket and held in her arms, putting his mouth about six inches from my left bicep. After he'd curled his lips to show me his pointy little teeth, I made sure I didn't spread beyond the seventeen-inch seat I'd purchased for the three-hour flight. There must be some poetic justice in sitting next to an arrogant little dog that wouldn't stay in his cage while on my way to try and put an arrogant old dog behind bars.

When my children were babies and toddlers I flew thousands of miles with them, praying that my little ones wouldn't disturb other passengers. Years ago, while on a military flight from Rhine Mein Air Force Base, Germany to McGuire Air Force Base, New Jersey, a recent widower with three young kids and a new baby were on the same flight. That poor baby was inconsolable. When we'd landed, collected our luggage, and made it through customs, we boarded an army bus that took us to Manhattan and dumped us out at the Port Authority at midnight, and the wailing baby still hadn't paused to take a breath. With three adults and four children and a mound of luggage on the curb, trying to hail cabs at that hour, was frightening and I wanted to cry. The patience that soldier dad demonstrated after almost twenty-four hours of travel should have earned him some kind of medal.

As a mother who's traveled with her own young children, I'm ashamed to admit that I do scan the waiting passengers to see if there are any potentially bothersome little guys who might sit next to me, but from now on I'll scan for small dogs with big personalities.

Ms. Vance caught me at the airport in Dallas with the details of a settlement offer for a few bucks. The airport hubbub was so loud that I could hardly hear myself think, but the word "offer" came through loud and clear. Rather than make a decision that I might later regret, I agreed to meet her at her office the next morning and do a little strategizing before court. My determination to hound my ex legally had never wavered. After six years, however, I'd become less interested in the elusive money and more interested in putting him in jail. I'd had more than enough of him, and accepting a settlement that involved monthly payments would keep me tied to him for years to come. On the other hand, Ms. Vance said, "I want you to have the money you deserve," so with reluctance I agreed to consider the court's decision, and we went to court with that goal in mind.

My determination to hound my ex legally had never wavered. After six years, however, I'd become less interested in the elusive money and more interested in putting him in jail. I'd had more than enough of him, and accepting a settlement that involved monthly payments would keep me tied to him for years to come.

Ms. Vance and her paralegal went off to hear the reading of the docket, or schedule, for that day's hearings, appearances, and arguments. When they returned to our waiting room they had news that we didn't want to hear. Roi's attorney had a sick child at home and had asked to have the trial rescheduled for the next day. That meant we'd have to reschedule our hotel and airline reservations. Ka-ching, ka-ching! It was about to become even more complicated, as Ms. Vance felt that if Gary could make it to the trial the next morning it would demonstrate a family's unified request for a jail sentence. To complicate things further, my son was attending an Army National Guard Conference in Richmond, Virginia, about two hours south of Dulles Airport. Relying on his trusty smartphone, he made a reservation to fly out of Dulles at *zero dark thirty*—the military term for half past midnight, or any other unpleasant time to be awake—which would put him in Dallas in time for the trial.

We returned to Ms. Vance's office to discuss the monetary offer made by my ex's attorney; that discussion took as long as it does to say, "Absolutely not." Roi's current hired gun most likely wasn't given an accurate accounting of his client's past legal troubles, so offering a small down payment followed by monthly installments must have seemed like the perfect solution to satisfy the greedy bitch.

With a computer at our disposal, we spent the afternoon in search of any information pertinent to the next day's trial. To seek a new smoking gun and not find one turned into a tiresome assignment. We were reminded that investigative work is tedious, so by the time we returned to the hotel around 7:00 pm, we were mentally exhausted and barely able to order room service.

It might sound bizarre that I was excited as we were on our way to court, but of course I wasn't the one being sued. The next morning, we once again passed the time in the very same waiting room Gary and I had hidden in two years earlier, and waited to be assigned to a judge. An hour later, Ms. Vance and her associate returned, visibly shaken. I'd never seen Ms. Vance speechless, but whatever happened at the docket reading must have been a major game changer. It took her a few moments to regain her composure and explain that three minutes before that day's docket was to be read, Roi's former bankruptcy attorney filed for Chapter 13 bankruptcy protection, which assured him yet again of a get-out-of-jail-free card. Nicole burst into uncontrollable tears, and that's when I realized she wanted her dad to make restitution even more than I did. Overnight, he'd gone over the head of his attorney, who, for personal reasons or a ploy, caused the trial to be postponed to the next day, giving Roi the opportunity to retain his former bankruptcy attorney. Granted, I harbor a negative opinion of that attorney for the way he handled the first bankruptcy case, so I didn't have high expectations for a positive outcome of this newest case.

Though we were down, we weren't out. Ms. Vance suggested we return to her office and have lunch while she called an attorney friend who represents clients in bankruptcy. Gary met us at her office, and once again Nicole broke down in tears, something my son had predicted. He was briefed and not at all surprised that his dad would be capable of pulling a rabbit out of the hat. When I informed him of the trial date he said, "Mom, that SOB has been able to deny everything the court has given you, so I wouldn't be surprised if he dropped dead the day before his trial."

Since that didn't happen, we'd go forward with a new strategy. What was a little more legal help at that point? Ms. Vance's colleague was another blessing in my collection of legal advisors. The two of them brainstormed about how to respond to the eleventh-hour filing for bankruptcy in order to keep Roi out of the local hoosegow. The word "fraud" was bandied about, just as it had been in his first filing by the federal bankruptcy attorney. Let's face it, Roi's a fraud and he's turned fraud into an art form. In an hour or so the two ladies of law had a plan and I had a few less dollars. At 9:00 a.m. the next morning my new filing would be presented at the beautiful old red-granite-and-limestone Bexar County Courthouse. The Romanesque Revival building is without a doubt far more charming than Virginia's contemporary Fairfax County Courthouse.

On our last day in San Antonio we took the opportunity to walk to the Alamo and wander around the courtyards and the enormous live oak, which was planted in 1912 and already forty years old at that time. It was a perfect day to visit the historic site and walk the surrounding area, as there were few tourists, and unlike the hot summer months when even the wind is hot, the temperature couldn't have been better. That evening, we enjoyed a walk along the network of walkways under trees adorned in twinkling lights that line the banks of the San Antonio River. Known as the Riverwalk, and just steps from our hotel, it's a smorgasbord of restaurants, bars, and tourist attractions where one could meet visitors from all over the world buying mementos.

On Monday morning, I was sure the judge was looking forward to getting his week off to a smooth start. By granting Roi's bankruptcy filing an automatic stay, he halted all actions by creditors, and my filing for dismissal was denied. That freed the judge from any responsibility for sending Roi back to state court and probably to jail. If my ex were a cat, he'd be close to running out of lives, and if he didn't follow the court ruling this time he just might. Jail will always be inevitable for him, until he's completed his obligation to me. It would have simply been inconceivable eight years ago that the divorce could reach the jailhouse steps not just once but twice.

Once again, the court required him to make a down payment of approximately one fourth of the unpaid alimony within five days; then a monthly payment would automatically be taken out of his bank account by the Chapter 13 trustee and deposited in my account. If the account fell below the amount necessary to make the payment, Roi would have two weeks to replenish the account before the bankruptcy court would dismiss his case without question and it would automatically return to the county court. So much for the standard court language, as it only has meaning if the person given the order honors his responsibility. My attorney was able to add her two cents to the ruling, and I'd just have to wait to see how the ruling would play out.

At last—a court order with teeth! Without enough disposable cash to satisfy the down payment, Roi was ordered to sign over his Lincoln MKZ to me and have his attorney deliver the car to Ms. Vance's office by five o'clock on February 18, 2015. I had a vision of Roi desperately hanging on to the bumper of his car as it was driven through the streets of San Antonio to Ms. Vance's, but that vision lasted only a moment. I presumed the attorney would show up by the stated hour and hand over the title and keys while making a hasty retreat. Divorce, however, dictates that nothing will be clean and simple or make sense, so an argument ensued over the license plates that the attorney was attempting to remove. A verbal knock-down-drag-out between the attorneys was averted, and in the end, Roi's attorney left with the plates, monogrammed with a configuration of distinguished veteran, yelling, "My client is very bitter about coming so close to jail."

> *Without enough disposable cash to satisfy the down payment, Roi was ordered to sign over his Lincoln MKZ to me and have his attorney deliver the car to Ms. Vance's office by five o'clock on February 18, 2015.*

Hey, dude, if your client had just followed court orders over the last six years, you wouldn't have been in the awkward position of delivering his car to his ex-wife! She'd have been paid off, and he'd be driving that car with her in his rearview mirror. Oh, but then you wouldn't have been able to charge for billable hours to drive it across town. I was spared the details of how the law firm negotiated the sale without license plates, but the loathsome behavior of Roi's attorney arose from pure vindictiveness.

I'll always question the ethics of a firm that would agree to represent a client who hadn't followed the stipulated repayment plan he'd agreed to under the Chapter 13 rules during the years 2013–2014 and again represent that unscrupulous client after filing Chapter 13 during 2015–2016. Maybe he duped that firm like he'd duped so many others. The attorney knew he was a veteran, and had perhaps heard the fabricated POW story and simply had compassion for him. I can't believe

I'm thinking something that stupid, however, when I've won every judgment and he's the one receiving protection from the law. I've lost faith in the justice system, and I'll view it with skepticism from now on. As an example, just look at the affluenza case: A judge sentenced a teenage drunk driver who'd killed four people and injured eleven others to probation because the teen had been raised in an affluent family and was too rich and spoiled to understand the consequences of his actions. That judge then conveniently retired, leaving Texas with one less judge with no good sense.

*I'll always question the ethics of a firm
that would agree to represent a client who
hadn't followed the stipulated repayment
plan he'd agreed to under the Chapter 13
rules during the years 2013–2014 and again
represent that unscrupulous client after
filing Chapter 13 during 2015–2016.*

How ironic for me to become the owner of his 2008 Lincoln MKZ, a vehicle that was purchased eight months before his affair, and a vehicle that caused friction between us. I didn't know he was looking for a new car, much less that he'd ordered one. How silly of me not to notice his three-year-old car was over the hill—and paid for, by the way. He described the new car and told me the price and its delivery date, so when it came in, I drove him to pick it up at a dealership we'd been doing business with for twenty years. The pretty, shiny black car was sitting there ready for him to drive off right after we signed for it. The signing didn't go well, however; as the salesman read over the contract, which included the cost, I heard a price very different from what Roi had told me. I question my hearing occasionally, but definitely not when we're discussing the cost of a new car. The salesman reiterated the price, and I turned to Roi and said, "You quoted me a lower price." He said, "No, you must have forgotten." Feeling belittled and embarrassed, I immediately excused myself, and as I walked away I said, "You sign for it," trying to maintain my dignity. On the other hand, it was the first time in our marriage that I hadn't kept my mouth shut and allowed him to get away with falsehoods. It was a huge "little" step for me to reveal a flaw in our marriage by calling him out in public. Chances are that salesman already knew his MO, if not that day, then surely when he flaunted his mistress on a later visit to the dealership.

How ironic for me to become the owner of his 2008 Lincoln MKZ, a vehicle that was purchased eight months before his affair, and a vehicle that caused friction between us.

For a fleeting moment I thought it might be fun to drive the car to Seattle and deck it out with my own monogrammed plates. My daughter and I had come up with some creative ideas, though choosing the most creative message would have been more challenging than getting rid of the car. In the end, I made a wise decision and sold it, which paid half my legal bill, allowing me a moment—and I do mean moment—of sweet justice.

When the first of May 2015 rolled around, it had been approximately three months since the court had notified me that I'd receive my first payment, and I was once again checking the mail, exactly what I didn't want to do. My anxiety level rose with each passing day, as I wondered if my ex was once again gaming the system at my emotional expense—precisely why I was willing to trade the alimony arrears for seeing him behind bars. By May 8, armed with the Chapter 13 case number, I called the United States Bankruptcy Court in Texas to inquire about the status of the first payment. They told me that the first check had been sent to Ms. Vance's office, and if I wanted to change the mailing address I would need to have the law firm handle it. Nothing is simple or inexpensive! The change of address was made, and by August 2015 I had five checks in my little hot hand, but they amounted to less than $5,000.

But wait—in October, a letter arrived from the Bankruptcy Court, Western District of Texas, instead of a payment. In legalese it stated that my ex was in default of the terms of the repayment contract he'd proposed in March 2015, and his dismissal hearing would take place on December 1. Roi's attorney argued that a dismissal would be detrimental to his client, and again a deal was struck with the court. The new plan was presented and approved on December 2, 2015; it allowed for reduced payments for several months, with increases over time. My bankruptcy attorney had already predicted that the court would dismiss the plan eventually, in due course, someday, sooner or later and that's exactly what happened.

Valentine's Day 2016 was a rainy, gloomy Seattle Sunday, the perfect type of day to shred outdated paperwork. I had the Sirius radio set on love tunes from the '50s and '60s, and I sang and swayed with the music as I shredded bank statements, investment accounts, and our final joint federal income taxes. I was down to the last documents when it dawned on me that I'd shredded about eight years of our financial life, from the time when the bottom line looked solvent. In the end, I filled a thirty-gallon plastic bag with shredded paper good for packing.

Speaking of finances, I hadn't heard from the bankruptcy court in almost three months, and my apprehension about the deal was on the rise. I've learned that the inexpensive way to obtain legal information is to go directly to the court, using the case number and contact information included on the original paperwork, rather than call the lawyer first. The trustee told me I'd receive the first check by the end of the month, February 2016. Uh-uh! In my most charming tone, I responded, "When can I expect an increase?" His reply was that I'd be paid pro rata each month, and that the payments would vary. My math skills are quite accurate when it comes to money, so a quick division of the amount owed and the pro rata amount gave me the number eighteen—eighteen years, that is. We usually think about coddling in reference to babies and toddlers, but the coddling afforded my ex and his ilk by attorneys, the federal bankruptcy court, and a court system that doesn't enforce court orders had me wondering if I was living in a Third-World country. I can assure you; I was held to a different standard and never coddled by anyone.

I hear the word" bankruptcy" almost daily, or perhaps I hear it because my former husband has involved me in his. It gives people, myself included, the idea that one files for protection and voila—every debt is somehow paid or erased! The rules for filing are very specific, and if the court approves the repayment plan, then the difficulty of making monthly payments begins. Being disciplined enough to make payments to the court over extended periods becomes burdensome. The attorney who went to bat for Roi and kept him out of jail will undoubtedly be paid. Accountability to his creditors is slim to none, even to me, a priority creditor. The success rate for completing a Chapter 13 repayment plan is less than 30 percent, especially when one has filed, twice, to stop a lawsuit offering an automatic stay and with no intention of actually completing the case.

The letter from the Federal Bankruptcy Court, Western District of Texas, arrived May 23, 2016 notifying me that the case had been formally dismissed. I only had to wait 15 months from the day he filed his second Chapter 13 until the court dismissed it. By the way we used to celebrate our wedding anniversary on May 23!

Figuratively speaking, I've chosen to write off my alimony. I no longer want a court, an attorney, or a judge to rule in my favor, which they did time after time, without an enforcement mechanism to deal with my con-man ex-husband. Also, I no longer want to pay taxes on the microscopic portion of what he did pay me, and finally, I can't trust a Texas judge to incarcerate him; maybe God will send him to a hot place.

If however, divorce raises its ugly head, you'll undoubtedly need a lawyer. To find a firm is as simple as using the Internet, but if you have a friend or acquaintance with a recommendation, use the Web to research that firm. Keep in mind that retaining a law firm is an expensive business decision. The emotional cost will be far greater than the financial, so choose wisely. Kick the tires, so to speak, before you sign the contract and pay the retainer. You must have a rapport with the attorney and be comfortable with the commute to their office. If you sense that the firm isn't going to become your new best friend, look for another—after all, we're talking about the rest of your life!

Keep in mind that retaining a law firm is an expensive business decision. The emotional cost will be far greater than the financial, so choose wisely.

Your family law attorney will guide you through the seemingly endless process of divorce. Assuming that all the players are ethical and follow through with the court's rulings, the divorce should end there. If, however, you're dealing with a cheater like my ex-husband, who with the support of his mistress was able to dishonor every order the court issued, be prepared for a lengthy ordeal. It will be shameful, an exhausting, disappointing event that leaves you drained. It will have cost too much money, and you'll have expended too much emotional energy, all perfectly predictable. I hate the statement "You just need some time." "Some time" is how long? From the moment my husband said, "I'm divorcing you," I never once thought I had time to wallow in fear over he and his mistress' desire to financially ruin me. I'm proud of how I've moved forward with dignity and accomplishing unimaginable hurdles. I'm not sure when my strength of character was first tested, but I do know when I grew a backbone.

Chapter Twenty-Eight Take-Aways

- You need to determine when enough is enough and if you have it in you, emotionally and financially, to continue fighting.

- I had no idea one could file for bankruptcy, have it dismissed, and a year later file again.

- Payment may come in an unusual form – your ex-spouse's car. While I never saw the car or the money from selling the car, my attorney did use the value of the car as payment for part of what I owed her.

29

Deutschland and An Officer's Wife

Flying out of Seattle on our wedding day fifty-three years ago, it never occurred to me that not only I but my whole life would change, and that Seattle would later become almost unrecognizable. I'm thankful that the Space Needle and Mount Rainier are landmarks the city still hasn't touched—yet! This time, to weigh anchor and leave my home will be heartbreaking, as it's not a decision I made because it was time to move to a smaller home or another location; rather, it came down to finances, a reality of divorce.

On May 23, 1963, I was a young woman leaving on an odyssey that would open doors to unimaginable places and experiences in the big new world, rather like freshman orientation week at Seattle University in September 1960, but without the beanie. I would describe myself as having a cheerful personality and a quick wit. I'm able to look at situations, even the divorce, with a sense of humor, though I can be shy and quiet.

Growing up, I was comfortable being at home, so I never wanted to go to camp or away to college. Instead I moved to Germany and learned how to take charge. I would need toughening up in order to handle the challenges I'd encounter in the next fifty-three years.

Instead I moved to Germany and learned how to take charge. I would need toughening up in order to handle the challenges I'd encounter in the next fifty-three years.

By the time we arrived at the Brooklyn Army Terminal I'd been a wife for a week, but as I walked up the gangplank among a sea of uniformed people, it hit me that this was what my future would look like as the wife of an army officer. The first nine days of June 1963 were spent pitching and rolling across the Atlantic Ocean to Germany. Navy regulations required that the stateroom, a nice big one with two bunks, decorated in navy gray, with one porthole, too high to see out of, be cleared by zero-eight-hundred hours, or 8:00 a.m. Sailors would come in to make up the bunks military-style, and after the drill sergeant's inspection we were able to return to our stateroom. I was so seasick I didn't care if the corners were tucked in at a 45-degree angle, but I didn't want my second lieutenant to be called on the carpet because of his wife, though the carpet looked exactly like gray linoleum. Lesson 1 was to learn to follow regulations, as they applied to me as well.

We disembarked from the ship directly onto a train that took us from Bremerhaven to Hanau, an overnight trip, and finally set foot on German soil. We sat on our luggage in the bahnhof (train station) till the battalion commander arrived to welcome us to the 6th Battalion, 40th Field Artillery. My lieutenant was very impressed that the colonel welcomed us. I, on the other hand, didn't know a private from a general, except that the general undoubtedly wouldn't look wet behind the ears, but who was I to judge? I had *clueless* written on my forehead. We spent a week with our sponsors while they helped us find an 'apartment-on-the-economy', as no quarters were available. Renting within the local community is termed 'on-the-economy'. Our sponsors were so gracious to total strangers as they moved into the baby's room so we could have their bedroom. Welcome to the military family.

Having not grown up in a community with clearly defined rules and expectations, I found the military lifestyle challenging at first. I needed to understand military culture as soon as possible in order to fit in. We moved into an apartment at 10 Friedrichstrasse, Hanau, Germany, that should have come with a decorator's warning: "Do not try this at home." I'd just completed a degree in interior design, and could see that no two walls were alike in the two-bedroom living/dining room apartment. Even the fabric used for draperies and upholstery was a mishmash of color and pattern—it was like the color wheel had spun out of control. Compared to the home I grew up in, the apartment was primitive. I had to carry buckets of hot water from the bathroom to the kitchen to wash dishes. I think it's possible that my mom thought I'd never learn to do dishes—but I'm a fast learner.

Having not grown up in a community with clearly defined rules and expectations, I found the military lifestyle challenging at first. I needed to understand military culture as soon as possible in order to fit in.

The few things that had been shipped from the States hadn't arrived, but somehow we had a transistor radio. It had to sit on the floor in the kitchen, leaning up against a pipe in order for us to hear the Armed Forces Network (AFN), an American military radio station that provided a variety of programs from news to current music. Each morning, one program was broadcast that catered to women. It was called *The Ironing Board Brigade,* which sounds ridiculous today, but political correctness hadn't taken over, and we all listened. It was the only English-language radio station, after all.

Some wives did claim they'd ironed fatigues in the 1960s, as they didn't come out of the dryer (if you had one) ready to wear. They needed to be pressed and creased in all the right places. Other wives went so far as to brag about spit shining their husbands' boots. I did iron fatigues, occasionally, as we weren't exactly flush with money for the cleaner's, but I drew the line at shining boots. It's no wonder that boots today are desert tan and lack any brilliance.

During our second week at our apartment, the battalion left for a week in the field. So, what to do? The answer was the beginning of how I would face obstacles for the rest of my life, though I wasn't, of course, giving the rest of my life any thought. I had the option of just staying in the apartment until my lieutenant's return and twiddle my thumbs as I wondered how I could correct the atrocious decorating, or I could walk to Pioneer *Kaserne,* or army post. I chose option number two, and executed the walk to the kaserne and back without getting lost, which gave me the confidence to walk the few blocks to downtown Hanau, look in store windows, and vow to return once I understood the deutschmark.

For $1,600 we bought a brand-new red Austin Healy Sprite, and we drove that cute little car all over Europe. It was liberating to have transportation. It didn't hold much, but we couldn't afford much. With a way to get around easily, I became an official member of the officers' wives club and the junior wife, assigned to Delta (D) Battery of the 6/40 Field Artillery Battalion. Even though I'd been to college and active in many organizations in my short life, I was unprepared for the hierarchy amongst officer's wives. My introduction to the pecking order began in D Battery. The battery commander was a major, and his wife, Jane, was in charge of two underlings, a first lieutenant's wife, Betty, and me, the wife of a lowly second lieutenant who'd been commissioned only six months earlier. Talk about wet behind the ears!

Jane and Betty outranked me, had been married longer than two months, and had been in-country for over a year— almost more important than rank—and, as you might guess, they knew the battalion gossip. The battalion constantly guarded the border between East and West Germany, and during those exercises, Jane and Betty had become fast friends. Betty would spend the nights at Jane's, as Jane lived in quarters known as the bowling alley, a large set of quarters with a very long hall and a bathroom big enough for a battalion party. They invited me to spend the night, and I did a few times; it was a way for me to get to know them and become a member of D Battery, and the truth is I was afraid to stay alone. Since I didn't know any of the other women in the battalion, it became Jane and Betty's mission to show me the ropes, in hopes they could influence me to agree with their assessment of the others.

They gave it their best shot, but I didn't want to be influenced by their malicious gossip. Believe me, they weren't the first gossipy wives in my army-wife career, or the first to believe the myth that "there's no rank among wives." Years later, I too became the subject of gossip, but I'll never forget Jane and Betty, and I thank them for the lesson they had no idea they'd taught me: namely, women who act like seventh-grade girls are not nice people—a quality I recognized in my ex-husband's second wife.

My military-lifestyle training was so subtle that I was unaware I was being taught valuable lessons that I'd need throughout my life. Fortunately for me, I've grown a backbone over the years, as that shy, quiet girl needed one. I've overcome shyness only to find that I'm occasionally surprised at what comes out of my mouth. It didn't happen overnight; it took place from year to year, experience to experience, but those first few years in Europe were the most valuable. I adapted to the military lifestyle and European culture, and became a fearless driver, unafraid to go anywhere, even driving around the L'Arc de Triomphe, in Paris, with my eyes wide-open. Each new assignment came with its own set of challenges, some weather related, as in the area known as Tornado Alley.

> *My military-lifestyle training was*
> *so subtle that I was unaware I was*
> *being taught valuable lessons that*
> *I'd need throughout my life.*

While I was growing up in earthquake country, drills that started in elementary school instructed us to drop, cover, and hold on. I've experienced several earthquakes, and they're almost over before you realize it's time to move the chairs and get under the table. The safety information I was given in case of a tornado was to get into a bathtub, preferably in a center room, and cover myself with a mattress. I tried to envision maneuvering our queen-size mattress down a narrow hall, taking a right turn into the bathroom, getting into the tub and pulling the mattress over me before the tornado blew our quarters into the next county. I'm thankful we never experienced even a tornado warning in the four years that we lived in any of the three states considered tornado territory, as the mattress plan wouldn't have worked in any of our living quarters.

Chapter Twenty-Nine Take-Aways

- You will find your strength through many avenues. I will be forever grateful for my ex-husband's career in the Army, as it truly taught me survival, strength, and a can-do attitude that I was unaware existed. We moved thousands of miles away from my comfort zone and it forced me to make the decision to "sink or swim." I decided I would take this amazing opportunity of living in a foreign country presented to me and make the best of it. Being an Army wife, especially of an officer who was often away from home for weeks at a time, pushed me to take on responsibilities of paying the bills, picking up the mail on post, grocery shopping, etc. These experiences gave me wings to fly! These experiences eventually translated into a strength of spirit that would serve me through Vietnam, Korea, moving fifteen times, the emotional turmoil of my daughter's premature birth, raising kids while my husband dedicated more time to work than family and eventually Bunny calling me that September afternoon and hearing "I'm divorcing you" from my now ex-husband. I probably wouldn't have believed anyone had they told me 56 years ago that my life would have taken the paths I have travelled, but despite the past very difficult ten years, I am grateful for it all.

30

Moving Onward and Upward

As I approached my new assignment, or what the military refers to as a PCS (Permanent Change of Station), I was overwhelmed with the enormity of the project. For nearly eight years, from the moment Roi said, "I'm divorcing you," I instinctively knew that my Seattle home would be in jeopardy; so, during those eight years I kept my eye on my investments (most of them losing value), and the excessive cost of the divorce. Luckily for me, the housing market in my neighborhood and Seattle in general was the only thing that gained value. Choosing a definite date, however, and marking the calendar was so final; knowing that I wasn't just moving to a three-year assignment was like being dumped all over again. On the other hand, I was blessed to have had eight years loving every minute in my perfect home without my ex.

Moving was a project I wanted to do on my own. Having watched the professional movers pack my treasures for fifteen major moves, I felt confident that I could pack them myself with precision. Over an eighteen-month period, I planned every step from start to finish in preparation for the last item to be placed in the moving van. I'm a list maker, but not particularly an organized list maker, so some of the things I needed to do were only in my head, and because I couldn't check them off it wasn't as rewarding as those on paper. My end goal was to do everything possible to keep the costs down, as the move was on my dime.

I started to collect a variety of different-sized boxes, like those that arrive from online stores, and shredded years of paperwork into thirty-gallon yard bags to use as inexpensive packing material. I frequented Home Depot so often I think the greeter thought I worked there. I needed dish-pack boxes, bubble wrap, yards of heavy-duty tape, and reams of newsprint wrapping paper. I wasn't looking for packing peanuts, but when I saw the anti-static variety online I ordered a bag. I highly recommend that stuff, as it stays where you put it, no muss no fuss. In the end I had packed and catalogued over a hundred boxes—and lost five pounds in the process.

Let's face it, moving is stressful whether you're moving across town, across country, or around the world. It's more complicated and emotional than packing boxes and putting your possessions on a truck. I interviewed several long-distance movers to make sure they had high standards, and selected the company that had moved us from Virginia to Seattle in 2004. I then chose a Realtor, and with that accomplished, added the packing day, the moving-out day, and my last three days in Seattle to the calendar.

> *Let's face it, moving is stressful*
> *whether you're moving across town,*
> *across country, or around the world.*

I'd kept the bill of lading for the move from Virginia to Seattle, which indicated that we'd shipped 13,000 pounds, so I knew I needed to reduce the weight. First of all, I mentally subtracted my ex's stuff, which was finally off my property, and then decided what pieces of furniture would go to a consignment store. I researched consignment stores and auction houses, and chose the consignment store, as the items would have up to a three-month exposure to buyers. An auction is a one- or two-day event, and the right people have to be there to bid on your pieces. In both cases, if your items don't sell within the stipulated time, you have two choices: pick them up or donate them. It's a little disappointing when the check arrives from either the consignment store or auction house to find out what others were willing to pay for your treasures. I was happy to give many things to a family member, and finally shared boxes and bags of donations to the Goodwill and the Society of Saint Vincent de Paul. In the end the new bill of lading indicated that I had reduced the weight by 4,000 pounds, no small feat!

Interviewing movers and realtors or packing and making donations are only a part of the whole saga. Stuff that's not donatable can be picked up by a local recycle company at a more reasonable price than the one with "JUNK" in its phone number.

If you've ever lived in government quarters, you'll never forget the signing in and signing out process conducted by the post engineers. The post engineer is the military's version of the civilian home inspector, who looks for structural or mechanical defects to protect the new owner, while the military inspection looks for a standard of cleanliness for the new occupant. I had the cleanliness drill down pat and had filled nail holes and touched up the paint where needed. Even though my home had had a major remodel in 2004 and was up to code in all areas, I was still worried about the invasive inspection and the cost, if any, for repairs.

By the time the home was empty, the FOR SALE sign was up, and my car was loaded for the return trip to Virginia, my daughter had arrived. We both felt numb. We'd driven over the mountains to take one last look at the ski areas where I'd spent so many Saturdays flying down the slopes as a kid. When my tears began to flow, it was time to change drivers.

We enjoy cross-country driving, and have done it so many times that we have our favorite route and the one that saves time. While I feel I'm capable of driving the 3,000 miles by myself, I wouldn't do it. We were about a hundred miles east of Council Bluffs, Iowa, when some jerk began to pace us; he moved in behind us, drove alongside of us, and cut in front of our car. This went on for about an hour, and put us on edge, but we didn't show intimidation or risk pulling off the interstate at a rest stop, as we felt safer on the road with other vehicles. The jerk finally gave up his dangerous game and sped away. Over the years, I've traveled thousands of miles across this country, but that was a first and a reminder that danger lurks even out on the wide-open plains of the West.

My home was on the market about five weeks and with each day my anxiety grew. I wouldn't have wanted to be in Seattle checking on it regularly, though being 3,000 miles away wasn't the answer either. Once the house was on the market, my realtor would email comments made by prospective buyers and their realtors, and I wasn't prepared for some of the criticisms. As an introduction to their expertise, my builder, Seattle Design Builders, had featured my home on Houzz, the online way to decorate your home by accessing millions of photos of interior design, home décor, and decorating ideas.

Though my realtor came highly recommended as an honest man, I needed that honest guy to be a pit bull, able to stand up to a buyer and his realtor who were pit bulls. Late one afternoon my realtor phoned to tell me about a prospective buyer whose realtor had visited the plumbing company I'd used to scope the sewer line of my home—strongly recommended for selling an older home in Seattle.

The prospect's realtor claimed that someone at the plumbing outfit told her I hadn't paid my bill. I gasped, and when I caught my breath, I shouted at my realtor, "You've got to be kidding! Someone is defaming my character."

I had divulged everything the realtor had requested of me, including the invoices from the plumbers. He said, "I don't remember you telling me you paid the bill." Fortunately for him, my daughter arrived from work and took over, her voice calmer than mine but very firm. Within minutes, proof of payment was on its way to Seattle, and she was on the phone with the plumbing company. The office manager assured us that they don't release client information, but the rumor had already spread to that realtor's client and my realtor. As it happened, I'd driven the $8,000 check to the company eight months before the malicious realtor's visit.

I believe that the realtor intentionally used a false representation of the facts or misleading allegations by concealment of what had been disclosed that deceives and is intended to deceive another. It's called fraud. The prospective buyer believed his realtor, not the date on my check.

She rehired my plumbing company in addition to two other companies. When the scoping was complete, the ninety-year-old pipe had been scoped five times in nine months, as my neighbor, who shared the pipe, had had it scoped within weeks of the scope I paid for. All five scopes determined that there were some cracks and some roots but no major water leaks. Ask any sewer guy in Seattle and he'll tell you it's predictable to find a crack in a sewer line.

Of course, it didn't end there. A letter from the prospective buyer arrived within days of the scoping, in which he and his realtor requested a price reduction based on the results. The bully buyer wanted the price of my home reduced by what the sewer repair would cost – we're talking thousands. The letter offered two options: 1) He would sue me; or 2) He would put the money for the sale into an escrow account until the sewer repair was complete, the buyer living in my home all the while. The sewer pipe is jointly owned by the neighbors, who'd accepted the condition of the pipe when they bought their home, and their remodel project was already in process. Chances are that they were already spending thousands and not up for sewer-gate. I considered saying, "sue me," as my hands were clean.

Anyone selling a home must be prepared for a challenge to the sale price, preferably a bidding war and not being threatened by an ethically challenged buyer and his realtor's slanderous intimidation to lower the selling price. Loyal friends in the neighborhood have reported that they haven't started the sewer repairs to-date. What happened to the urgency of needing it repaired? That realtor and her client were nasty shady people.

> *Anyone selling a home must be prepared for a challenge to the sale price, preferably a bidding war and not being threatened by an ethically challenged buyer and his realtor's slanderous intimidation to lower the selling price.*

I had really hoped to create a relationship with the buyers of my family home, to be able to share the history with the hope that they would take care of it and love it as my family had for 80 years. Moving onward and upward is what I wished for myself and my military and civilian sisters who have endured a cheater and been abandoned. The challenge is for all of us to move forward smartly.

Chapter Thirty Take-Aways

- Never let the difficult times keep you down for too long. They're not worth it!

- Like Marvin Gaye sang, "Ain't No Mountain High Enough." You'll find that you can surmount peaks taller than you ever imagined.

- One of my favorite songs by Whitney Houston, "One Moment In Time" and the old Army slogan, "Be All You Can Be," are truly mantras I lived by throughout the entire divorce journey, all eight years!

31

The Ex-Husband Strikes Again

Returning to Virginia has been a challenge for me as I love the grandeur of the Pacific Northwest and most especially the humidity free summers. Throughout 2017, Nicole and I dealt with the complexities of building a new home together, finally moving in the spring of 2018. Gary, his wife and Disco, the Lab, live nearby in the same community and I admit, I love being close to them.

As you know, moving is stressful (now there's an understatement). Then, of course, you need to unpack the treasures and put them somewhere. Perhaps, you might even have to make several trips to the big hardware store for shelving and floor paint. Painted floors in the storage and garage areas just make the treasures look more valuable. None of this happens overnight, and months later you're still trying to figure out where to put the stuff or where to find things. This all occurs while remembering your last master closet where there was room to spare, in contrast to the "new" closet built for a little girl, described on the blueprints as the "Princess Suite." My kids have a new designation for the room and it's very clever, just not fit to print.

We advertised the packing boxes on line several times and never had to take them to the curb or to a recycling facility.

By the end of the last chapter you might have thought that my divorce story had ended and that I had moved forward smartly, which I have for the most part. Yet, there is nothing like an ex-husband who exudes shameless boldness to throw a monkey wrench into your new life.

> *Yet, there is nothing like an ex-husband who exudes shameless boldness to throw a monkey wrench into your new life.*

Our divorce became official on January 31, 2010 and I was awarded 49% of my ex's retirement pay. For seven years, I regularly received my portion of the retirement from Defense Finance Accounting Services (DFAS). I depended on that payment each month, considering he chose not to make the alimony payments.

Yet, in the mail of December 9, 2017 a small pay stub arrived from DFAS. When I say small, I mean a slip of paper 8"X 3" stating EFFEC-TIVE WITH CHECK DATED DEC 29 2017, YOUR ENTITLEMENT WILL BE CHANGED AS FOLLOWS: $247.80. No other information was provided.

I immediately called DFAS to find out what it meant. When I explained why I was calling I was either transferred to another office or was advised to call another number all together. After 45 minutes or so, someone in another division informed me that there had been a pay increase. That sounded plausible and I hung up thinking that $247. 80 would be a nice increase and I didn't give it another thought until I checked my bank statement January 9, 2018.

Geez Louise, where did the $1,100 go?

I was again on the phone with DFAS as I wanted to know how in hell the payment was reduced without some form of notification. This time I was told that it was due to a garnishment. Legally, a garnishment is defined as a debt owed by a debtor to a plaintiff creditor. I can't help wondering who the plaintiff creditor might be as I've taken him to court more than once as a priority creditor and was awarded back spousal payments; however my ex, the debtor, paid nothing and I am still owed thousands.

Calling a government agency is one of the most unpleasant phone calls to make. You are passed around like something that smells bad; no one wants to talk to you much less respond to your questions, assuming that they can even answer them. If they do know the answer to a question, then they act like it's a state secret so that you hang up not knowing anything further than when you first began the phone call.

Although you're positive it has everything to do with the ex!

Once again, it was time to call my attorney, Dem. He was glad to hear from me, although not why I was asking for help. Before he could say much, he said "Do you realize it's our 10th year anniversary?" Talk about bizarre; some marriages don't even last that long and he should know as he helps dissolve them.

I parted with the retainer and the little pay stubs along with a collection of past legal papers. Since everyone is owed due process as outlined in the 14th amendment, we were obliged to send the ex a letter requesting an explanation of the dramatic reduction in my portion of his army retirement. Dem and I did not anticipate a reply to the letter and the ex-did not disappoint us. Next, Dem wrote a letter to DFAS in the hope that the letterhead would be taken more seriously than if I had used my monogrammed stationary. About a month later I received a response identifying two U.S. Codes that in my opinion, answered nothing. The paralegal's letter said, "Should you have questions regarding this matter, please contact me." Dem encouraged me to call; however, when I dialed the number the message said, "This is a service number. If you want to get in touch, send an email."

The DFAS Paralegal Specialist did reply to my email stating. "Please be advised that all payments to the former spouse under the Act are based off of the retiree's disposable pay. Therefore, it is gross pay less any authorized deductions. In final decrees issued after February 3, 1991, authorized deductions include: VA Waivers, indebtedness to the United States, Survivor Benefit Plan, and any portion of retired pay which may be based on disability. If the retiree receives any portion of money from the VA it is deducted from their pay because the VA pays him directly. He has authorized deductions for VA waiver of $3245.28. Therefore, $3751 - $3245.28 x 490 % = $247.80. DFAS does not pay him."

He may have serious health problems. However, I do not think his ethical problems can be treated by the VA. In 2010 qualifications for PTSD made it easier for veterans to apply for VA disability benefits. Today many are claiming PTSD (Post Traumatic Stress Disorder, a disorder officially recognized in 1980) as they leave active duty. Roi left the service in 1983 when PTSD was not a common disorder but due to the injuries he sustained in 1967 in Vietnam, he most likely qualifies for the current benefits.

I questioned my attorney about the 1991 ruling and he responded, "Yes, this was the law and is standard in the calculation of disposable pay. Orders have to be written to account for the reduction in VA Waiver, meaning DFAS will reject all Orders that say that a former spouse is paid from the gross. That is why when you have agreements to pay from the gross; you have to specify that the former spouse's share shall not be reduced. That is what your Agreement says. However, in order to get the differential if pay is reduced, you have to get that directly from the retiree, or seek a garnishment order from the VA."

If the 1991 agreement was discussed as the two attorneys were typing up the Marital Agreement in 2009 I do not remember that conversation. It was at the end of an exhausting nine hours back and forth with two contemptible men, namely Roi and his attorney. While I have a memory like a steel trap, the complete details of the Marital Agreement are not fully ingrained in my brain.

I would have to be a resident of fantasyland to believe that I could garnish his VA account or go after him personally. Though he raised his right hand and agreed to act in accordance with court rulings, my ex-husband has proven that he is incapable of respecting court orders. Like Robert Tew says, sometimes walking away has nothing to do with weakness and everything to do with strength.

To my military and civilian sisters, divorce is complicated and picking yourself up after being sucker-punched will be your first hurdle. Depending on how long you have been married, you will need a lawyer to help you navigate the process that can only be more complicated if a mistress is involved. I recommend that, at a minimum, consult with a lawyer to understand your rights. More often than not, an initial meeting will be free.

*To my military and civilian sisters,
divorce is complicated and picking
yourself up after being sucker-
punched will be your first hurdle.*

As you look back over the whole process your attorney might say "you have won all your cases." While that may be true legally, its natural to question if your ex has chosen not to follow court orders and you are not receiving alimony or child support, it's natural to question if you are really winning; just know that you do deserve a gold medal.

I hope that by sharing my experience, you will have an idea of what you might encounter along the divorce road. I would consider it a miracle to be able to tell you that when your divorce is wrapped up, the alimony and child support will be in the bank, the kids will be going back and forth happy, healthy and successful, and the lawn will look like the gardener just left. Again, that only happens in fantasyland. Take time to have a laugh or two, persevere and be proud knowing you have handled all the crap that came along.

*Take time to have a laugh or two,
persevere and be proud knowing
you have handled all the crap
that came along.*

No need for revenge. Just sit back and wait. Those who hurt you will eventually screw up themselves and if you're lucky, God will let you watch. God may have already let me watch the foreclosure of my ex's home.

*No need for revenge. Just sit back
and wait. Those who hurt you
will eventually screw up themselves
and if you're lucky, God will
let you watch.*

Chapter Thirty-One Take-Aways

- You need a lawyer, no matter how the situation begins.

- Divorce is complicated from start to finish.

- You are the only one who can chase your ex for alimony and child support.

- Should your child support be in arrears for over 2 years or behind by $10,000, the violation is considered a felony.

- Waiting to be given a court date and then appearing in court takes months and feels like forever.

- Your ex could apply for increased VA benefits that will ultimately reduce your portion of the military retirement and, unless your ex gives you a heads-up, you will be caught off guard—in other words, screwed.

- The divorce is all about money and he has money power over you.

- If a new partner is involved, please keep in mind that someone else is influencing your ex.

Glossary

341 Meeting/Meeting of the Creditors
The Meeting of Creditors (341 Hearing) In both Chapter 7 and Chapter 13 bankruptcy, the debtor is required to attend a meeting of creditors, also called the 341 hearing. The meeting of creditors is not a court hearing.

Abandonment
In law, abandonment is the relinquishment, giving up or renunciation of an interest, claim, civil proceedings, appeal, privilege, possession, or right, especially with the intent of never again resuming or reasserting it. Such intentional action may take the form of a discontinuance or a waiver.

Alimony/spousal support/maintenance
a husband's or wife's court-ordered provision for a spouse after separation or divorce.

Appraiser
A person whose job is to assess the monetary value of something.

Army Criminal Investigation Command (CID)
As the U.S. Army's primary criminal investigative organization and the Department of Defense's premier investigative organization, the U.S. Army Criminal Investigation Command, commonly known as CID, is responsible for conducting criminal investigations in which the Army is, or may be, a party of interest.

Arrears
Money that is owed and should have been paid earlier.

At-fault State vs. No-fault
A fault divorce may be granted when the required grounds are present and at least one spouse asks that the divorce be granted on the grounds of fault. Only some states allow fault divorces.

"No fault" divorce describes any divorce where the spouse asking for a divorce does not have to prove that the other spouse did something wrong. All states allow no fault divorces.

Attorney vs lawyer

An attorney, or attorney-at-law, is a person who is a member of the legal profession. An attorney is qualified and licensed to represent a client in court.

A lawyer, by definition, is trained in the field of law and provides advice and aid on legal matters.

Bankruptcy

When a company or person is bankrupt, a court of law gives control of the finances to someone who will arrange to pay as much as possible of what is owed.

Bankruptcy Trustee

A trustee is an independent contractor (not an employee of the bankruptcy court), who is appointed to in effect oversee your bankruptcy case. They are essential to the operation of the bankruptcy system. A trustee will be appointed in almost every bankruptcy case except for Chapter 11 reorganizations and Chapter 9 municipality cases. The bankruptcy trustee's duties depend on the type of case he or she is appointed to administer.

Billable Hours

Billable hours refer to time worked on business matter that will be charged to a client according to a contractual rate. Billable hours in the context of legal representation is often charged in tenths of an hour.

Brats

"Military brat" and various "brat" derivatives describe the child of a parent or parents serving full-time in the United States Armed Forces and can also refer to the subculture and lifestyle of such families. The term refers to both current and former children of such families.

Carabinieri

Term used for Italian police.

Chapter 13 vs 11, 7

Different types of bankruptcy. Chapter 11 is open to almost any individual or business without any specific income or debt-level limits. Both Chapter 11 and Chapter 13 let you keep certain assets you might lose under Chapter 7 bankruptcy.

Chutzpa

Chutzpah means fearlessness. It takes chutzpah to stand in front of the whole class and announce that you are a better writer than William Shakespeare. Chutzpah is a Yiddish word meaning "impudence or gall."

Clean hands vs Dirty Hands

Unclean hands, also referred to as the clean hands or dirty hands doctrine, is a type of legal doctrine that operates as a defense to a complaint. If the defendant can prove that the plaintiff has unclean hands, i.e., acted unethically, then the plaintiff's complaint will be dismissed.

Command General Staff College

The United States Army Command and General Staff College at Fort Leavenworth, Kansas, is a graduate school for United States Army and sister service officers, interagency representatives, and international military officers.

Contempt of court

Contempt of court, often referred to simply as "contempt", is the offense of being disobedient to or disrespectful toward a court of law and its officers in the form of behavior that opposes or defies the authority, justice and dignity of the court.

Daddy Warbucks

Someone who is rich enough to pay for someone else's expenses, either in a large lump sum or over a long time.

DD214

The DD Form 214, Certificate of Release or Discharge from Active Duty, generally referred to as a "DD 214", is a document of the United States Department of Defense, issued upon a military service member's retirement, separation, or discharge from active duty in the Armed Forces of the United States.

DEERS

Defense Enrollment Eligibility Reporting System (DEERS) is a computerized database of military sponsors, families and others.

Defense Intelligence Agency (DIA)

The Defense Intelligence Agency is an intelligence agency of the United

States federal government, specializing in defense and military intelligence.

Deposition
A deposition is the taking of an oral statement of a witness under oath, before trial. It has two purposes: To find out what the witness knows, and to preserve that witness' testimony. The intent is to allow the parties to learn all of the facts before the trial, so that no one is surprised at trial.

DFAS
Defense Finance and Accounting Services (DFAS) provides payment services to the United States Department of Defense.

Divorce from bed & board
Unlike absolute divorce, a divorce from bed and board is a fault-based legal action. Despite its name, a divorce from bed and board does not dissolve the marriage: rather, it is a court-ordered decree of legal separation. In this separation, the matrimonial bonds still exist, so neither spouse has the right to remarry.

Edith Ann
A character on the former TV show, "Laugh-In". Sitting on an outsized rocker and dressed as a 6-year-old named Edith Ann, who observed the passing world with that special combination of innocence and mischief.

Equal Distribution/Common Property State
In a Community Property State, marital property is divided 50-50. In an Equitable Distribution State, marital property is divided equitably, based on a variety of factors.

Garnish
A court order directing that money or property of a third party (usually wages paid by an employer) be seized to satisfy a debt owed by a debtor to a plaintiff creditor.

Inspector Clouseau
Inspector Jacques Clouseau is a fictional character in the farcical The Pink Panther series.

Judge Advocate General (JAG)
The Judge Advocate General's Corps is the branch or specialty of a military concerned with military justice and military law.

La viva Loca
La vida loca is Spanish for "the crazy life."

Lawyer vs Attorney
An attorney, or attorney-at-law, is a person who is a member of the legal profession. An attorney is qualified and licensed to represent a client in court.

A lawyer, by definition, is trained in the field of law and provides advice and aid on legal matters.

Maintenance
Can be awarded to a spouse/civil partner for their own benefit and/or for the benefit of a dependent child who is under the age of 18, or 23 if the child is in full-time education. Another word for alimony.

Marital Agreement
A marital agreement refers to any agreement between spouses involving division and ownership of marital property. A marital agreement is relevant prior to the filing of an action for dissolution of marriage or for legal separation.

Meeting of the Creditors
The Meeting of Creditors (341 Hearing) In both Chapter 7 and Chapter 13 bankruptcy, the debtor is required to attend a meeting of creditors, also called the 341 hearing. The meeting of creditors is not a court hearing.

Modus operandi
A modus operandi is someone's habits of working, particularly in the context of business or criminal investigations, but also more generally.

Motion for enforcement
File a Motion to Enforce and/or for an Order to Show Cause. This kind of motion asks the judge to hold the other parent in contempt of court for not following the court order. The judge can punish the other parent with sanctions, fines, and/or jail.

Motion to Dismiss
A motion to dismiss is a formal request for a court to dismiss a case.

Net Worth
In a nutshell, your net worth is really everything you own of significance

(your assets) minus what you owe in debts (your liabilities). Assets include cash and investments, your home and other real estate, cars or anything else of value you own.

No-fault vs. at-fault state
The difference between a fault and a no-fault divorce is the grounds for the divorce. In the first case, the spouse filing the divorce claims the other spouse is responsible for ruining the marriage, while in the other case no blame is placed on either party. State laws vary greatly. The difference between a fault and a no-fault divorce is the grounds for the divorce. In the first case, the spouse filing the divorce claims the other spouse is responsible for ruining the marriage, while in the other case no blame is placed on either party. State laws vary greatly.

NeoNatal Intensive Care Unit (NICU)
A hospital ward or department equipped and staffed to provide intensive care to dangerously ill or premature newborn babies.

OK Corral
Shootout at the O.K. Corral. On October 26, 1881, the Earp brothers face off against the Clanton-McLaury gang in a legendary shootout at the O.K. Corral in Tombstone, Arizona.

Opposing Council (OC)
That is, the plaintiff's legal counsel and the defendant's legal counsel would be referred to as opposing counsel because they are on the opposite sides of the case.

Paralegal
A person who perform tasks requiring knowledge of the law and legal procedures.

Paramour
A lover, especially the illicit partner of a married person.

PCS
A PCS move is basically a move between one duty station and another, or between your final duty station and home of record upon retirement or discharge.

Pendente Lite
A Latin term meaning "awaiting the litigation" or "pending the litigation" which applies to court orders which are in effect while a matter (such as a divorce) is pending.

Primary Creditor
A principal creditor is the party who has a claim against the debtor that is far greater than the debt owed to any other creditor, and in some instances, to all other creditors combined.

Post-Traumatic Stress Disorder (PTSD)
A mental health condition that's triggered by a terrifying event — either experiencing it or witnessing it. Symptoms may include flashbacks, nightmares and severe anxiety, as well as uncontrollable thoughts about the event.

Quitclaim Deed
A quitclaim deed is a legal instrument that is used to transfer interest in real property.

Rest and Recuperation (R&R)
Military slang for rest and recuperation, is a term used for the free time of a soldier.

Repayment Plan
Standard means regular payments—at the same monthly amount—until the loan plus interest is paid off. Referencing bankruptcy repayment plan.

Retainer
A fee that the client pays upfront to an attorney before the attorney has begun work for the client.

Rule to Show Cause
The enforcement mechanism is through a contempt action, commonly called a "Rule to Show Cause." A rule to show cause asks the family court to hold the opposing party in contempt until he or she complies with the provision of the court order at issue.

Survivor Benefit Plan (SBP)
Allows a retiree to ensure, after death, a continuous lifetime annuity for their dependents.

Separation Agreement/Marital Agreement
An agreement on all the issues you and your spouse need to resolve before getting divorced, such as the division of marital property (assets and debts), child custody, visitation and support issues, and Temporary Maintenance and Post-Divorce Maintenance (commonly known as 'alimony or spousal).

Sisty Ugler
Originally referring to the characters in Cinderella, this fun little phrase can be brought out whenever you must refer to a friend. (referenced my sister-in-law)

Spousal support/maintenance/Alimony
A husband's or wife's court-ordered provision for a spouse after separation or divorce.

Stolen Valor Act of 2005 & 2013
Term applied to the phenomenon of people falsely claiming military awards or badges they did not earn, service they did not perform, Prisoner of War experiences that never happened, and other tales of military derring-do that exist only in their minds.

Subpoena
A writ ordering a person to attend a court.

Traumatic Brain Injury (TBI)
TBI is a neurological disorder caused by trauma to the brain. When PTSD and TBI coexist, it's often difficult to sort out what's going on.

The Jeffersons
An American sitcom that was broadcast on CBS from January 18, 1975, to July 2, 1985.

Tricare
is a health insurance program for military members, their dependents, retirees, and some survivors & former spouses. To use Tricare, you must be listed in DEERS as being eligible for military health care benefits.

Tumbleweed
a plant of dry regions that breaks off near the ground in late summer and is tumbled about by the wind, thereby dispersing its seeds.

Uniformed Services Former Spouse Protection Act (USFSPA)
The USFSPA also permits former spouses to continue receiving commissary, exchange, and health care benefits after a divorce in certain cases.

In order to qualify for continued benefits a former spouse must show that the service member served at least 20 years of creditable service, that the marriage lasted at least 20 years and that the period of the marriage overlapped the period of service by at least 20 years. A former spouse who meets these requirements is known as a 20/20/20 former spouse and is entitled to full commissary, exchange and health care benefit.

Resources

These websites, organizations and books provide a place to start or to find more detailed information for those contemplating or going through the divorce process. It also provides helpful information for those in difficult relationships.

The early references relate to military information. Those that follow provide similar information but for a general audience.

Although Nancy Stevens did not experience domestic violence in her journey, she knows that it is often a part of relationships headed for or involved in divorces. Therefore, she has offered several websites as resources here to help those who do.

Domestic Violence in the Military
WomensLaw.org
https://www.womenslaw.org/laws/federal/domestic-violence-military/all

Free Legal Assistance
Military.com.
https://www.military.com/benefits/military-legal-matters/legal-assistance-and-jag/free-legal-assistance.html

Managing the Divorce Process
MilitarySource.mil
https://www.militaryonesource.mil/financial-legal/legal/family-legal-issues/managing-the-divorce-process

Finding a therapist in your geographic area
www.GoodTherapy.org

Finding an attorney in your geographic area
www.lawyers.com

Finding a Private Investigator
https://www.einvestigator.com/private-investigator-associations/

Legal information – articles, locating attorneys
www.nolo.com

Divorce therapists
https://www.psychologytoday.com/us/therapists/divorce

Divorce counseling
https://www.regain.us/advice/divorce/divorce-counseling-what-to-expect-and-are-there-benefits/

When Georgia Smiled:
https://www.whengeorgiasmiled.org/

Domestic Violence
WomensLaw.org

Support for Victims of Domestic Violence
National Network to End Domestic Violence
www.nnedv.org

Immediate help for domestic violence
National Domestic Violence Hotline - 1-800-799-7233 (SAFE)
https://www.thehotline.org

Domestic Shelters – online searchable database for shelters in your geographic area
https://www.domesticshelters.org

Post-Traumatic Stress
National Institute of Mental Health
https://www.nimh.nih.gov/health/topics/post-traumatic-stress-disorder-ptsd/index.shtml

Books

Chapman, Gary. *The 5 Love Languages, Military Edition: The Secret to Love That Lasts.* Chicago, Ill., Northfield Publishing, 2017.

Fahey, Maryjane and Caryn Beth Rosenthal. *Dumped: A Guide to Getting Over a Breakup and Your Ex in Record Time!* South Portland, Maine, Sellers Publishing, 2012.

Manfred, Erica. *He's History, You're Not: Surviving Divorce After 40.* New York, New York, Globe Pequot Press, 2009.

Schneider, Esq., Stacy, *He Had It Coming: How to Outsmart Your Husband and Win Your Divorce.* New York, New York, Gallery Books, 2003.

Schorn, Tracy. *Leave a Cheater, Gain a Life: The Chump Lady's Survival Guide.* Philadelphia, Penn., Running Press Books, 2016.

Stark, Vikki. *Runaway Husbands: The Abandoned Wife's Guide to Recovery and Renewal.* Montreal, Canada, Green Light Press, 2010.

Williams, Pat. *Character Carved In Stone.* Grand Rapids, Mich., Baker Publishing Group, 2019.

www.ingramcontent.com/pod-product-compliance
Lightning Source LLC
LaVergne TN
LVHW052019080426
835513LV00018B/2079

What early readers are saying.

"Some divorce books are entertaining or emotional while others instructional and advisory. *Now What?*, by Nancy Stevens, is both. It's the first book to pick up for a person contemplating divorce—especially a military divorce. Unfortunately, what Nancy went through happens all too often. That's why this is a must read to arm one's self prior to battle. There are nuggets all throughout the book like "tenacity and perseverance and cogency can pay off". *Now What?* should be read before hiring an attorney or diving deep into the divorce process."

—John T. Winkler, Attorney at Law

"Nancy is heart-breakingly honest in writing about the pain of her divorce, but she also shows great humor and gives very practical advice to people who find themselves in the same predicament."

—Ann Bilodeau, Former Development Director, Stanford University

"Nancy Stevens is a raconteur of the first order. The descriptions of her marital journey through its inception, demise and beyond, evoke such vivid real-world imagery, the reader immediately begins to walk in her shoes. Join Nancy as she experiences the pain, the headache, the education, the downright absurdity and yes, even the love and loyalty, that one finds in going through a divorce. The most valuable lessons a person going through a divorce can be found bound within these pages."

—Demian J. McGarry, Virginia Family Law Attorney

"I have to say that I have laughed and cried. I am so proud that we were able to serve a small role in your success! I am ready for the NEXT book!"

—Lisa Vance, Law Offices of Lisa A. Vance, P.C.

"Painful and hilarious"

—Candice Maillard, Editor, Chatsworth, CA.

"The author has a delightful sense of humor that makes this a very entertaining read."

—Lesia Stanchak, Business Owner

"You laid it all out—the good, the bad and the ugly. It is a most important guide to understanding the past, present and future of the personal journey known as divorce. There are so very many who will benefit from your fine book—and understand better that they are not alone in their long journey. The advice in the "take aways" at the end of each chapter are so informative and educational...priceless."

—Patricia Gallo-Stenman author, mother of 3 and fellow divorce journey traveler